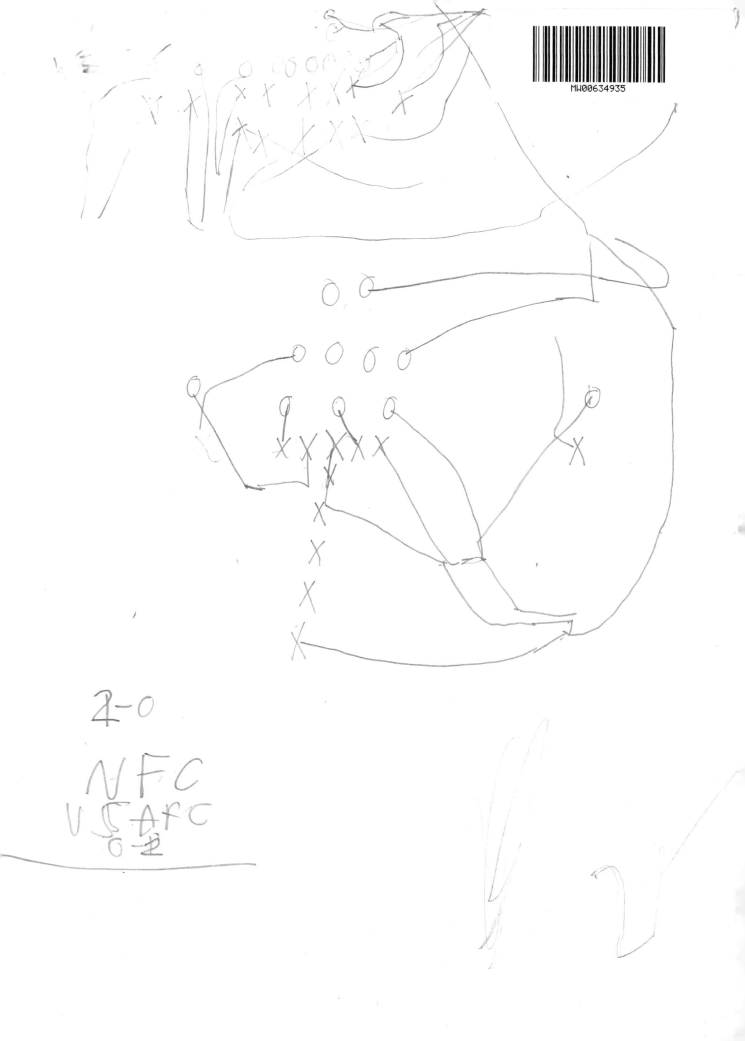

2-0

NFC
vs AFC
0-2

LEGENDS OF ALABAMA FOOTBALL

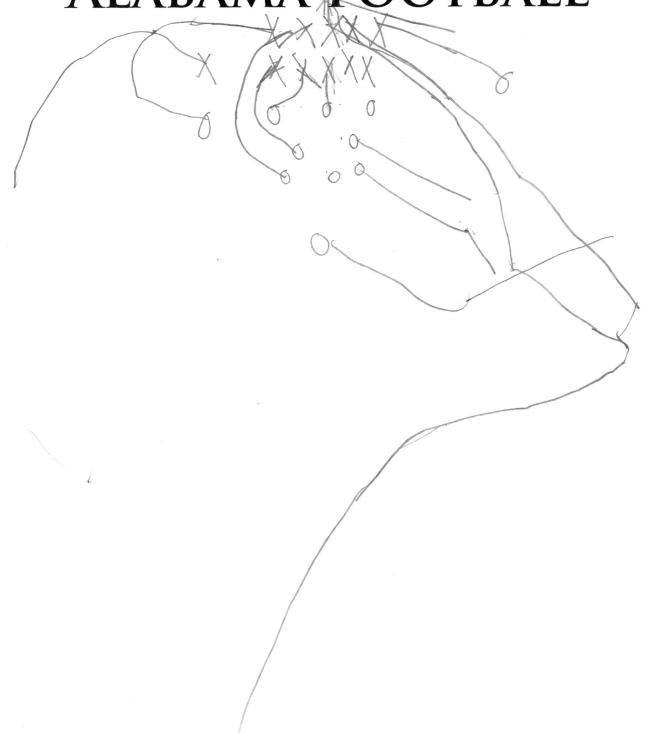

LEGENDS OF ALABAMA FOOTBALL

Joe Namath, Ozzie Newsome, Mark Ingram Jr., and Other Alabama Stars

RICHARD SCOTT
WITH JASON MAYFIELD

FOREWORD BY JAY BARKER

SPORTS
PUBLISHING

Sports Publishing books may be purchased in bulk at special discounts for sales promotion, corporate gifts, fund-raising, or educational purposes. Special editions can also be created to specifications. For details, contact the Special Sales Department, Sports Publishing, 307 West 36th Street, 11th Floor, New York, NY 10018 or sportspubbooks@skyhorsepublishing.com.

Sports Publishing® is a registered trademark of Skyhorse Publishing, Inc.®, a Delaware corporation.

Visit our website at www.sportspubbooks.com.

10 9 8 7 6 5 4 3 2 1

Library of Congress Cataloging-in-Publication Data is available on file.

ISBN: 978-1-61321-444-2

Printed in Canada

To my Dad:

For teaching me to respect the past,
Live with purpose in the present and
Look with hope to the future.
And for all those games of catch.

—RS

CONTENTS

Foreword..vii

Preface to the New Edition..viii

Introduction..xi

The Coaches
Wallace Wade...1

Frank Thomas...7

Paul "Bear" Bryant..15

The Players
Johnny Mack Brown...27

A.T.S. "Pooley" Hubert..33

Fred Sington..39

Johnny Cain...45

Millard "Dixie" Howell...51

Don Hutson..57

Harry Gilmer...63

Vaughn Mancha...69

Bart Starr..75

Billy Neighbors...81

Pat Trammell...87

Lee Roy Jordan..93

Joe Namath...99

Ken Stabler...109

Johnny Musso..117

John Hannah..125

Ozzie Newsome..131

Marty Lyons...137

Barry Krauss..143

Don McNeal..149

Dwight Stephenson..157

Jeremiah Castille..165

Tommy Wilcox...171

Cornelius Bennett..177

Derrick Thomas..183

Bobby Humphrey..189

Shaun Alexander..195

Acknowledgments..200

Epilogue...201

FOREWORD

I don't think I can remember anytime when I wasn't an Alabama fan. From the time I was small, my dad and I talked about Alabama football and coach Paul "Bear" Bryant and went to the games.

I remember when I was five years old playing youth football. We'd throw wet washcloths in a plastic baggie so we could wash off after games and then get to the Alabama games in Birmingham on time. Sometimes we went to Tuscaloosa, but part of the fun of having the Alabama games in Birmingham was being able to play your own game and then go to see two or three games a year. That was at a time when you could actually walk up and buy tickets at the ticket office.

Every kid who was an Alabama fan wanted to play on Saturday and then go watch the legends you wanted to be like and dream about maybe one day having a chance to put on that crimson jersey. I used to tell my friends that one day I was going to play for Alabama, and they would all laugh.

I used to rush home from church on Sunday so my dad and I could sit in front of the television with our Coca-Cola and Golden Flake potato chips and watch *The Bear Bryant Show* and listen to him talk about some of those great players in the 1970s, the Steadman Shealys and Jeff Rutledges and Major Ogilvies and the players who won the back-to-back national championships. I'd sit there and think about one day I'd like to hear Coach Bryant say, "The other day I saw Jerome and Barbara Barker up in the stands and had a chance to say hello to Jay's parents."

That never happened because Coach Bryant passed away a few years later, but two of the greatest things that have ever happened to me deal with the color crimson. One is my relationship with Jesus Christ and the crimson blood He shed and the other is the crimson jersey, having a chance to finally wear that and win a national championship.

One of the things that a lot of people don't understand about Alabama football is that it becomes even more than a passion for people. I don't want to say religion, but it does become a family affair. It's passed down from your grandparents to your parents, your uncles and your aunts, and they all get involved. They're talking about it Friday and Saturday before the game and Sunday afternoon after the game and it just becomes such a big part of your life.

It's that passion that creates legends. You become a legend based on what people are passionate about. There are outstanding players at different colleges all over the country, but they're not necessarily legends. It's the program, it's the state, it's the fans that allow you to reach that legendary status. It's the fans who fall in love with the players, and the kids who wear your jersey number and dream about one day wearing the crimson jersey.

I don't think you can realize how important Alabama football is to people until you've been there as a player. I thought I understood how big it was as a fan, but it's totally different once you get there. I don't want to equate football with war, but if you've ever heard veterans talk about war, it's totally different than the way people talk about it who haven't experienced it.

For me, this book brings back a lot of great memories of watching those older players and thinking about wearing that crimson jersey and the possibility of one day being thought of as one of those legends. I think it will mean a lot to Alabama people. It connects the generations and allows the granddad to tell his son and his grandson about the legends he followed. He can say, "Hey, go read this book and see what these guys meant to me. Today's players are good, but these guys were pretty good back in my day as well."

Reading *Legends of Alabama Football* connects the past with the present and shows how this phenomenon of Alabama football got its start. These are the people who established the tradition and created the legendary status that the rest of us had to live up to and got to be a part of through the years.

—Jay Barker, Alabama quarterback, 1991-94

PREFACE TO THE NEW EDITION

In the 10 years since this book was first published, the legends of Alabama football mourned the loss of several of its own and rejoiced at the addition of three national championships.

Some of the men who built the Crimson Tide legacy have passed away. Former All-America center Vaughn Mancha passed away in 2011 at the age of 89. Former All-America lineman Billy Neighbors passed away in 2012 at the age of 72. Longtime assistant coach, athletic director, and former player Mal Moore died at the age of 74 in 2013. Moore's legacy is examined further in this book's epilogue.

To preserve the immediacy and research of the original book, little was changed in the coach and player biographies. Here's a brief update on the legacy of each in 2014:

Wallace Wade: Wade made a name for himself at Duke University, and Duke announced the launch of a $250 million athletics initiative with plans to expand and accessorize Wallace Wade Stadium. The current coach at Duke is David Cutcliffe, a 1976 Alabama graduate and student assistant under Bear Bryant.

Frank Thomas: In 2006, the university erected a statue honoring Thomas's national championship legacy. Thomas's statue sits alongside those of Wade, Bryant, Gene Stallings, and Nick Saban on the Walk of Champions entering Bryant-Denny Stadium.

Paul "Bear" Bryant: Bryant's legacy continues to live on in the work of his former players. Among the notables: Ozzie Newsome, general manager of the Baltimore Ravens; Joey Jones, head coach at South Alabama; and Bill Battle, Alabama's current athletic director. In 2006, Alabama wore houndstooth trim on its jerseys in a game against Ole Miss to commemorate the 25th anniversary of Bryant's 315th win.

Johnny Mack Brown: Official Johnny Mack Brown comics are still selling on eBay, Brown's movies are now available on Netflix, and Brown has been honored with several awards for his work on the screen. He was posthumously awarded the Golden Boot Award for his work in Westerns in 2004, and in 2008, he was inducted into the Hall of Great Western Performers in Oklahoma. A Johnny Mack Brown Film Festival was held in his hometown of Dothan in May from 2004-2011.

A.T.S. "Pooley" Hubert: A.J. McCarron is just the latest player to live up to Hubert's legacy in the No. 10 jersey. In 2005, Hubert's former players gathered at Waynesboro High School in Georgia for a reunion and to raise money for a memorial to Hubert.

Fred Sington: The Kiwanis Club of Birmingham continues to award the Fred Sington Award to a deserving large school football program.

Johnny Cain: Cain's name continues to come up whenever an all-time best list of punters is put together. Cain's 1962 Ole Miss team met for a 50th-year reunion to celebrate its perfect 10-0 season.

Millard "Dixie" Howell: Recent winners of the Dixie Howell Memorial MVP award for the annual spring game, A-Day, include two-time winner and current running back T.J. Yeldon, Trent Richardson, Mark Ingram, Marquis Maze, and Greg McElory.

Don Hutson: In 2012, the NFL Network named Hutson the greatest Green Bay Packer of all time. In 2005, a family donated an authentic No. 14 Hutson jersey to the Packers. The jersey had been discovered in a trunk of old uniforms at the lodge where the Packers stayed during training camp.

Harry Gilmer: Gilmer still lives on his 57-acre farm in O'Fallon, Mo., and told the *St. Louis Dispatch* in 2010 that he would watch the Bama-Texas BCS game "from start to finish."

Vaughn Mancha: Mancha passed away in 2011, leaving behind his wife, Sibyl, three children, and four grandchildren. Mancha remained active in Florida State athletics as a member of the Hall of Fame selection committee.

Bart Starr: The NFL annually gives The Bart Starr Award to a player of outstanding character. In May 2013, work began to extend Bart Starr Drive in Green Bay as an effort to develop local businesses. Starr continues to give motivational speeches throughout the country.

Billy Neighbors: Neighbors passed away from a heart attack at the age of 72 in 2012. In 2011, he and many of the members of the 1961 team attended a 50th reunion for that championship season. The team was recognized on the field prior to kickoff.

Pat Trammell: The Dr. Patrick Lee Trammell Sr. Excellence in Sports Medicine Program is an endowed fellowship and chair in honor of Trammell. It started in 2008 though a partnership with the University's School of Community Health Sciences and the Department of Intercollegiate Athletics.

Lee Roy Jordan: Jordan and John Hannah were named to the 75th anniversary Orange Bowl team in 2008. In 2010, following A-Day, future NFL players Marcell Dareus and Mark Barron were named recipients of the annual Lee Roy Jordan Headhunter Award.

Joe Namath: Namath graduated December 15, 2007, with a degree in interdisciplinary studies from the University at the age of 64. He became a grandfather in 2007 when his daughter Olivia gave birth to a daughter, Natalia.

Ken Stabler: Stabler's XOXO Foundation in 2013 revived an invitational golf tournament in Point Clear, Alabama, to benefit the Ronald McDonald House Charities of Mobile. A part of the proceeds also went to the Ashley Harrison Memorial Scholarship Fund. Harrison was a victim of the 2011 Tuscaloosa tornadoes. In 2009, The Snake was the grand marshal at a NASCAR event in Northern California. His voice has been gone from the Alabama radio booth since 2007 and has been dearly missed by some of the team's biggest fans.

Johnny Musso: Musso was on the field and a part of the ceremonies in 2011 before the North Texas game to honor the 1971 regular season undefeated Tide. Musso's No. 22 was worn by Mark Ingram when Ingram won the Heisman Trophy in 2009.

John Hannah: Hannah and Lee Roy Jordan were named to the Orange Bowl's 75th anniversary team in 2008. Hannah attended a reunion of the Crimson Tide All-America players in 2012 and told the *Tuscaloosa News* the lineman that played most like he did in the 1970s was future NFL first-round draft pick Chance Womack.

Ozzie Newsome: Newsome continues to lead the Baltimore Ravens as one of the NFL's most successful general managers. He owns two Super Bowl rings as a GM (2001 and 2013). He is also a member of the first "Ring of Honor" class the Cleveland Browns named in 2010, and he is always mentioned as a top candidate to lead the Crimson Tide as a future athletic director.

Marty Lyons: Lyons was inducted into the College Football Hall of Fame in 2012. He was inducted into the Tampa Bay Sports Club Hall of Fame in 2007.

Barry Krauss: Krauss was inducted into the Alabama Sports Hall of Fame in 2007. In 2012, he was named the recipient of the James Keller Award for his work with the Marty Lyons Foundation in fulfilling special wishes for children and teens with life-threatening or terminal illnesses. Since 2004, he has served as an analyst for the New York Jets Radio Network.

Don McNeal: McNeal was inducted into the Alabama Sports Hall of Fame in 2008. In 2010, McNeal was on hand at Bryant-Denny Stadium to welcome his nephew, Penn State quarterback Robert Bolden. McNeal said prior to the game that he wanted his nephew to do well, but for the Tide to win. Bolden, a freshman at the time, threw for 144 yards in a 24-3 Alabama win. The following year in Happy Valley, Bolden threw for 144 yards again in a 27-11 Alabama win. McNeal still serves at New Testament Baptist Church in south Florida as a counseling pastor.

Dwight Stephenson: Stephenson was named the Walter Camp Man of the Year in 2005 for his work in public service. He was inducted in 2011 into the Hampton Roads Sports Hall of Fame for his contributions to sports in southeastern Virginia. His son completed his college playing career at Notre Dame in 2007.

Jeremiah Castille: Castille currently serves as a chaplain for the Crimson Tide, and the Jeremiah Castille Foundation annually awards a scholarship to a deserving high school student. He was inducted into the Alabama Sports Hall of Fame in 2005. His son Tim finished his playing time at Alabama in 2006 and played four seasons in the NFL for the Arizona Cardinals and Kansas City Chiefs. Son Simeon finished his playing days in 2007 and played one year with the Cincinnati Bengals.

Tommy Wilcox: Tommy Wilcox Outdoors continues to air regionally and nationally. Among his guests have been such Crimson Tide legends as Ken Stabler, Mal Moore, Sylvester Croom, Scott Hunter, Mick Shula, Bobby Humphrey, Brodie Croyle, Barry Krauss, and Nick Saban.

Cornelius Bennett: Bennett was inducted into the College Football Hall of Fame in 2005. In addition to his annual golf tournament for charities in Birmingham, Bennett serves as the chairman of the NFL Players Association's Former Players Board of Directors.

Derrick Thomas: Thomas was elected to the NFL Hall of Fame posthumously in 2009. He has yet to be named to the College Football Hall of Fame, despite receiving the Butkus Award in 1988 and holding the NCAA records for single-season sacks (27) and career sacks (52). Cornelius Bennett told a local Birmingham TV station in 2013 that he will continue to boycott the Hall because of the snub.

Bobby Humphrey: Humphrey was head coach of the Birmingham Steeldogs of the Arena Football League 2 from 2000-2005. Humphrey is vice president of business development for Bryant Bank. Humphrey's sons and daughters are budding football and track talents at the high school and collegiate level.

Shaun Alexander: Alexander was the NFL MVP in 2005 and was named to the NFL's 2000s All-Decade Team. He was just the eighth player in NFL history to score 100 rushing touchdowns. He finished his career with limited work with the Washington Redskins in 2008.

INTRODUCTION

Like most successful traditions, Alabama's history of winning is no accident. Someone had to start with a vision. Someone had to construct a plan. Someone had to make a commitment to building a winning program.

Long before Coach Paul "Bear" Bryant ever climbed his tower and took Alabama to new levels of achievement, before Wallace Wade and Frank Thomas brought Alabama football to national prominence, someone had to decide that Alabama would be a football power.

That someone was Dr. George Hutcheson "Mike" Denny, the University of Alabama's president from 1912 to 1936, and then again from 1941 to 1942. Yes, the same sports fan whose name graces Denny Chimes and Bryant-Denny Stadium, grand reminders of Denny's legacy to the University. Denny also is credited with being the first to call the University "The Capstone."

Alabama's history of football success is another monument to Denny's legacy. Would Bryant have ever come to Alabama from Arkansas to play and coach football if Denny had not decided to make football a high priority at the university, designed to attract students and build the institution's reputation? How about Joe Namath, Shaun Alexander and other Crimson Tide legends who came to Alabama from other parts of the United States?

It's easy to debate that point in retrospect, but there's no argument that Denny knew what he was doing in 1923 when he had the vision to hire Wade, a 32-year-old Vanderbilt assistant and Brown University graduate and a rising up-and-comer in the expanding world of college football. If Denny had not hired Wade, someone else would have. Fortunately for the University, Wade was the right man at the right time.

Alabama had already experienced a measure of national achievement in 1922 against John Heisman's University of Pennsylvania heavily favored stalwarts. After Georgia Tech beat Alabama 33-7 and then lost to Navy 13-0, Penn defeated Navy 13-7. That explains why legendary sportswriter Grantland Rice picked Penn to win by 21 and most sportswriters assumed the Crimson Tide had traveled to Philadelphia by train to play the part of sacrificial lamb. Instead, Alabama coach Xen Scott, relying on his own Northern connections, had Penn well scouted and the Tide well prepared. The result was a 9-7 Alabama victory that put the Crimson Tide in the national spotlight for the first time.

That same fall, Scott fell ill. He lost 35 pounds and defied a doctor's advice not to travel to Philadelphia. *The Birmingham News* reported that Scott had decided to resign on October 6, a month before the Penn game, and later had to be persuaded into finishing the season. That season turned out to be his last. Soon after, Scott died of cancer.

When Denny began his search for a new coach, he originally attempted to hire Vanderbilt coach Dan McGugin. It's hard to imagine a Vanderbilt coach from today's era turning down a chance to coach at Alabama, but McGugin instead recommended Wade. After spending two years coaching the Vanderbilt linemen and helping the Commodores win 16 out of 18 games, Wade was ready to become a head coach.

LEGENDS OF ALABAMA FOOTBALL

WALLACE WADE

COACH 1923-1930

In 1980, during a reunion of the 1930 national championship team, coach Paul "Bear" Bryant introduced Wallace Wade to his team by saying, "Men, I'd like you to meet coach Wallace Wade, the man who is most responsible for the University of Alabama football tradition. In many ways, he is the reason I'm here and the reason you're here."

Wade was a stern, strict disciplinarian who refused to accept anything but perfection. That may have made him difficult to play for at times, but those qualities also pushed the Crimson Tide football program down the right path. Finding tough, athletic, hard-nosed kids willing to pay a high price for success wasn't a problem in Alabama in the 1920s, so Wade simply brought discipline and direction to a program on the verge of major success.

During one afternoon practice, Wade was called away to answer a long-distance tele- phone call. After completing the call, Wade showered and left for home. Meanwhile, the assistant coaches and players continued to practice well into the evening. Finally, an assistant coach called Wade at home and asked what he should do about practice. Wade paused and answered, "Yes, well, let them go in. It's dark now."

Wade didn't waste any time establishing himself or his no-nonsense methods at Alabama. While former coach Xen Scott was popular and affable with his players, Wade struck fear into the hearts of his new charges.

After Wade's first few months on the job, *The Birmingham News* wrote, "The spirit of Wallace Wade is already an institution around the Crimson stronghold. There has been a change in the football routine in Crimson town. Xen Scott, fine little tutor that he was, was more or less of the easygoing school. Long practices were not the rule under his regime. Firm, yes, but in the milder sense of the word. But Wade is different. And the warriors who were in harness under Scott were but one day finding this out.

"The writer strolled out to Denny Field in the early afternoon just to see if there were any changes since the last trip. 'Too early yet,' ran our thoughts, 'for the football boys.' It was not yet 2:30.

"But instead of just a football field and bleachers, he found almost the entire squad ready on the practice grounds. The coaches were not out yet and didn't show up for almost half an hour. But the Crimson jerseyed lads were hard at it, nonetheless."

Fans and sportswriters did not expect much from Wade's first team, but the Crimson Tide still went 7-2-1, including impressive Southern Conference wins over Ole Miss (56-0), LSU (30-3) and Georgia (36-0). Suddenly high expectations evolved into mounting pressure for success in 1924.

According to the *International News Service*, "Over in Tuscaloosa, students and alumni are feeling comfortable. They view prospects for the season through a rosy haze. Nothing but a string of unbroken victories is expected of them and Alabama's chances of coming through the season undefeated never were better than this year. Tuscaloosa is all prepared to celebrate."

The Tide gave Tuscaloosa plenty to celebrate about that season, winning eight games and the Southern Conference championship. Only a 17-0 loss to Centre College of Kentucky in the eighth game of the season ruined Alabama's perfect record. After years of football prowess in the Northeast, Midwest and Pacific, the South was finally catching up to its regional rivals, led by Wade's Crimson Tide.

In a *Birmingham News* story that fall, Wade made it clear that the South was on the right track to challenge for national respect and recognition. "Sectionalism in football is rapidly disappearing, due to the interchange of coaching ideas. Coaching schools are being held and attended by coaches in all parts of the country. Coaches are coming into the South from other sections; also coaches are carefully studying the football books put out by the leading coaches of the West and the East.

"More men are devoting their entire time the year round to the study of football. This and many other conditions are putting the standard of football of the South on a plane with that in other sections."

Wade also pointed out the special qualities that Southern football brought to the gridiron.

"In spite of those conditions, Southern football continues to retain some distinctive characteristics. This fact must be recognized from the fact that few coaches who have come to Southern universities from the West or East have been successful until they have become familiar with conditions by a year or two of experience in this section.

"There is more sentiment in Southern football; the coaches appeal to the affections of the players. There is less driving and more loyal conscientious effort. The Southern coach holds a higher position in the hearts of his players and of the entire student body than does the coach of the North. Instead of being called by the affectionate term of 'Coach,' as the Southern coach is, the Northern coach is often called by his first name and is too often treated with very little respect."

Southern football teams, Wade noted, were also employing greater use of the forward pass, making considerable progress in defensive strategy and skill and playing before bigger crowds in better stadiums. Even the newspapers, Wade insisted, were playing their part by covering the games more acutely and accurately, and even adding photos to illuminate their stories.

For all those developments, nothing did more to elevate the status of Southern football than Alabama's success in 1925. Led by future College Football Hall of Fame backs Johnny Mack Brown and Pooley Hubert, the Crimson Tide allowed only seven total points in the regular season and rolled to nine consecutive victories, including a 7-0 win over previously undefeated Georgia Tech and a 27-0 victory over Georgia before destiny came calling from the Pacific coast.

Before long, the rumor mill began to mention Alabama as a possible contender for the Rose Bowl, the only bowl in college football at the time. Skeptics doubted Alabama's legitimacy as a candidate for the Rose, due to the 2,800-mile distance between Tuscaloosa and Pasadena and the general lack of national respect for Southern football. Reports suggested the invitation would go to Tulane, Colgate, Dartmouth or Princeton, and Wade himself didn't believe the rumors until an official representative of the Tournament of Roses came to Birmingham with an official invitation for the Crimson Tide to play Washington.

Even as Alabama prepared for its journey west, scribes and football insiders didn't give the Tide much of a chance to beat Washington and bruising back George Wilson. Cal coach Andy Smith, following a 7-0 loss to Washington, insisted the Huskies were "one of the greatest football aggregations

that I have ever seen, and I believe they are as strong as any team in the country."

Of course, Smith had never seen Alabama before. Throughout the prolonged train trip to California the 22 Alabama players focused on football and academics, at Denny's insistence. The academic progress of the players may be lost to history, but *The Birmingham News* reported "There isn't a player on the train who can't tell you the name, weight, disposition and a few other little things about every player eligible on the Washington team."

Wade, too, was able to give his full attention to the game after putting an end to rumors of his departure by signing a five-year contract. The University never announced his salary, but newspaper reports at the time claimed he could have gone to Oregon or Washington State for as much as $25,000 per year. With that behind him, Wade kept the players on track all the way to California, making only a brief stop at the Grand Canyon before stopping for practice in rolled up trousers in Williams, Arizona.

After leaving Tuscaloosa on December 19, the team finally arrived in Pasadena on December 24 and became immediate celebrities, especially Brown and Hubert. After four days of waging war with distractions, Wade circled the wagons on December 28 and put an end to all outside activities. The players ate their meals in a private hotel dining room and were instructed to avoid the lobby.

Alabama's focus didn't impress western writers who insisted the Tide had no chance against the Huskies, and those predictions looked pretty smart when Washington took a 12-0 lead into halftime. Then Alabama charged back in the second half, scoring all 20 of its points during a seven-minute period in the third quarter after knocking Wilson out of the game with an injury.

Alabama held on for a 20-19 victory that gave the Crimson Tide its first national championship, forever changing the perception of Southern football and putting Alabama on the road to national prominence. "Tuscaloosa, Alabama, which Western fans didn't know was on the map," *The Los Angeles Evening Herald* wrote, "is the abiding place of the Pacific Coast football championship today."

To further prove its point, the Crimson Tide went 9-0-1 in 1926, allowed 27 total points and returned to the Rose Bowl once again, tying Stanford 7-7 and winning another share of the national championship.

Alabama stumbled to five, six and six wins over the next three seasons before Wade's best team finished the 1930 regular season 9-0 and earned a trip to the 1931 Rose Bowl. Wade had started his second team throughout the season in an effort to wear down opponents psychologically and physically, and the second team never allowed a point. In all, the entire Alabama team allowed only 13 points all season. In fact, Wade was so confident in his team during the week before the Rose Bowl that he vowed to start his second team once again. He followed up on his promise and the Crimson Tide still beat Washington State 24-0 on New Year's Day and won the University's third national championship.

The Crimson Tide also lost something special that day. Wade had coached his last game at Alabama, having decided to resign the previous April so he could become the head coach at Duke. Wade still had one more season left on his contract when he made his decision and insisted on honoring his commitment, giving him one last chance to return to the Rose Bowl and finish his Alabama tenure on top. He did just that with a 61-13-3 record and a third national title.

At the time *The Birmingham News* reported that Wade gave no reason, and over the course of his life Wade rarely talked about his decision in public. Friends and former players attributed Wade's departure to two basic reasons. One was his tendency to take criticism personally, especially during the 1927, 1928 and 1929 seasons. In *The Crimson Tide: A Story of Alabama Football*, Hoyt "Wu" Winslett, who played defensive end for Wade in 1925-26, said, "He talked to me in 1930 about his situation. They were criticizing him and he couldn't take criticism. And they offered him a good deal at Duke."

The other reason was Wade's desire to be more than just a football coach. When Duke president William P. Few originally contacted Wade for help with Duke's search for a new coach, Wade presented two names before offering his own services. Few didn't entice Wade with money or the opportunity to revive a dormant football program. Instead, he gave Wade the chance to build a total athletic program, including intramural activities for all students. Wade also wanted to return to a private university after his experience at Vanderbilt.

Wade went on to earn a place in the College Football Hall of Fame and the National Football Foundation Hall of Fame, as well as the Alabama, Tennessee, North Carolina, Brown University and Rose Bowl Halls. He also earned military honors for his participation in both World Wars.

Back where it all started, Wade remains

a legend at the University of Alabama as the coach who led Alabama to national football notoriety.

"He called a team meeting just before the first game [in 1930] and it was an emotional one. His remarks lit a fire under us," said All-American running back John Henry "Flash" Suther in *Bowl Bama Bowl*. "Coach Wade said it would be his last year at Alabama, because some of the radicals in the state didn't care for the way he was running things. Then he gave us all a challenge.

"'Gentlemen,' Coach Wade said, 'I'm gonna win this damn championship this season, and if you want to be a part of it, you can. If not, get out of here now.'

"Well, we got with it. I mean we really buckled down and worked for him. You know the rest. But the end of the year, those radicals were begging Coach Wade to stay and it's obvious what he told them.

"Coach Wade was like a blood-thirsty army officer. We all wanted to hate him, but when it got down to it, we loved him. He was a helluva coach who developed us into an outstanding team in 1930."

FRANK THOMAS

COACH 1931-1946

The best thing about Wallace Wade's resignation in April 1930 and his decision to honor the final year on his contract is that it gave University president George H. "Mike" Denny plenty of time to find a new football coach to perpetuate Alabama's growing reputation as a national football power.

By the time the football team left Tuscaloosa for the 1930 Rose Bowl, Denny had already found his man in Frank Thomas, a Georgia assistant under coach George Woodruff and former Notre Dame player under the legendary Knute Rockne.

Thomas got a head start on the job by traveling with the team to California, with Wade's approval. In fact, it had been Wade who had first recommended Thomas to Denny.

"There is a young backfield coach at Georgia who should become one of the great-est coaches in the country," Wade wrote to Denny upon his resignation. "He played football under Rockne at Notre Dame. Rock called him one of the smartest players he ever coached. He is Frank Thomas, and I don't believe you could pick a better man."

History backs Wade's opinion, but Thomas still had to pass one more test with Denny. When Thomas, accompanied by Atlanta newsman Ed Camp, met with Denny and Alabama supporter Borden Burr in Burr's office on July 15, 1930, Denny threw down the gauntlet in front of Thomas.

Denny told his prospective new coach, "Mr. Thomas, now that you have accepted our proposition, I will give you the benefit of my views, based on many years of observation. It is my conviction that material is 90 percent, coaching ability 10 percent. I desire further to say that you will be provided with the 90 percent and that you will be held to strict accounting for delivering the remaining 10 percent."

After Thomas and Camp left the meeting, Thomas said, "Those were the hardest and coldest words I ever heard. Do you reckon his figures are right?"

Camp answered that he believed the numbers might be a little off, "but there is no doubt the good doctor means what he says."

Mean it he did, and Denny knew how to get what he wanted. He did his part, and fortunately for Thomas and the University, Thomas did his part as well, delivering three

Coach Wallace Wade (left) and coach Frank Thomas (right)

trips to the Rose Bowl, as well as trips to the Cotton, Orange and Sugar Bowls. Under Thomas, Alabama also set the standard for its regional rivals by winning the first ever Southeastern Conference championship. In 15 seasons under Thomas, Alabama won two national championships and four SEC titles and finished 115-24-7.

Thomas became accustomed to success as a prep star in Chicago and as a quarterback at Kalamazoo College (1919) and Notre Dame (1920-22), where he once roomed with George Gipp, the Fighting Irish star immortalized in Rockne's "Win One for the Gipper" speech in the movie, *Knute Rockne All-American.*

Thomas, the youngest of six children born to Welsh immigrants in 1882, probably would have followed in his father's footsteps as a Chicago ironworker if so many area ironworkers had not been laid off when Thomas was in high school, or if his own coach, Floyd Murphy, had not set an example that Thomas wanted to follow.

"He made me want to get an education—something my father didn't have," Thomas said. "He inspired me to become a coach, to follow in his footsteps."

Murphy's influence not only inspired Thomas to earn a law degree at Notre Dame, but to pursue a coaching career that would take him to Georgia straight out of law school in the spring of 1923. By the time Thomas arrived in Tuscaloosa after the 1930 season, he was determined to succeed and had his own ideas about how to make it happen. After all, this was a player of whom Rockne had once said, "It's amazing the amount of football sense that Thomas kid has. He can't help becoming a great coach some day."

Thomas discarded Wade's single wing for Rockne's Notre Dame box offense and went to work building his own success. His first three teams went 9-1 in 1931, 8-2 in 1932 and 7-1-1 in 1933 before Thomas finally hit the jackpot in 1934 with a team that went 10-0 and beat Stanford 29-13 in the Rose Bowl. Led by stars such as Dixie Howell, Don Hutson and Riley Smith, the Crimson Tide won a fourth national championship.

While Hutson earned national acclaim and unanimous All-America status for his play at end in 1934, it was "the other end," a rugged young man from Morrow Bottom, Arkansas, named Paul Bryant, who came to symbolize the toughness the raw-boned southern boys brought to Pasadena.

The year after Thomas won his first Rose Bowl, the Tide slipped to 6-2-1, but it wasn't because the team wasn't tough enough. Bryant did his part when he suffered a broken leg in the first quarter of the third game of the season and returned in the third quarter and finished the game. The Crimson Tide lost that game to Mississippi State, and Bryant ended up with a cast and crutches the next week. Despite his injury, Bryant returned the following week to play at Tennessee and played until the game was out of hand in a 25-0 victory over the Vols.

Bryant wasn't the only hard-nosed player Alabama produced during Thomas's tenure. In fact, his teams were loaded with hardy rural boys willing to pay a high price for victory. All-America guard Leroy Monsky played in the 1938 Rose Bowl with 14 stitches and a drain on his eye after colliding with a teammate in practice during a stopover practice on the way to California. He rejected the protection of a face bar on his helmet because it limited his vision and got knocked out in the first quarter while tackling 224-pound Cal quarterback Johnny Meek. The hit tore his face open again, but he returned in the second quarter and played the rest of the game.

"All of us had that kind of fight in us," Monsky said.

That quality made Thomas's 1937 team his most treasured squad, or, as he called them "The greatest kids I've ever coached." His 1934, 1941 and 1945 teams may have been more talented and more famous, but his 1937 and 1944 teams played with a special determination that made Alabamians, and even a transplanted Yankee like Thomas, proud to be Southerners.

"This is the durndest team I've ever coached," Thomas told West Coast reporters before the 1938 Rose Bowl. "All the boys believe they are red hot and there was nothing grown out here can cool them off. They felt the same way through the season.

"I tell you one thing: the Rose Bowl customers are going to see the fightingest Alabama team that ever came out here. It may not be the most powerful or most versatile, but this bunch can really get down on the ground and fight it out with you.

"The boys are ready to play anytime, anywhere. They could ring the starting bell at four o'clock tomorrow morning and five minutes later every one of those boys would be there fully dressed and ready for the kickoff.

"The Civil War will be just one way they will fight. They won't get around to the Civil War until late in the third period. Before that one is reached these kids will have fought the Seven Years War, the War of 1812, the Spanish War, all of the expeditionary excursions into Mexico, and the Crimean War."

That Crimson Tide team finished 9-1 and won the SEC championship but lost in the Rose Bowl for the first time. Alabama suffered a 13-0 defeat to a superior Cal, but it didn't change Thomas's opinion of his team.

"You lost, but I'm proud of you just the same," Thomas told his players. "You showed amazing fight. ... You fought your hearts out, and I'm just as proud of you as I've ever been of any team I've coached."

The 1941 team became another source of tremendous pride for Thomas. When that team finished 9-2 and won the national championship by beating Texas A&M 29-21 in a 1942 Cotton Bowl clouded by the December 7 attack on Pearl Harbor, the season came as no surprise to Thomas.

"This should be a good season," Thomas had said before the 1941 season. "We have a lot of power. If we don't win, there'll be something wrong."

Alabama produced another winner in 1942, going 8-3 and beating Boston College 37-21 in the Orange Bowl, but like many colleges and universities, Alabama did not field a team in 1943 when World War II took its toll on male enrollment throughout the nation.

After Thomas devoted the 1943 season to leading War Bond drives and serving as the president of the Tuscaloosa Exchange Club, it didn't take long before he started making plans to resume the football program in 1944. Thomas admitted it would be difficult but also told the University's athletic committee that he could build a team "that will not disgrace the University." Despite initial concerns, the

Frank Thomas directs practice from his trailer.

committee approved his plan and Thomas quickly recruited a team comprised mainly of 17-year-old freshmen and army rejects (4-Fs), including Harry Gilmer, a 155-pound halfback from Birmingham's Woodlawn High School.

With Gilmer leading the charge, the team Thomas called his "War Babies" went on to win five games, lose one and tie two others before earning a surprise invitation to play Duke in the Sugar Bowl. During bowl preparations Thomas started showing obvious signs of fatigue that he dismissed as stress over the thought of his young team playing a Duke team loaded with war veterans and navy trainees. Despite the obvious age differences between the two teams, the Tide held its own in a 29-26 loss. Alabama doesn't have a history of accepting moral victories for close losses, but this was one time when the Crimson Tide made an exception and celebrated its effort in a losing cause.

"I've never been prouder of any team I've coached," Thomas said.

The 1945 season also produced a special team, for reasons both glorious and sad. The War Babies returned for their sophomore season a little older and much wiser. The Crimson Tide also welcomed back several players returning from the war, as well as assistant coach Harold "Red" Drew. Between the brash young returnees and the veterans, the Tide set a school record with 430 points and won all nine of its regular-season games on the way to another invitation from the Rose Bowl, this time to play Southern California.

"Haven't my War Babies grown up?" Thomas told his wife in the days before the bowl. "These are the greatest kids I've ever

coached. I'm sure they'll do just as fine a job against Southern California as my 1935 team did against Stanford."

The Tide not only lived up to Thomas's possible expectations against USC, but also surpassed them by taking a 27-0 lead before USC even gained a first down, forcing Thomas to pull back in the second half to avoid a more embarrassing result. Alabama came up short in the national championship voting to Army (remember, it was 1945) and never made another trip to the Rose Bowl, only because the Rose Bowl opted to pursue a Pac 10-Big Ten alliance. Thomas, though, left a legacy of class by the way he handled Alabama's final bowl trip to Pasadena.

"There's a great coach," USC coach Jeff Cravath said, pointing toward Thomas. "I'll never forget what he did today. If he had wanted to name the score he could have."

If only regaining his health had been that easy for Thomas. Instead of renewing his strength in the off season, he found himself growing more and more tired and battling the effects of dangerously high blood pressure.

He tried to fight high blood pressure by watching his diet, giving up cigarettes and getting more rest. Despite his best intentions, he was forced to give up many of his civic-related business and charitable interests. Thomas also spent the summer visiting with medical specialists in North Carolina and attempted to follow a strict rice diet. He even spent most of the 1946 season in bed and got out of bed to conduct many practices while riding in a trailer because he could no longer stand for long periods of time.

No matter what he did to follow his doctor's orders or how hard he pushed himself to be the coach he had always been, it wasn't enough to allow him to continue coaching like he wanted to.

"It was my hardest and least enjoyable season," Thomas said after a 7-4 finish in 1946.

On the Wednesday before the season came to an end, Thomas met with University president Dr. Raymond Paty who encouraged him to resign for the sake of his health, promising Thomas he could continue as athletic director. At age 48, Thomas retired from coaching, a decision he would always regret.

"I have thought a million times since what a foolish decision I made," Thomas said.

Thomas's health deteriorated slowly but surely, eventually forcing him to resign as athletic director. In 1951, he became a charter member of the College Football Hall of Fame. On May 10, 1954, Thomas died in Druid City Hospital in Tuscaloosa.

His legacy, however, remains very much alive. Even as the men who played for "Coach Tommy" grow older and pass on, Thomas's role in Alabama's winning tradition remains unshakeable.

"We know Coach Thomas was not well, but he was not the kind of man to complain or quit," Hal Self, Alabama's quarterback in 1954-56, said in *Bowl Bama Bowl*. "He was some fellow. Even when he was sick, he worked hard until he could work no more. We all loved him for it, too."

PAUL "BEAR" BRYANT

COACH 1958-1982

Time has a way of turning simple men into mythological heroes. It also has a way of tearing down statues and reducing heroes to rubble. History scholars know Abraham Lincoln wasn't nearly the valiant icon he is made out to be, especially when it came to matters of racial equality. Over time, John F. Kennedy's legacy has been tarnished by infidelity and deception. Somewhere in the vast gray landscape between god and mortal man, both men rose to celebrated heights of fame, with their strengths and weaknesses in tow.

Such was the case for Paul William "Bear" Bryant, widely regarded as a god in college football circles and throughout the South. Some even capitalized the G and believed that, yes, he really did walk on water. Yet, more than 20 years after his death, it's all too easy to latch on to his faults and mistakes and wonder if he was something less than who and what he appeared to be.

He could be mean and harsh, with a tongue that could slash and gut anyone who crossed or disappointed him. He smoked excessively, drank too much at times and was often driven to extremes by his obsession with winning. He could be cold, calculating and cutthroat, as well as mysterious, aloof and arrogant. He could also be tender, gentle, humble, charming, charitable and compassionate and often times directed acts of kindness to former players, players' families and fans with quiet and unassuming dignity.

Like most men, he wrestled with demons and genuinely believed in God. Somewhere in between the length, width and breadth of his accomplishments and the depths of his imperfections, Bryant is seen, through the hearts and mind of his players, coaches and coaching peers, as a man who rose above other men in a way that inspired, drove and lifted many, conquered some and intimidated others.

"I'm just a simple plow hand from Arkansas," Bryant once said, "but I have learned over the years how to hold a team together. How to lift some men up, how to calm others down, until finally they've got one heartbeat, together, a team."

With all due respect to Eddie Robinson, Joe Paterno and Bobby Bowden, three coaches who went on to win more games than Bryant in their careers, no college football coach built winning football teams better than Bryant, whose list of accomplishments almost requires its own chapter.

As a head coach for 38 seasons, Bryant broke Amos Alonzo Stagg's record of 314 victories and eventually finished with 323. From 1958 to 1982 at the University of Alabama, Bryant's teams won national championships in 1961, 1964, 1965, 1973, 1978 and 1979, and 13 Southeastern Conference titles. Under Bryant, Alabama earned 25 winning seasons and played in 24 consecutive bowls, including seven Sugar Bowls, five Orange Bowls and four Cotton Bowls. It's no wonder Bryant once said, "I ain't nothing but a winner."

Bryant himself was selected the National Coach of the Year three times, and the SEC Coach of the Year 10 times. In three seasons as a Crimson Tide player, six years as an assistant coach at Alabama and Vanderbilt, one year as the head coach at Maryland, eight years as the Kentucky head coach, four years at Texas A&M and 25 years at Alabama, he finished 384-100-25, for a winning percentage of .799.

Three former coaches, Bum Phillips, Duffy Daugherty and Jake Gaither, have been cred-

ited with a famous saying about Bryant, but regardless of the source the statement proved to be all too true, "He can take his'n' and beat you'rn', and he can take you'rn' and beat his'n'."

It didn't take long for Bryant to separate himself from the pack as a child, even as the youngest boy in a family of 12 in the utter poverty of rural Arkansas. He was born on September 11, 1913, in Moro Bottom, a three-square mile plot of land where seven families lived near Moro Creek in southern Arkansas.

His father, William Monroe Bryant, tried to farm but was often ill. His mother, Ida Kilgore Bryant, must have been somebody special, because Bryant said, "I was a mama's boy." In fact, when he filmed a commercial for South Central Bell in which the script called for him to say, "Call your mama," Bryant drew on the memory of his late mother and added his own ad lib, "I wish I could call mine." His addition made the final cut.

In 1924, the family moved to nearby Fordyce, a town of 3,600 people, and Bryant quickly developed a reputation as a rugged young man willing to fight and able to win. When he was 14 he wrestled a bear at a carnival and earned a nickname that became both a symbol and moniker throughout his life. He went on to play in the first football game he ever saw and had cleats screwed into the only shoes he owned, and wore them everywhere he went.

Bryant found his way to Tuscaloosa in the rumble seat of Alabama assistant coach Hank Crisp's Ford in 1931, and even though he wasn't much for school, he knew how to succeed in other fields. He went on to become student body president and married one of the most popular girls on campus, Mary Harmon Black, in June of 1935, even though coach Frank Thomas forbid his players to marry during their playing careers. Bryant simply kept the marriage a secret and went on about the business of becoming a hard-nosed player who played with a broken leg during his senior season. All-American Don Hutson may have been the Crimson Tide end with all the glory, but Bryant, at six foot three, 210 pounds, was a tough cuss who knew how to block, tackle and win.

"I'll never forget going to the Rose Bowl," Bryant said, speaking of the 1935 Rose Bowl when the Tide beat Stanford and won the national championship. "I remember everything about it. We were on the train and Coach Thomas was talking to three coaches and Red Heard, the athletic director at LSU. Coach Thomas said, 'Red, this is my best football player. This is the best player on my team.' Well, shoot, I could have gone right out the top. He was getting me ready. And I was, too. I would have gone out there and killed myself for Alabama that day."

Those qualities were so obvious to Thomas that he helped Bryant get into the coaching business by sending him up to Union College in Jackson, Tennessee in 1936, to install Alabama's version of the Notre Dame box offense. The job only paid $170 a month, but Bryant knew he wanted to coach and he had to support a wife who by then was pregnant with their first child, Mae Martin. At the time even a little money was better than the unsteady life offered by pro football, so Bryant took the job. Later that year, a spot opened up on Thomas's staff and Bryant returned to Tuscaloosa at $1,250 a year.

Bryant spent four years learning his trade, even to the point of giving his players bruising lessons in blocking and tackling, but eventually became tired of being the lowest man on Thomas's totem pole. In 1939 he left for Vanderbilt, where coach Red Sanders gave him a raise and more responsibility. After two seasons he was all set to become the 28-year-old head coach at Arkansas until World War II got in the way. Bryant spent his service time in the Navy, and even though he did go overseas he served most of his time in a fitness program and coached the football program at North Carolina Preflight in Chapel Hill.

By the time the war was over, Bryant was convinced he was ready to become a head football coach. When Maryland gave him that chance in 1945 he brought 17 Navy players with him and they went 6-2-1. "You had to have something inside you to play for Coach Bryant," Maryland quarterback Vuc Turyn said in Coach: The Life of Paul "Bear" Bryant. "He wasn't interested in how much talent you had. He wanted to know if you were willing to throw everything you had on that practice field every day. He was going to push you until you either became a player or you quit."

Enough players bought into Bryant's methods that the Terps probably would have been even better the next year if Maryland president Curly Byrd hadn't angered Bryant by firing one assistant coach and allowing a player to return to the team after Bryant kicked the player off for a rules violation.

Bryant quit, despite having a wife and two children, but his gamble quickly paid off when Kentucky came calling with an immediate offer via telegram. Bryant's impact in Lexington was just as immediate. When former NFL and

Kentucky standout George Blanda first saw Bryant walk into a team meeting, he remembers thinking, "This must be what God looks like. He'd walk into the room and you wanted to stand up and applaud."

Bryant gave the Wildcats plenty to applaud. In eight years at Kentucky Bryant did things no Kentucky coach has ever done, before or since, by going 60-23-5 and taking the Wildcats to four bowls and the school's first SEC championship. During that time Bryant came to realize he would never be more important at Kentucky than basketball coach Adolph Rupp and started looking around. He almost became the Arkansas coach in 1952, but eventually left for Texas A&M in February 1954, based on a phone interview and a gentlemen's agreement.

It was at Texas A&M where Bryant took his first team off to a dusty old army base near the remote town of Junction, Texas, for a preseason war of attrition that saw more than 100 players arrive and only 29 return to form Bryant's first team. The 10-day test of fortitude has since been the subject of a melodramatic ESPN movie. The movie often stumbles over its factual inaccuracies, particularly its portrayal of Bryant as callous and inhumane, but the demands were very real for the players.

"It became a test of your physical and mental endurance," said Jack Pardee, who went on to become a star linebacker in the NFL and the head coach of the Houston Oilers. "It was hot as hell and it was as demanding as hell ... and some guys just couldn't take it."

The ones who could take it won only one game that fall. They went on, however, to form the foundation of a team that went 7-2-1 in 1955 and 9-0-1 in 1956, beating archrival Texas

34-21 and winning the Southwest Conference title. Bryant's 1957 team won its first eight games and climbed to No. 1 in the nation when rumors started to fly about the possibility of losing Bryant to Alabama. With the Crimson Tide well on its way to a 2-7-1 record, the speculation was all too logical for folks on both sides. Incoming University President Frank Rose, former Tide standout Fred Sington (then president of the Alabama Alumni Association) and athletic committee chairman Ernest Williams met with Bryant on the sly in Houston, but the secret nature of the meeting didn't last long. By the time the day-long meeting ended, both sides had come to an agreement that Bryant would be the football coach and athletic director, and reporters were waiting outside the door.

While the news was greeted with enthusiasm back in Alabama, it hit hard in College Station, and the Aggies went on to lose their next game 7-6 at Rice. A&M would finish the season with an 8-3 record, including a 9-7 loss to Texas and 3-0 loss to Tennessee in the Gator Bowl, but it was too late to turn back the clock. Bryant would always resent losing a chance at winning the national championship that year, but he didn't spend much time looking back. As he said when he announced his move to Alabama, "Mama called," and mama was not to be denied.

Neither was Bryant. If anyone thought 10 days in Junction was hellacious, Bryant took his new team to another level of stringent demands throughout the first half of 1958, starting with a grueling off-season conditioning program. Players knew they were in trouble when they entered the gymnasium at the top floor of Friedman Hall and found the walls lined with garbage buckets for vomiting. Once again, Bryant set about separating the survivors from the rest of the players who had gone 4-24-2 in three seasons under J.B. "Ears" Whitworth.

Lineman Dave Sington recalled, "He told us, 'I'm not worried about whether I'm going to win or lose. I know I'm going to win. I know that. And I'm not worried about my assistant coaches. I know they're winners. And I'm not worried about whether Alabama is going to win. I know that. The only thing I don't know is how many of you in this room are winners, and how many of you will be with us.'"

Bryant wasn't cruel for the sake of his ego or reputation. He knew Alabama needed a major change in attitude, starting at the top and permeating throughout the coaching staff, the support staff, the players and facilities. As guard Don Parsons had said after encountering Bryant for the first time at a team meeting, "He looked like a man on a mission, and before he reached the front of the room you could sense that everyone was beginning to feel new hope."

Bryant didn't waste any time feeling sorry for his new players or worrying about the ones who left the program. Instead he turned his attention to a freshman class that included future Alabama standouts Pat Trammell, Billy Neighbors, Tommy Booker, Jimmy Sharpe, Bill Rice, John O'Linger and Billy Richardson.

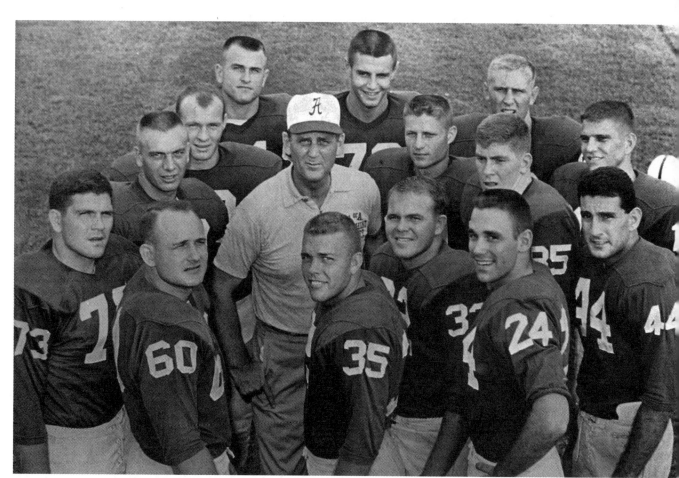

Coach Paul "Bear" Bryant and his seniors in 1961

Four veterans had showed up late for Bryant's first team meeting months before, only to be kicked out of the meeting. When the freshman arrived for their first meeting with their new coach, they all showed up on time.

Bryant advised them to call their mamas and write home at least once a week, and then issued both a warning and a promise.

"Look around at the guys sitting next to you," he said. "Chances are, four years from now, there's probably going to be no more than a double handful of you left. But if you work hard and do the things I ask you to do, you can be national champions by the time you're seniors."

The change in attitude would be almost immediate, but the change in Alabama's football fortunes would take some time and recruiting. Bryant's first Alabama team went 5-4-1 and failed to play in a bowl only because Bryant was dissatisfied with an offer to play in the first Bluegrass Bowl in Louisville. Bryant would later regret his decision not to play in the bowl, only because it would have offered his team more practice time, but it was the only time his teams would ever finish a season without a bowl trip.

The next year the Tide improved to 7-2-2, but lost 7-0 to Penn State in the Liberty Bowl. The Tide followed with an 8-1-1 season in 1960 with a 3-3 tie with Texas in the Bluebonnet Bowl. All of this set the stage to fulfill Bryant's promise to his first recruiting class.

"In 1961 we had the best team in college football," Bryant said. "We had 16 or 17 players, the nut of the team, and all 16 or 17 were leaders."

Led by junior linebacker Lee Roy Jordan, Alabama allowed only 25 points in 1961. The offense, led by Trammell, scored 297 and the Crimson Tide finished 11-0, beating Arkansas 10-3 in the Sugar Bowl and winning Alabama's first national AP championship and the program's first national title of any kind since 1941. Bryant also earned National Coach of the Year honors.

"Regardless of who was coaching them, they still would have been a great team," Bryant said. "I said early in the season that they were the nicest, even the sissiest bunch I've ever had. I think they read it, because later on they got unfriendly."

The season put Alabama back on the national map and put Bryant at the top of the coaching world, two places where the Tide and Bryant would spend most of the next 21 seasons.

It didn't take long for Bryant and the Tide to return to the national championship scene again, winning it all in 1964 and 1965. Alabama followed with a 12-10-1 "slump" in 1969-70 that had Tide fans wondering if Bryant had passed his prime and led Bryant to accept the Miami Dolphins head coaching job for a few hours before he changed his mind. Instead, Bryant dug in, made the necessary adjustments, switched to the wishbone offense and led the Tide to three more national titles in 1973, 1978 and 1979.

If Bryant was past his prime, it didn't show on the field in 1978 and 1979, especially when the Tide made its infamous goal-line stand to beat Penn State 14-7 in the 1979 Sugar Bowl.

"There's only one team that could have made those plays, and that was Alabama," Bryant said. "There was only one team that could have stopped Penn State on the goal line, and that team was Alabama. It was a time of champions."

Bryant's era was an era of champions for Alabama, a time when the Crimson Tide became synonymous with winning, both in the sports world and college football. In the college football world, he held a special place among coaches and fans, even the ones he beat on a regular basis. Those who hated or feared him still respected him, and those who admired him often did so with a certain distance reserved for American heroes such as Douglas MacArthur and John Wayne.

"Even his peers in the coaching business felt in awe of him," Paterno told author Keith Dunnavant in *Coach: The Life of Paul "Bear" Bryant*. "He had such charisma. Whatever it is that makes great generals, he had it. Tons of it. He was just a giant figure."

He remained a giant figure among his assistant coaches and players throughout his life, during both the good times and the tough times. No one demanded more of his coaches and players than Bryant, but it didn't diminish their respect or reverence for him.

"Whatever he had, whatever it was, he had a lot of it," said Mal Moore, who played and coached under Bryant and now serves as Alabama's athletic director. "He had something about him that people simply didn't have or don't have."

Some of what Bryant had was simply his ability to intimidate and impose his will on people. Defensive back Tommy Wilcox, who played for Alabama from 1979-82, remembers a game in which Mississippi State quarterback John Bond was running all over the Tide in the first half using the option. Bryant came in at halftime, approached the chalkboard and told defensive coordinator Ken Donahue what changes needed to be made.

"Coach Donahue looked at him and said, 'Coach, we don't have that defense,'" Wilcox recalled. "Coach Bryant said, 'you've got about 10 minutes to find it' and turned around and walked away."

Donahue not only made the necessary adjustments, but the Tide went on to shut Bond and the Bulldogs down in the second half and win the game 20-12. Further proof that when Bryant spoke, mountains moved or the earth stood still for Crimson Tide coaches and players.

"We were scared to death of him," said John Hannah, an All-America tackle in 1971-72 who went on to become one of the greatest offensive linemen in NFL history and a member of the pro and college halls of fame. "We always said you could always tell an assistant coach at Alabama because he had one eye on the field and one on the tower.

"We were practicing one day and Coach Bryant fell asleep in the tower and we kept on practicing and practicing and finally the horn fell off his leg and made a sound and he woke up and said, 'Take it in.' On the way in [running back Johnny] Musso looked at me and said, 'Damn, I'm glad he wasn't dead. We'd have never gotten off the field.'...

"He was tough. He was a great man and I admire him and love him, but let's call a spade a spade."

Defensive lineman Marty Lyons remembers a game in which Alabama beat Southern Miss decisively, only to have Bryant walk into the locker room and say, "I don't know what you guys are celebrating for. You embarrassed the red jerseys."

"I was rooming with [defensive lineman] Bob [Baumhower] then and I said, 'Bob, didn't we just win?' Coach Bryant made us go out the very next day and play the game completely over.

"He talked about the people who made those red jerseys proud and told us we had a responsibility to wear them the same way and he held everyone accountable for wearing them that way."

Yet, for all of the fear he struck in the hearts of coaches and players, Bryant somehow managed to inspire intense devotion and loyalty from those same people. Quarterback Ken Stabler remembers how he would just stare at Bryant, walking on the field, entering the locker room, and just being intimidated by his mere presence.

"There was something about him ... that was different from everybody that made us always want to please him," Stabler said. "You'd do anything you could to make him slap you on the ass and say, 'Way to go' or recognize you in front of the rest of the team."

That desire to please Bryant was evident in the way his players practiced and played.

"People always ask, 'What is it like to play for Coach Bryant?' It's hard to explain that unless you've been around him and seen the effect he had on people," Stabler said. "We would play teams that were always bigger, always faster, always more of them and we always won. That was because of Coach Bryant. He outcoached the other guy. He outmotivated the other guy."

Only age and failing health could dim Bryant's impact. From 1980-82, Bryant's teams won 27 games, lost eight and tied one and won one more SEC championship, but his health

and age were starting to work against him, especially in recruiting.

"Coaching is a young man's game," Bryant said before the 1982 season. "You never see old men winning championships. All these people are recruiting better than we are."

Bryant eventually found he could no longer look a recruit in the eye and promise he would be there throughout the player's career. Opposing programs, especially Auburn and its new coach, former Alabama assistant Pat Dye, were telling recruits that Bryant's days were numbered.

"There's no telling how many good players we lost with that line," said Clem Gryska, Alabama's recruiting coordinator and an assistant from 1960-76.

"Kids wanted to play for him, but they were afraid he would retire while they were playing."

It had to happen someday, and that fateful day he decided to retire finally came in 1982. Years of smoking, drinking, stress and long hours were taking their toll on his health, and with Stagg's record having fallen, Bryant appeared to be running out of goals and the energy to pursue them. In his later years, he had become more reflective on religion and family. He let his veteran coaching staff do more of the coaching and delegated more and more authority.

On December 15, 1982, two weeks after Alabama closed out its regular season with a 23-22 loss to Auburn and Dye, Bryant sent shockwaves across Alabama, and the national college football landscape, by announcing his retirement, his intention of staying on as athletic director for a few more months and the hiring of former Alabama wide receiver Ray

Perkins as head coach.

"There comes a time in every profession when you need to hang it up," Bryant said. "And that time has come."

Perhaps the only thing more disappointing for Bryant than retiring was the painful knowledge that Alabama's president, Dr. Joab Thomas, refused his input and his recommendations for a new coach. Suddenly, the most successful coach in college football was no longer wanted and needed by an administration who ignored him when he suggested it hire one or two former assistants, Gene Stallings or Mal Moore.

Bryant coached one more game, leading Alabama to an emotional 21-15 victory over Illinois in the Liberty Bowl. He tried to deflect the sentiment of the moment by saying, "We won in spite of me," but his players and coaches had fought their hearts out for him one more time, knowing they would never get another chance.

Now Bryant had to face something he had not encountered since he was a boy back in Arkansas: life without football. He had once joked that he'd "croak in a week" without coaching. Unfortunately for those who loved him, he came painfully close to fulfilling that prediction.

Unbeknownst to all but his closest confidants, Bryant had suffered a minor stroke and heart failure in the previous three years. When he was rushed to Druid City Hospital complaining of chest pains on the evening of January 25, 1983, doctors intended to keep him overnight for observation and release him the next day.

On the morning of the 26th he visited with Perkins and gave him a hard time for visiting him when Perkins should have been out recruiting. He also made sure the son of a former Kentucky player would receive a University of Alabama scholarship under the plan Bryant established and funded. That afternoon he was sitting up in bed eating lunch when he went into cardiopulmonary arrest at 12:24. By 1:30 p.m., he was pronounced dead.

On January 28, Bryant was laid to rest at Elmwood Cemetery in Birmingham. Eight players from his final team—Tommy Wilcox, Paul Ott Carruth, Walter Lewis, Jerrill Sprinkle, Mike McQueen, Paul Fields, Jeremiah Castille and Darryl White—served as the pallbearers.

"He literally coached himself to death," former Ohio State head coach Woody Hayes said at the funeral. "He was our greatest coach."

At age 69, Bryant's death left a gaping hole in the state of Alabama, the University of Alabama and in his coaches and players that has never been filled. Coaches will come and go, but time continues to prove that Bryant was truly one of a kind.

It's easy to remember him now for his hard-nosed approach, his demands for discipline and his intimidating persona. For former players and coaches, though, he's more likely to be remembered for the way he loved his own, long after they had left Alabama.

In addition to establishing the Bryant Scholarship, he also brought the Alabama football program into a new era of integration in 1971, at a time when the state needed someone of prominence to point the way to the future.

"No one has done more to promote racial harmony in Alabama than Bryant," Auburn University history professor Wayne Flint wrote in *Alabama: The History of a Deep South State*.

Coaches still recall how he demanded total loyalty but didn't want "yes men." He wanted them to speak their minds, and if they could better their lives and careers by becoming a coordinator or head coach, he was often the first to support their decision.

Players recall surprise visits to pro football training camps, as well as telephone calls and telegrams to congratulate them on important events or accomplishments. When they returned to Tuscaloosa for visits, he treated them like long-lost sons.

"Coach Bryant was the most tenderhearted man I've ever been around," said longtime Alabama trainer Jim Goosetree, who passed away in 1999. "But he didn't want anyone to know it."

Sometimes he couldn't help himself. Baumhower, who played for Bryant from 1974-76 and then went on to a successful NFL career with the Miami Dolphins, returned to Tuscaloosa to watch spring practice after his rookie year. When Bryant spotted Baumhower down below, he told him to climb the tower. Baumhower was wary of whatever fate await-

ed him at the top, but when he arrived he witnessed a different side of Bryant than he was accustomed to.

"He started asking all these questions. He wanted to know how my mom and dad were doing, if they were still in this business, still doing this, still doing that," Baumhower said. "I was amazed at how much he knew about things I had no idea he knew about. He even asked me, 'Are you still dating that cheerleader?' I said, 'Yeah Coach, we're still seeing each other. She comes down to see me in Miami every once in a while. She's living up in Memphis now.'

"Before I could finish he said, 'I know where the hell she's living. Who do you think helped her get that job up there?' He knew all about who I was dating. He knew about my family. He knew so much that I didn't know about and that impressed me so much because you didn't see that as a player. You didn't know how closely he followed you.

"Then I saw the other side. He really, really cared about us. He kept up with us. We'd get notes from him, or phone calls. That was really, really special. He really cared. Coach Bryant just had that knack."

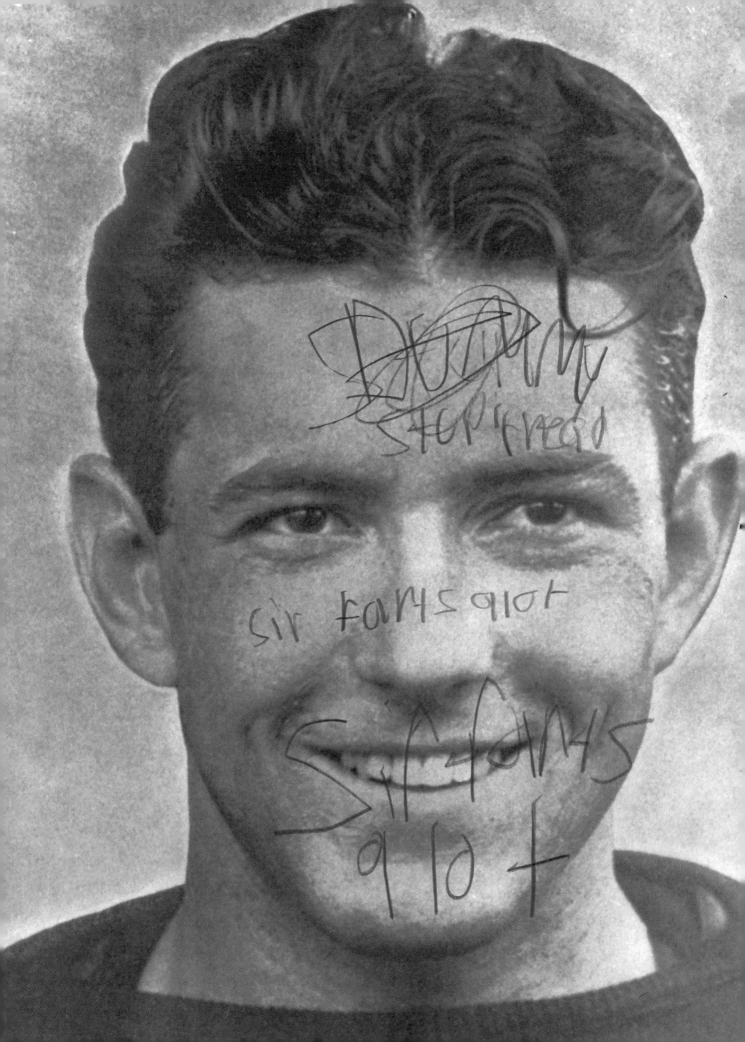

JOHNNY MACK BROWN

HALFBACK 1923-1925

The Alabama players who made the monumental trip to California for the Rose Bowl in December 1925 became instant celebrities with local reporters and photographers, eager to see the rugged young rubes from far-off Alabama. For most of those players, the fleeting fame of Hollywood lasted only as long as their trip to Pasadena and had to be packed away in suitcases and trunks for the long haul home.

For two Tide standouts, backs A.T.S. "Pooley" Hubert and Johnny Mack Brown, the flashbulbs burned more frequently on that trip. For one, the fame lasted a lifetime—and beyond.

"Hubert and [Johnny] Mack Brown will have enough experience posing for the cameramen to enter the movies after their stay here," wrote Zipp Newman of *The Birmingham News*.

Newman turned out to be prophetic about a handsome halfback Brown, who rode his Rose Bowl stardom to a lengthy career as a silver screen cowboy.

In the days of Gene Autry, Roy Rogers and Hopalong Cassidy, when any kid with a nickel could walk down to the theatre on a Saturday and see two "dusties," a serial and maybe a cartoon or two, Brown rode the range as a cinematic hero, mostly in B-movies.

Today, the connection between Hollywood and Dothan, Alabama, is as convenient as a trip to the local Movie Gallery for a DVD rental. But in 1904, when Johnny Mack Brown was born to clothing merchants John Henry and Hattie Brown, Dothan was a far cry from the current corporate home of retail giant Movie Gallery.

Brown, the second son among nine Brown children, took to hunting, fishing and a variety of sports at an early age, graduated from Dothan High School in 1922 and moved on to the University of Alabama, becoming the first of four brothers to play football for the Crimson Tide.

Brown's first season at the Capstone only hinted at the greatness to come. Playing under first-year coach Wallace Wade, the Tide won seven of 10 games in 1923 and Brown contributed his only touchdown in a 55-0 runaway over Ole Miss. His biggest play of the season actually came on defense when he set up the winning touchdown in a 7-0 victory over Sewanee with an interception in the closing minutes of the game.

"The Dothan Antelope" shared the ball with a crowded backfield as a junior in 1924, but despite the presence of talented backs such as Hubert, Andy Cohen and Dave Rosenfeld, Brown still scored nine touchdowns as Alabama won eight games and lost just one. He also proved to be one of the key differences between victory and defeat in many of those games, including a 99-yard kickoff return for a touchdown against Kentucky, a 65-yard interception return for a touchdown against Georgia and an interception return of 58 yards against Furman.

It's no wonder longtime Alabama assistant Hank Crisp said of Brown, "I don't know what kind of step he has, but it's something to see. He can jump sideways and still not lose forward speed. One man will not hem him in."

That continued to be true in 1925 as Brown and Hubert led the way to Alabama's first undefeated season. In Alabama's biggest regular-season game of the year, Brown's teammates cleared a path on a punt return by knocking down all 11 defenders and a referee, with Hubert himself putting two Georgia

Tech players on the ground. Brown did the rest, racing 55 yards for the only score in a 7-0 win that helped convince Rose Bowl officials to invite the Tide west.

"I could have walked into the end zone," Brown said.

Five weeks later in Pasadena, on New Year's Day, 1926, Brown ran into history by scoring two of his team's touchdowns in a 20-19 "upset" of highly favored Washington.

The outcome shocked West Coast fans and reporters, but it came as no surprise to Wade and his players.

"We were nothing but little country boys in our sophomore year, but Coach Wade made something out of us and to the Rose Bowl we went," Brown later told Rube Samuelsen, author of the 1951 book, *The Rose Bowl Game*.

Not only were the Tide players not intimidated by their surroundings or the predictions that accompanied their Christmas Eve arrival, but they were less than enamored with the growing legend surrounding Washington star George Wilson.

At first, Brown told Samuelsen, the players were "suckered in" by all the Wilson hype, but Brown wasn't buying it.

"Superman, my eye," Brown said. "He's only one guy, isn't he?"

Brown was only one guy, too, but he also had players such as Hubert, Grant Gillis, Hoyt "Wu" Winslett and Bill Buckler on his side. It was Brown, however, who helped spark Alabama's comeback from a 12-0 halftime deficit. Hubert got Alabama moving with the Tide's first touchdown before Brown struck, hauling in a long pass from Gillis at the 25-yard line and racing the rest of the way for a 63-yard touchdown.

"All I had to was sidestep one man and I was across," Brown said.

Brown's second touchdown came one play after Alabama recovered a fumble on the Washington 33-yard line. Hubert pointed to Brown in the huddle and told him to run as fast as he could toward the goal line. Brown did just that, and Hubert did the rest.

"When I reached the three, I looked up," Brown said. "Sure enough, the ball was coming down over my shoulder. I took it in stride, used my stiff arm on one man, and went over carrying somebody. The place was really in an uproar."

The Tide, Brown in particular, finally convinced the critics who had doubted Southern football.

"That Mack Brown was all they said of him and more," Wilson said. "He was about the fastest man in a football suit I have bumped up against."

Seattle newspaper reporter George Vernall, who also served as head linesman during the game, said, "Johnny Mack Brown has the sweetest pair of feet I have ever seen."

The *Denver Post* wrote, "A figure in football that is a flash, Brown could carry a ball through any team on earth. Great speed, wonderful side stepping and at the same time that persistent Alabama interference. There are few more attractive players."

Ed Danforth of *The Atlanta Journal* also wrote, "The South will outdo itself in welcoming Mack Brown home. It should. He has written Dixie all over California."

While it would be fun, and probably more interesting, to believe the myth that Brown was quickly whisked away by Hollywood talent scouts to the nearest studio following the game, the truth is that he returned to Alabama with his team and became an assistant coach before the movie business gave him a shot.

Professional football was a possibility for Brown, but Champ Pickens, an Alabama alumnus who also happened to be a promoter and author, had bigger, better visions for Brown than a brief career in the fledgling pro leagues of the era.

Brown had already split some of his time on the Alabama campus between the football field and bit parts in university theatrical productions, and had already caught the eye of one Hollywood insider. During Brown's senior season, Alabama played Kentucky in Birmingham around the same time a movie company was filming a movie called *Men of Steel*. Several members of the production company received sideline passes to the game, including actor-director George Fawcett. He was immediately impressed with Brown, met with him after the game and offered to arrange a screen test. Brown turned down the opportunity, but his curiosity got the best of him a year later when Alabama returned to California for the 1927 Rose Bowl.

Brown, then a part-time assistant at Alabama, an insurance agent and newly married to his college sweetheart, the former Connie Foster, accompanied the team to California at the request of Pickens. He produced a favorable screen test, signed a movie contract with MGM and soon landed a part in his first movie, a silent movie titled *Bugle Call*. He earned several more supporting roles before he received his first starring role opposite silent screen star Mary Pickford in *The Coquettes*.

Who knows what a serious disciplinarian such as Wade must have thought of one of his best players becoming an actor, but Wade was said to have quipped, "He has to make a living doing something."

Early in his career Brown dabbled for a time in dramas, romances and comedies, but when silence turned to sound, Brown's rugged good looks and Southern accent made him a natural for Westerns. In the heyday of Westerns, Brown went on to star in more than 160 films over 40 years, mostly as a cowboy hero willing and able to fight injustice. He even brought out the best of the title character in *Billy The Kid*, a 1930 movie that held its world premier at the Bama Theatre in Tuscaloosa.

"In contrast to an array of jolly, happy-go-lucky singing cowpokes," wrote University of Alabama English professor Philip Beidler, "Mack Brown's character image was always

From left: Assistant coach Hank Crisp, Johnny Mack Brown and coach Wallace Wade

one of a rough, tough, no-nonsense hero, eager to bring about justice with a quick fist or trigger finger."

Over the course of his career, Brown appeared in movies with well-known stars such as John Wayne, Wallace Beery, Greta Garbo and Joan Crawford. Away from the big screen, Brown was considered a Southern gentleman who knew how to treat people, both the famous and those behind the scenes. Following the completion of a movie, he was known for telling members of the crew, "Thanks for letting me make this film with you."

None of this would come as a surprise to those who knew him at Alabama. Winslett once told *The Tuscaloosa News*, "The beautiful part about Johnny Mack was his attitude. He knew he was a great football player, but he was the most humble individual I have ever been around. There was no arrogance about him, absolutely no egotism.

"After he left Alabama and became famous he never forgot all of us folks back home. I admired him for that."

Brown continued to make Alabama proud of him throughout his life, even taking time to scout Stanford before the 1935 Rose Bowl.

He met the team in New Mexico armed with charts and diagrams and Alabama went on to win 29-13 on its way to a 10-0 season and the school's fourth national championship.

Brown also attended the legendary 1971 Alabama-USC game at the Los Angeles Coliseum in which the Tide unveiled the wishbone and upset the Trojans 17-10. Brown had become a regular fan of USC football by that time, but his heart wasn't divided that day.

"I'm very loyal to USC," he said before the game, "but in this game I'm an Alabama man."

Alabama's first true national football star went on to receive both a star on the Hollywood Boulevard Walk of Fame and induction into the College Football Hall of Fame, as well as a place in the Rose Bowl Hall of Fame. Brown died in 1974, leaving behind a wife, four children and an impressive legacy as both a football player and movie star.

"Am I surprised Johnny Mack made it big?" Winslett said. "You know, I am. I knew he was something special in football, but I had no idea he could do much of anything else. Johnny Mack made us all mighty proud of him."

Johnny Mack Brown (left) and Pooley Hubert

A.T.S. "POOLEY" HUBERT

FULLBACK 1922-1925

There he is, in a wrinkled black-and-white photo from 1925 buried in the archive files at the University of Alabama's Coleman Coliseum. Despite the fact that the wrinkle runs right across his face and through his shoulders, he's easy to spot. He's right there in the foreground, the one player in the backfield with no helmet. His jaw is set firm, his eyes set on fierce and determined and his shoulders squared for impact as he surges forward to make the lead block on a sweep.

He is Allison Thomas Stanislaus Hubert, better known to his teammates, family, friends and history as "Pooley," Alabama's second All-American and one of the primary reasons why Alabama emerged as a national college football power in the 1920s.

In his four years at quarterback, fullback, linebacker and defensive back for Alabama, Hubert led the Crimson Tide to some of the most significant wins in the early history of the program, including the 1926 Rose Bowl victory over Washington that put Alabama on the national map.

"He was the greatest player I ever coached in over 40 years," said Hank Crisp, longtime Alabama assistant coach and athletic director. "There was never a more fierce competitor. He was a born leader and at his very best when the going was tough. He was just as good on defense as offense."

Born in 1901, Hubert's versatile skills and overall ability made him a natural prospect when he graduated from high school in Meridian, Mississippi. Life and the United States Army had other plans for Hubert, though, so he served in World War I before he returned and turned his attention toward college and football.

Princeton offered Hubert a scholarship, but he arrived too late to prepare for entrance exams. With Princeton off his list, Hubert changed directions and headed south for Virginia for a couple of weeks, but found he didn't particularly like it. His next choice was Georgia Tech, where Hubert said he "stayed around for two or three days, but I was too late and they didn't let freshmen play."

Instead of running Pooley off, Tech coach Bill Alexander did something that would be unheard of today: he recommended Hubert try the University of Georgia. Alexander's suggestion seemed like a good idea until Pooley ran into a transportation problem.

"I asked him if the Southern Railway went to Athens and he said no," Pooley said. "So I asked him what was the next school on the Southern and he said Alabama."

Hubert arrived at Alabama as a tackle until Crisp saw something special in the 20-year-old freshman and moved him to the backfield, where he could take more of an on-field leadership role. His first game in the backfield came in Alabama's historic 9-7 win at Penn in 1922.

Hubert lettered as a freshman, but his combination of age and athleticism finally kicked into a higher gear during his sophomore season, coach Wallace Wade's first at Alabama. By the time he was a 24-year-old senior he was known among his teammates as "Papa Pooley."

As Alabama's field general, Pooley did most of the Crimson Tide's passing and stood out so notably on defense that southern writers considered him "the greatest defensive back ever." With his running and passing, Hubert led the Crimson Tide to a 31-6-2 record from 1922-25, scored 38 touchdowns, served as captain, was twice selected All-Southern

Conference and earned All-America honors in 1925. In Alabama's 7-0 defeat of Georgia Tech in 1925, Hubert paved the way for Johnny Mack Brown's 55-yard punt return for a touchdown by knocking two Georgia Tech players to the ground, propelling Alabama to its first Rose Bowl game.

For all of the attention West Coast football fans and writers focused on Brown, Hubert's flashier teammate, most knowledgeable sportswriters of the time quickly surmised the Alabama-Washington match up as a battle between Hubert and Husky All-American George Wilson.

It was Wilson who got the better end of the confrontation in the first half, as Washington took a 12-0 lead into halftime as Alabama appeared to be living up to its pre-game role as a lightly regarded underdog to the more reputable Huskies. In *Talk Of The Tide*, Johnny Mack Brown sized up the dire nature of the situation, and Hubert's swift, decisive response.

"I'll never forget coming onto the field and looking up and seeing about 58,000 people at the Rose Bowl," Brown said. "All of the Alabama players were pretty well awestruck by this, and as the game started we fell behind 12-0. Had it not been for Pooley Hubert, the score would have probably been worse than that early in the game.

"Hubert made most of the tackles in the first few minutes. I can still see old Pooley [who was several years older than the rest of the guys on the team] as he made a tackle to save a touchdown and jumped up. His helmet was twisted around, he readjusted it and turned to the ref and said, 'Time out, Mr. Ref!'

"The other 10 of us were squatting there

looking up at the big crowd and not knowing exactly what to do, and we saw Pooley walking toward us with a very businesslike look on his face. He walked up to us and put his hands on his hips and said, 'Now, just what the hell's going on around here!' That somehow resurrected the Alabama team and we got together and managed to play pretty well."

It was Hubert who led the comeback charge. Just 190 pounds at the time, Hubert had been instructed in the first half by Wade to avoid running the ball against Washington's bigger players.

"Pooley, I want you to get in there and run the game as you think it should be run," Wade said. "But don't run with the ball yourself or they'll kill you. Remember, those Washington players once knocked out [Stanford star] Ernie Nevers."

Then again, Nevers didn't have Hoyt "Wu" Winslett on his team. Winslett, so nicknamed by Hubert because of his Asian features, collided with Wilson early in the second half and sent the Washington star to the bench. At that point, Hubert took control of the game with a change of heart from Wade.

"Go ahead Pooley, full steam ahead," Wade told Hubert at halftime. "Run yourself all you want. It's tough out there, but you can handle it."

Handle it he did, leading the Crimson Tide to three quick touchdowns in the next seven minutes. With the ball at the Washington 41-yard line Hubert got his team pointed in the right direction by taking Wade at his

Pooley Hubert scores in the 1926 Rose Bowl.

word, carrying the ball on five consecutive plays for 26, 10, one and three and finally one yard for the touchdown.

Alabama got the ball back quickly and scored just as suddenly when Grant Gillis threw a long pass to Brown, who raced away from the defense for a 63-yard touchdown. With the extra point, Alabama led 14-12.

After Alabama's Ben Ennis recovered a Washington fumble near mid-field, Hubert took over once again, directing Brown to go out for a pass and run as hard and fast as he could toward the goal-line. When Brown reached the three-yard line, he looked up, caught a perfect pass from Hubert and scored to put Alabama ahead 20-12.

Wilson returned to the game and Washington scored another touchdown, but the rules didn't allow for a two-point play at the time. Besides, Hubert wouldn't have

Pooley Hubert (far right, without helmet)

allowed it. By the fourth quarter, he was practically willing the Tide to victory. Jeff Coleman, the longtime business manager for the athletic department, recalled one point in the game in which Hubert pointed directly at Wilson and said, "We're coming right over you!"

"He did it, too," Coleman said.

With the victory, Alabama finished 10-0, earned its first national championship and brought newfound national recognition to Southern football and the state of Alabama. In the process, Hubert secured his place in Alabama football lore.

"Seldom have the spectators at these annual New Year's Day struggles been privileged to see the performance of such marvelous individuals as George Wilson and Pooley Hubert," wrote Paul Lowry of the *Los Angeles Times*. "Nobody made a mistake in naming Wilson an All-American, but how in the world they overlooked Hubert on the first team is a mystery."

As for Hubert, the end result came as no real shock.

"It was quite a surprise that we even had the opportunity to go to the Rose Bowl," Hubert said. "We had some indication that we might get to, but we were afraid to even hope.

"It was a right pleasant trip going out there, but coming home was the best part about it, because we had been out there representing the South. We never thought about losing."

It was that kind of attitude that made Hubert such a special player in the opinion of his coaches and teammates.

Wallace Wade called him "undoubtedly one of the greatest football players of all time. Pooley was the greatest team leader and field general that I ever coached in my long career. I'll never forget my touchdown twins: Hubert, one of the greatest quarterbacks I've ever seen, and Brown, the kid with the hands of a magician."

In the early 1950s, Brown himself said, "Pooley was a great football player and a great leader. I haven't seen Pooley in about 16 years, but if he walked in that door over there, I'd get up and go hug him. I really love that man."

Hubert remained busy with football following his Alabama career, moving on to a semi-pro career in Ironton, Ohio and Ashland, Kentucky, and playing professional football with the New York Yankees of the American Football League, where he called the signals and often blocked for legendary halfback Red Grange.

When his playing career came to an end Hubert turned to coaching, serving as the head coach at Mississippi Southern Teachers College (now Southern Mississippi) from 1931-36 and even coaching the basketball team during that period. He left Mississippi to become the head coach at Virginia Military Institute, where he coached from 1937-46.

When he finally retired from coaching, he moved to Waynesboro, Georgia, where he raised peaches and coached high school football at a local academy. He was the fifth Alabama coach or player to join the College Football Hall of Fame in 1964 and was inducted into the Alabama State Hall of Fame in 1972.

FRED SINGTON

TACKLE 1928-1930

I n a different era, when novelty songs were popular and college football was a bit more innocent, a football player could become famous overnight if someone regaled his triumphs in song.

Such was the case with Fred Sington, who played at Alabama from 1928-30. The irony of Sington's musical claim to fame is that the 1930 song "Football Freddie" by Rudy Valle celebrated his football prowess, but came nowhere close to matching Sington's actual resume.

In real life, Sington was a dominant lineman on both sides of the ball as well as a Phi Beta Kappa student who went on to become a Major League baseball player, a college football assistant, a college football official, the owner of his own sporting goods stores and an active civic leader who tried to squeeze every ounce out of his 88 years.

By the time he died in 1998, Sington appeared to be a member of every charitable, civic and alumni board from Birmingham to Tuscaloosa and his name seemed to be connected to numerous sports- and civic-related awards in the Birmingham metropolitan area. Perhaps it just looked that way because Sington refused to go down without a fight in his later years, much as he had done as a University of Alabama athlete and student. As *Birmingham News* sportswriter Clyde Bolton once wrote, "Fred Sington is a role model for adults."

"I just like to get involved," Sington said in his later years. "I'm proud of my city, my university and my state. I don't mind working to get others to like it, too."

Sington was an easy fellow to like because of his enthusiasm for life and fervor for all things football, especially Alabama football.

Perhaps his love for the university came naturally, given the fact that his father, Max, worked for a popular Birmingham furniture store that installed most of furnishings in the University's Morgan Hall in 1911. Sixteen years later, after a successful four-sport athletic career at Birmingham's Phillips High School, Max and Halley's second son would go on to attend classes in that same building.

Sington's older brother, Herbert, stepped on a nail at age eight and died of lockjaw, so Fred was the first of the Sington children to attend college. At that time, attending the University was a major challenge for a kid with few financial resources, so Sington also played in the band as a freshman in 1927.

"It was purely economic for me," Sington said. "I got to make all the trips and got two tickets for the games. I didn't have a nickel."

Of course, football was Sington's first priority in the fall, and it became quickly obvious that he had a special knack for the game.

"The freshman always ran the other team's plays against the varsity," Sington said. "Ten days prior to the varsity game with Georgia in Birmingham, we played the Georgia freshmen in Rome, Georgia. ... During the first half we were pretty ragged. The game was tied 7-7 at the half.

"Coach [Shorty] Propst was really upset with us. Matter of fact, he wouldn't even take us to the dressing room. He took us over under some bleachers and he was giving us down the country about how we were playing.

"We just looked at each other during Propst's harangue. We knew we were better than that, and I finally stood up and asked to speak. I told Coach Propst that for the past two weeks all the freshman team had done was run Georgia's plays against the Alabama varsity. I said we hadn't run our own plays in so long we'd almost forgotten them. All of the guys were nodding in agreement, and I asked Coach Propst if we could just go out there and run Georgia's plays. After a pause Coach Propst said, 'Let's try it.'"

The result was three quick touchdowns, a one-sided victory for the Alabama freshmen and a new facial scar for handsome young Fred Sington.

"You wore canvas pants with steels staves in those days," he said. "The canvas got torn in one of the Georgia men's pants and the steel stave hit me in the face. It was like a knife and it peeled off half my face.

"Well, a few days later we're having a big pep rally in the lobby of the Tutwiler Hotel [in downtown Birmingham] for the varsity game with Georgia. I'm in the band now, standing there with my white pants and red cloak and saxophone—with my face half ripped off.

"And I hear some guy behind me whisper to somebody, 'Hey, look at that big guy. He ought to be playing football.'"

Sington was at his best on the football field as an active six-foot-two, 230-pound lineman who ranked among the fastest and best overall athletes on the team. He played tackle on defense and made a habit of busting through the line to disrupt plays in the backfield. On offense, he was called the running, or "whipping" guard who pulled out and led the way on sweeps. He was at his best as a senior against Tennessee when Sington spent the entire day harassing Volunteer passer Bobby Dodd, helping Alabama win 18-6.

Performances such as that one led to All-America honors and numerous accolades.

Famed sportswriter Grantland Rice said of Sington, "He was alert, fast, aggressive, and in addition he was capable of many outside duties. Tackles such as Sington rarely come along." Legendary Notre Dame coach Knute Rockne called Sington, "the greatest lineman in the country."

In addition to his talent, Sington was also wiling to pay the price to play for coach Wallace Wade, even though that price was often exceedingly high for Alabama players. Of the 128 players who came to Alabama with Sington in 1927, only 10 played as seniors in 1930.

Wade demanded single-minded devotion to football, and Sington recalled how Wade would cruise around town in his Chrysler, keeping a close eye on his players and attempting to chase away any possible distractions.

"If I saw him coming and there were any co-eds around, I would cross the street," Sington said. "He didn't like seeing his players with girls."

One spring when Sington was playing baseball for Alabama he threw a no-hitter against Mississippi State, only to have Wade call him into his office after the game. Instead of congratulating Sington, Wade told him, "Son, I just want you to know football is first."

Wade ruled his entire program with an iron fist, even in the spring. After training six days a week for six weeks in the spring of 1928 the players thought they were done until the summer. Instead, Wade gathered his team around and told them spring football had gone so well that the players should consider practicing for another two weeks. Wade even asked for a vote, but his was the only one that counted and the Tide practiced for two more weeks.

When the Tide traveled to Pasadena for the 1931 Rose Bowl, Wade was all business, not even allowing his team out of the hotel to watch the Rose Bowl parade. The day before the game, though, Wallace announced the team would go on an outing.

"We did go on a little trip—out to an orange grove," Sington said. "We picked two oranges each and came back. That was his big outing."

Wade's strict regimen didn't prevent Hollywood from noticing Sington's rugged, square-shouldered good looks. After Johnny Mack Brown's initial success in the movies, Sington had to seriously consider a $500 offer to sign an actor's contract until Wade and University president George Denny reminded him of his scholarship and his academic goals. If he had dropped out to enter the movie business before the end of his senior year, he would not have graduated or completed his Phi Beta Kappa requirements.

Of course, Wade's demands had their rewards. Those survivors went on to form the nucleus of an Alabama team that went 10-0 in 1930, won the Southeastern Conference championship and then the national championship by defeating Washington State 24-0 in the Rose Bowl.

When Wade left Alabama following that season, Sington thought so much of his coach that he joined Wade at Duke as an assistant coach, spending four years under him. Sington also signed a professional baseball contract and spent his summers working his way up the baseball ladder. Starting his professional career on the mound before emerging as a power-hitting out fielder, Sington played with the Atlanta Crackers and the

Chattanooga Lookouts before landing in the Major Leagues with the Washington Senators and the Brooklyn Dodgers.

Sington seriously considered the possibility of playing both professional football and baseball when the Washington Redskins came calling, but Senators owner Clark Griffith wouldn't allow it, Sington countered with a request for a raise. This time, Griffith gave in.

"I think I could have played both sports," Sington said. "I was the second fastest man on the football team at Alabama."

When his athletic career ended in 1939 after six years in the big leagues Sington began to channel his energies in a wide variety of areas, mostly through his civic service and contributions to sports in the state of Alabama. He put those activities on hold

Fred Sington (second from the right) and coach Frank Thomas (far right)

during World War II when he entered the United States Navy as a lieutenant junior grade and served from 1942-46, spending some of his time coaching the Navy Zoomers football team in Norman, Oklahoma.

When the war ended he returned home to Birmingham to start the first of a series of successful sporting goods stores that stretched from Homewood to Huntsville. He eventually became known as "Mr. Birmingham" and "The Mayor of Fifth Avenue" for his active role in local causes, including serving breakfast at the Salvation Army on Christmas mornings, and still found time to became a football official in the SEC and some professional games.

Along the way he played an active role in the hiring of Paul "Bear" Bryant as Alabama's head football coach in 1957, served as president of the University of Alabama Alumni Association twice and collected more trophies and awards than most men can even imagine.

Sington was inducted into the College Football Hall of Fame in 1955 and joined the Alabama Sports Hall of Fame in its first year, 1972. In 1967, he received the Distinguished Alumnus Award from the University of Alabama and was chosen Birmingham's Man of the Year in 1970. Four years later, Fred was inducted into the Southern Athletic Hall of Fame. He also was inducted into the Alabama Business Hall of Fame in 2000.

Additionally, Sington worked overtime to bring the Hall of Fame Bowl to Birmingham. In 1991, the press box at Birmingham's Legion Field was named in his honor, an appropriate tribute considering his accommodating relationships with the state's sportswriters and broadcasters. The state of Alabama still presents the Fred Sington Trophy to the state's top male and female athletes.

The list goes on and on, just as Sington seemed to keep going and going, even toward the end of his life. As he said in his later years, "As long as the Lord will let me work, I'm going to work."

JOHNNY CAIN

FULLBACK 1930-1932

It's easy for myths to become legends as the decades pass, when the people at the center of such folklore have long since passed, unable to cut through the fable and get to the facts.

Such is the case with Johnny Cain, one of the all-time great backs in Alabama football history. With a name like Cain and fleet feet, the nickname "Hurry" or "Hurri" was an obvious choice.

The origin of the name isn't quite as obvious. Several printed sources claim it came from coach Wallace Wade, sending Cain into a game and yelling "Hurry Cain!"

That story makes sense, but the origin isn't as original as the story from Cain's prep career at Sidney Lanier High School in Montgomery. According to the story, Cain was returning to the huddle after a practice play at less than top speed when his coach yelled, "Hurry up Cain!" A Montgomery newspaper writer, present at practice, also attended the Poets' next game and watched Cain score three touchdowns against Greenville.

The next day, the headline read, "Hurry Up Cain Hurries Up!"

Whether the nickname came from his high school or college days doesn't really matter. What does matter is that Cain was an All-America fullback, linebacker and punter from 1930-32, in an era of 60-minute two-way football. History also recognizes him as the punter on Alabama's All-Century team, as well as a member of the College Football Hall of Fame and the Alabama Sports Hall of Fame.

As *Birmingham News* sportswriter Zipp Newman wrote, "He could run, block, punt and play defense—the best all-around back I ever saw." In a 1967 letter promoting Cain for the College Football Hall of Fame, Newman also wrote, "From all the great backs I have seen play since 1913 I rate Johnny Cain the greatest all-around back I ever saw. ... He is one of the South's all-time long and accurate punters—a coffin-corner specialist. He was a fine deceptive left-handed passer. He ran with a hip-swinging motion—terrific in a broken field. He was a fine power runner. I never saw a more deadly tackler."

Not bad for a guy who once had to move positions during his college career because he was too modest to give himself the ball enough.

After an all-state prep career Cain became the only sophomore starter on the Crimson Tide's undefeated 1930 national championship team. He was fast, strong and talented, but he did possess one shortcoming that eventually forced first-year coach Frank Thomas to move him from quarterback to fullback in 1931. It turns out Cain was simply too humble to call his own signals, and Thomas needed the ball in Cain's hands.

The move paid off immediately the next week when Cain scored three touchdowns against Ole Miss and went on to earn All-America honors and lead Alabama to a 9-1 season. As a senior in 1932 he opened the season with nine touchdowns in the first four games before suffering a knee injury that would keep him out of three games and limit his availability throughout the remainder of the season.

Cain secured his individual place in Alabama history as a senior in 1932 when he squared off in a dramatic duel with Tennessee star Beattie Feathers. In today's game, punting is practically seen as a turnover at the conclusion of a failed offensive possession. In Cain's day, a punt was seen as more of a weapon to improve field position and bury offenses deep in their own end of the field. Coaches often

chose a "quick kick" on third down instead of a pass attempt.

Both Feathers and Cain entered their showdown at Birmingham's Legion Field carrying a reputation as the South's best punter, and both had the credentials to back it up. They put those reputations to the test on October 15 when a frigid downpour turned both coaches, Alabama's Thomas and Tennessee's General Robert Neyland, more conservative than ever.

As the Crimson Tide and the Volunteers battled for position and frequently punted the sloppy ball away on first and second down, Feathers punted 21 times for an average of 43 yards. Cain responded by punting 19 times for an average of 48 yards, despite a 12-yard punt following a bad snap that bounced in his own end zone. Cain saved a possible touchdown or a safety by snagging the low snap, but unfortunately for Cain and his teammates, Feathers and the Vols took advantage of the short punt and scored three plays later, giving Tennessee a 7-3 victory in one of the greatest punting exhibitions of the era.

Cain went on to earn All-America honors once again that season, despite being limited by a knee injury. His knee injury often forced him to play a limited role, but he still came off the bench to run 51 yards for a touchdown in a 24-13 victory over Ole Miss. After a 9-6 victory over Virginia Tech, newspaper accounts praised Cain for "being worth his weight in gold even with a bum knee."

In a game against St. Mary's in California on December 3, Cain closed out his Alabama career with the game's only touchdown, racing 71 yards for a score and a 6-0 Crimson Tide victory. Cain's performance moved one West Coast sportswriter to write, "There have been longer runs in Kezar Stadium than the 71-yard touchdown dash by captain John 'Hurri' Cain, but none more spectacular than the weaving display of ball toting put on by the compact 183-pounder who has been rated the greatest the old South has ever given to American college sport."

Cain completed his senior year with his third consecutive all-conference honor and tied with Feathers for the Southern Conference scoring lead with 72 points, even though he played in only nine games compared to 10 for Feathers. He also finished with

26 touchdowns in 24 varsity games, but more important he completed his career with an impressive 27-3 record.

When his playing career came to an end Cain spent two years as a coaching aide under Thomas and then spent the 1935-36 academic year as a coach at his high school alma mater. He moved on to become the head coach at Southwestern Louisiana Institute in Lafayette in 1937, winning four Southern Intercollegiate Athletic Association championships and never finishing lower than second in the Louisiana Intercollegiate Conference before serving in

From left: Johnny Cain, Jake Gibbs and Archie Manning

Archie Manning (left) and Johnny Cain

the military for four years as a lieutenant commander in the Naval Preflight Program during World War II.

Cain returned to Southwestern Louisiana to coach in 1946 and served as athletic director in 1947 before new Ole Miss coach Johnny Vaught hired him as his backfield coach in 1947.

During his career at Ole Miss, Cain coached some of the best SEC players of the time, including Charley Conerly, Jake Gibbs and Archie Manning. Cain and Manning became good friends during their days as travel partners on the college football banquet circuit when Cain served as Manning's chaperon at Vaught's insistence.

Sometimes, Manning confesses, being the only player with a chaperone could be a little embarrassing. On the way to a promotional trip to Chicago for *Sport* magazine before Manning's senior season, Cain lectured Manning about representing Ole Miss, warning him against drinking alcohol and staying out late. When dinner started and players began to order, Stanford quarterback Jim Plunkett, Notre Dame quarterback Joe Theisman and Ohio State quarterback Rex Kern all ordered alcohol and Manning, seated next to Cain, ordered iced tea. Cain then proceeded to order a double bourbon.

"I looked at him and Coach Cain said, 'Do as I say, not as I do,'" Manning says, laughing. "Coach Cain was a sweet guy. I was crazy about him. He had a great sense of humor. His wife, Britt, also had a great sense of humor

and they always seemed to have a good life together."

For all that humor and good will, the one thing Cain did not and would not do is talk about his playing days at Alabama. That same modest man who would not call his own signal enough didn't allow himself to brag on his playing days.

"You could tell he was a great athlete," Manning says. "He was up in years when he was coaching us, but you could tell by the way he carried himself and walked with those bowed legs that he was a great athlete.

"We heard about what a good player he had been at Alabama, and on these trips I'd try to get him talking about it a little, but he was very humble and it was hard for me to get anything out of him. I never heard him say anything about how good he was."

Manning's suspicions about Cain's college football career were finally rewarded when Cain accompanied Manning to Birmingham for an awards dinner. "This was 1969, and it was obvious Alabama people still thought a lot of him," Manning says. "All the Alabama people were glad to see him and he was very popular there."

Cain continued to coach football at Ole Miss until 1972. During his tenure at Ole Miss, the Rebels won six SEC titles and a national championship. He also coached the Ole Miss men's tennis team from 1957-73 and served an administrative assistant in the athletic department from 1972 until his retirement in 1974. He died in 1977 at the age of 68, in Memphis.

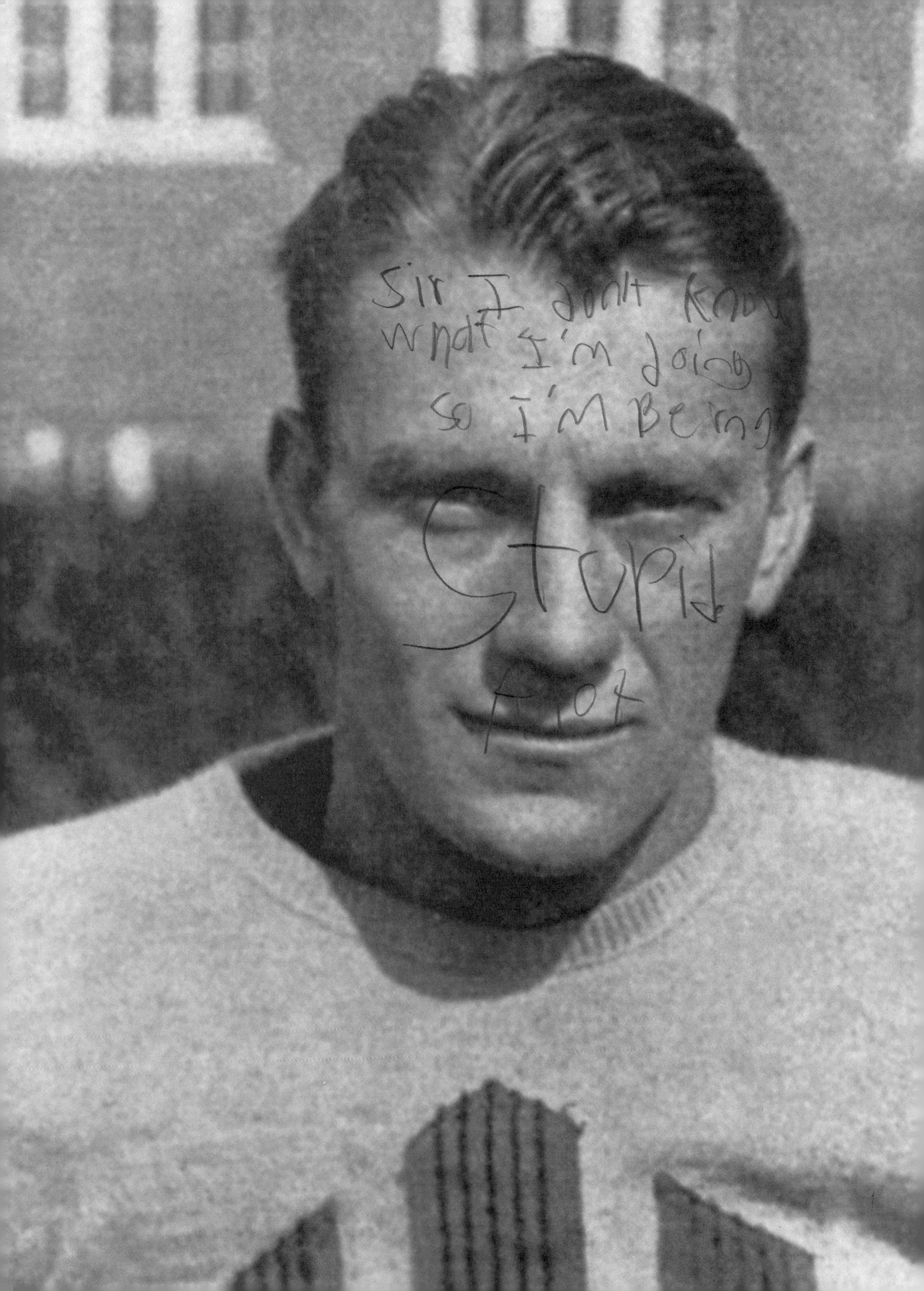
Sir I don't know
what I'm doing
so I'm Being
Stupid
Alex

MILLARD "DIXIE" HOWELL

HALFBACK 1932-1934

If Millard Filmore "Dixie" Howell was worried about playing Stanford in the 1935 Rose Bowl, he wasn't showing it in the hours leading up to the game. As the coaches and players gathered on the team busses outside the Pacific Palisades Hotel, Howell was nowhere to be found. Eventually, coaches sent players up to Howell's room to find him and bring him back.

When they got there, they found him busily involved in a craps game in his room.

"Howell was a pretty cool fella," said Kavanaugh "Kay" Francis, a center at Alabama from 1933-35. "We had a lot of faith in him."

Howell repaid that faith time and time again during his career at Alabama, particularly on that day when he led Alabama to a 29-13 victory over Stanford, a triumph that would give the Crimson Tide its fourth national championship and change college football forever.

In an age when teams rarely passed the ball, and usually only in cases of desperation or deception, it was Howell who teamed up with All-America receiver Don Hutson to make the forward pass a dangerous weapon, earning the nickname "The Human Howitzer" from famed sports writer Grantland Rice.

Howell, though, was more than just a passer. As the left halfback in Coach Frank Thomas's Notre Dame box offense, Howell passed, ran, kicked and did whatever it took to give his team a chance to win.

"He was a perfect triple-threat man," Francis said. "He could do it all. Even when we got behind and we were taking some lumps, we knew he could pull it off."

Confidence was never a problem for Howell, born October 12, 1913, and raised in Hartford, Alabama, a small town just southwest of Dothan that also produced Baseball Hall of Fame pitcher Early Wynn. He must have believed in himself, because he certainly didn't create much of a stir when he arrived on campus.

"Howell reported for the frosh team as a 150-pound end in 1931. Physically, he was everything but impressive looking," Thomas wrote in a 1954 letter to *The Atlanta Constitution*. "However, he had been recommended to use by one of our alumni who we had a great deal of faith in judging an athlete."

Howell's career got off to a slow start when he suffered a broken leg during the second week of his freshman year. Thomas then moved Howell from end to halfback the next spring. "I couldn't see a 150-pound end trying to block 215-pound tackles," Thomas wrote. "He showed great speed and was an excellent punter but didn't show much promise as a forward passer."

Howell didn't play much until injuries to two other left halfbacks left Thomas with no choice. "This gave Howell a chance to run behind the number-one line and he took advantage of it," Thomas wrote. "His running and punt returns were a big factor in winning the game. From then on he was the number-one left half."

Thomas went on to write that Howell had all the natural qualifications for a good halfback, with his speed and his "unusual ability to follow his interference." More than anything, though, Howell had the special something that separates champions from mere great athletes.

"His mental reactions were the thing to my mind that made him great," Thomas wrote. "He had the ability to see and realize the situation a split second ahead of the usual player.

George Gipp, one of Notre Dame's greatest whom I had the pleasure of playing with, had the same quality. ... To me Howell had something that few athletes possess—a touch of genius in his make-up."

Howell's make-up also came with a large helping of mischief. When the team reached Pasadena for the 1935 Rose Bowl, Alabama's practices were surrounded by large numbers of reporters and photographers, most of who were just getting in the way. Assistant coach Hank Crisp became so frustrated that he offered two dollars to anyone willing to knock over one of the newspapermen. Howell called a pass and threw deep to end Paul Bryant, who did his part by plowing into a reporter. When Bryant returned to the huddle for his two dollars, Howell made him split the money.

Howell also developed a craving for hot tamales on the trip. After months of following Thomas's dietary regime, Howell insisted, "I want six hot tamales, win, lose or draw. I've been thinking about them so much out here that I've got to be dreaming about them. I dreamed about hot tamales last night. That is, I dreamed about one hot tamale. It was as big as [Alabama tackle] Bill Lee. I mean, it was too big for a football player and not big enough for a hippopotamus. The coach won't let us eat tamales now, but as soon as that game is over—well, you watch."

Perhaps Howell didn't wait until after the game, because reports from game day suggested he didn't look well the morning of the game. Of course, that didn't stop him from playing craps, or football.

Howell not only went out and led Alabama to victory, but he also played the best game of his career. In the second quarter he returned a punt for 25 yards, passed to Hutson for 17 yards, ran twice for 10 yards each and then followed with a five-yard run for a touchdown that tied the game 7-7. After passes to Hutson and Bryant set up a field goal by Riley Smith, Howell followed with a 26-yard punt return and a 67-yard run for a touchdown for a 16-7 lead. In that quarter he also completed all six of his passes for 19, 13, 15, three, 25 and five yards as Alabama ran off 22 unanswered points.

"We had been a good passing team all year," Francis said. "We certainly didn't catch them by surprise with our throwing. They knew we could pass. But Howell had a great game. He was a combination of speed and shiftiness—and of course, he had some pretty good blocking, too."

Howell finished Stanford with a 59-yard touchdown pass to Hutson in the fourth quarter. For the game, he totaled 239 offensive yards and 74 more yards on returns. For all the attention afforded Hutson, it was Howell who won the MVP award, prompting Bill McGill of *The Atlanta Constitution* to write, "No team in the history of football, anywhere, anytime, has passed the ball as Alabama passed it today. And no man ever passed as did Dixie Howell, the swift sword of the Crimson attack."

Brian Bell of *The Associated Press* wrote, "Howell, doing everything a football player is called on to do, was the outstanding player on the field. He passed, ran, kicked, intercepted passes, and backed up the ends and tackles in the open."

Rice added to the accolades, writing, "Dixie Howell ... blasted the Rose Bowl dreams of Stanford today with one of the greatest all-around exhibitions football has ever known."

The game may, or may not have, also brought more of the same Howell high jinks. On his 67-yard scoring run Howell appeared to thumb his nose at Buck Van Dellen, the last Stanford defender in pursuit. West Coast sportswriters assumed it was true and called it an unsportsmanlike gesture. Howell denied it then and denied it throughout his life, saying he was only waving at Van Dellen.

Ten years after the incident, Howell told *Los Angeles Times* sportswriter Vincent X. Flaherty, "Nobody who saw that movie [game film] believes me. ... I saw that movie, too, and I'll be darned if it didn't look like I thumbed my nose. It must have been the angle of the camera."

The writers never bought his story, but Howell didn't spend much time worrying about it. He moved on by signing a professional baseball contract with the Detroit Tigers that winter and joining the Tigers in Lakeland, Florida, for spring training.

"He was a great athlete," Alabama teammate Jim Whatley said. "He could have been a star in basketball, but he didn't want to play it. With baseball, he was just great. ... He was cocky enough to do anything he wanted on the athletic fields."

What he could not do, however, was overcome a head injury that ruined his career. During a 1935 spring exhibition game against Cincinnati in Lynchburg, Virginia, Howell was playing pepper with some teammates when a foul ball off the bat of slugger Johnny Mize hit him in the head. He was hospitalized for a week before the Tigers sent him down to Birmingham, then to Beaumont, Texas. He spent the fall coaching at the University of Mexico, in Mexico City and married the former Peggy Taylor.

He returned to baseball the following spring and played that year with Portland and Toledo and spent the fall coaching the backfield for the University of Loyola in New Orleans. After spending the 1937 baseball season in Memphis, he decided to give pro football a shot. He signed with the Washington Redskins, but spent the entire season on the bench behind a future Hall of Famer named Sammy Baugh.

Howell went on to play three more seasons of baseball in Beaumont and Oklahoma City, but his football playing days gave way to a new career in football as the head coach at Arizona State Teachers College. When he took over in Tempe, he inherited Arizona State's first black player, Emerson Harvey, who was immediately concerned about the possibility of racism. Instead, "He was completely fair with me," Harvey told ASU historian Dean Smith. "He was a great coach, and a good friend."

Howell coached Arizona State to a 23-15-4 record from 1938 through 1941 and managed one pro baseball season in Albuquerque before he joined the U.S. Navy in August 1942. By the time he was discharged in 1945, he had risen to the rank of lieutenant. Following the war, he returned to coaching at the University of Idaho, where he went 13-20-1 from 1947 through 1950.

Howell became successful in private business in California when his coaching career came to an end, but he remained dedicated to the University of Alabama by participating in fund-raising campaigns and organizing alumni groups on the West Coast until he died all too soon in 1971 at the age of 58, due to cancer.

Howell was inducted into the College Football Hall of Fame in 1970, and the Alabama Sports Hall of Fame in 1971, but his most personal honor came when Bryant honored his old teammate with his own award. The MVP of the annual spring A-Day game is given the Dixie Howell Award, named for the player his old coach, Frank Thomas, once called "The greatest player I ever coached."

Alabama's All-Time First Team

Hometown · Hartford, Ala.

ALL S.E.C. '33-'34

ROSEBOWL STAR   1934
ALABAMA 34 STANFORD 13

'BAMA ASSISTANT COACH

1934 Record
RUSHING · 114 TRIES   = 668 YDS.
PASSING · 35 out of 61 = 489 YDS.
TOTAL YARDS   1157 YDS.

Pro·Baseball
DETROIT TIGERS

MILLARD "DIXIE" HOWELL
BACK   WT. 160
ALL·AMERICAN
                                    1934

Don Hutson photo, autographed for Paul "Bear" Bryant

DON HUTSON

END 1932-1934

G o deep. No, deeper. Farther. Way past the era of Jerry Rice and Steve Largent. Past the days of Lance Alworth and Fred Biletnikoff. Keep going, past the age of Elroy Hirsch and Tom Fears. Way back to a time when the forward pass was the vestige of the few, far and in-between.

Then stop, at Don Hutson, at the beginning. At the place where passing became more than an occasional deception or novelty act and receivers became more than blockers. At the place where passing became a reality and receivers became dangerous weapons in the right hands. There you will find Hutson doing things no one receiver had ever done before, in college or professional football, and you will find arguably the best, or at least the most innovative receiver in the history of football.

As a college player at Alabama, the success of Hutson and quarterback Dixie Howell changed the way college football teams looked at the forward pass, making the pass more of a necessity, even if it remained a necessary evil for many coaches. As a pro with the Green Bay Packers, Hutson's impact made passing a regular part of the game by the time he retired in 1945.

How good was Hutson? When *Sports Illustrated*'s Peter King began extensive research for his book *Football: A History of the Professional Game*, he entered his search for the greatest player of all time with the assumption that his work would lead him to Jim Brown. Instead, his exploration took him to Hutson, who dominated his era more unlike any player in the game's history.

"He had all the moves," Green Bay teammate Tony Canadeo once said of Hutson. "He invented the moves. And he had great hands and speed, deceptive speed. He could go get the long ones; run the hitch, the down-and-out. He'd go over the middle, too, and he was great at getting off the line because he always had people popping him.

"To me, he made the passing game what it is today and I don't think anybody can argue with that. Pass patterns and routes he ran were modeled after him."

What Hutson's place in the annals of football history often fails to mention is that he came astoundingly close to being left out of football altogether.

He was a standout baseball player at Pine Bluff High in Arkansas, but didn't become a first-string football player until his senior season. Even then, at six feet tall and just 150 pounds, college coaches had a difficult time seeing him as a two-platoon player.

Hutson had baseball and track in mind when he followed a high school teammate to Tuscaloosa. A partial baseball scholarship awaited him, but he couldn't shake the football bug and walked on to the football team where he initially had a difficult time matching up with bigger, stronger ends such as Paul Bryant, Ralph Gandy and Jimmy Walker.

"When [Hutson] was a freshman or a sophomore, he was so inept that the Arkansas group—Bryant and Foy Leach and Happy Campbell and some others—called a special meeting and set him straight," recalled Jim Dildy, who played tackle from 1931-33. "They told him, 'Look, you'd better your butt in gear. You're not going to embarrass the guys from Arkansas.'"

Perhaps it took a while for the message to take hold. Or, maybe the coaches just failed to notice Hutson's growth and progress. Either way, Hutson spent most of his first three years at Alabama as an outstanding centerfielder and sprinter, but he sat the bench and did little of note on the football field.

"Don didn't make all that much of an impression when he made varsity as a sophomore," said Buck Hughes, an Alabama fullback from 1931-33. "As I recall, he played just enough to earn a letter in 1932 and 1933. Now 1934, that's another story."

For Hutson, it was the start of a senior story that would end up on college football's biggest stage, the 1935 Rose Bowl.

In the fourth game of his senior season, Hutson, by then weighing nearly 180 pounds, caught fire against Tennessee by catching a 33-yard touchdown pass from Dixie Howell and scoring another touchdown on an end-around, leading the Crimson Tide to a 13-6 victory. Against Kentucky, his 22-yard reception from Howell set up one score and his 20-yard end-around provided another score as Alabama won 34-14.

In the seventh game of the season, a 40-0 victory over Clemson, Hutson did his part by catching three touchdown passes from Howell. In a 40-0 defeat of Georgia Tech the next week he caught three more touchdown passes and scored yet another on another end-around. His performance convinced Tech coach Bill Alexander of his worth as an All-America candidate.

"All Hutson can do is beat you," Alexander said.

Even Hutson's coaches and teammates had to admit they were surprised by the sudden revelation.

"Don had the most fluid motion you had ever seen when he was running," said Bryant, who was soon to be known as "The Other End" at Alabama. "It looked like he was going just as fast as possible when all of a sudden he would put on an extra burst of speed and be gone."

"I guess the main reason [Hutson had not played before 1934] was that he played so effortlessly and with such grace, the coaches thought he was loafing," said Harold "Red" Drew, then an assistant under coach Frank Thomas and later the Crimson Tide's head coach. "It turned out he could catch any ball thrown near him. He had big hands and was relaxed at all times. He was hard to notice. ... We made a mistake."

Hutson spent his entire 1934 season correcting that mistake, earning All-SEC and All-America honors and saving his best for last. In the 1935 Rose Bowl against Stanford, he caught six passes for 165 yards and two touchdowns, leading Alabama to a 29-13 victory and the Crimson Tide's fourth national championship. The combination of Howell-to-Hutson combined for 211 yards in a performance that Drew called Hutson's "greatest day."

Hutson's college success didn't exactly set professional football on fire. He received only three professional football offers, including contracts from the Packers, the Chicago Bears and the Brooklyn Dodgers.

"The Bears were coming off a championship year, and [owner and coach George] Halas wrote me a two-page letter telling me what a privilege it would be to play for the Bears," Hutson said in a 1988 interview. "It sounded like I was going to have to pay Halas to play for the Bears. In the last sentence, he got down to the gist of the letter. He said if I made the team, he would pay me $50 a week."

Instead, Hutson signed contracts with both the Packers and Dodgers. NFL president Joe Carr decided that the team that mailed its contract to the league office first would get Hutson. Both contracts were postmarked the same day, but the Packers won out because

their contract had been postmarked was seventeen minutes earlier.

It all worked out for the best for Hutson. Not only was Curly Lambeau, Green Bay's vice president, general manager and head coach, prepared to take a few risks and throw the ball, but he also paid Hutson $300 per game. That amount was considered so exorbitant at the time that the Packers allegedly paid him with two checks each week to avoid embarrassment. Lambeau must have known what he was doing, though, because he had watched Hutson practice in person before the Rose Bowl.

Hutson didn't take long to start earning his paycheck. In his second regular-season professional game in 1935, the Packers took their first possession of the game on their own 17-yard line, with Hutson starting and lining up for his first play on the team's left side.

"Our wingback, Johnny Blood was wide to the right," Hutson recalled. "And our right end lined up as what you'd call a tight end today. The Bears had never seen that [formation] before. Nobody had. Our coach, Curly Lambeau, dreamed it up the night before.

"I went down the middle as a decoy. Arnold Herber dropped back to pass. Blood was the league's leading receiver. He was also the signal caller. The ball was supposed to go to him."

Instead, the ball went to Hutson, who had faked out former Tennessee star Beattie Feathers with a move to the outside and a cut to the inside. Hutson hauled in Herber's pass in stride and took it the rest of the way for an 83-yard touchdown reception. The Packers went on to beat the Bears 7-0 and a star was born. Hutson was soon running roughshod through the league, with his 9.7-second 100-yard dash speed, sure hands and his ability to elude defenders and run precise routes no one had ever seen before. He is widely credited with inventing routes such as the Z-in and Z-out, the button hook, the comeback and the hook-and-go.

"He would glide downfield," Lambeau said, "leaning forward as if to steady himself close to the ground. Then, as suddenly as you gulp or blink an eye, he would feint one way and go the other, reach up like a dancer, gracefully squeeze the ball and leave the scene of the accident—the accident being the defensive backs who tangled their feet up and fell trying to cover him."

Before long opponents were devising entire defenses around Hutson, double- and triple-teaming him in ways defenses had never been forced into before. Halas went out of his way to design defenses aimed at containing

Paul Bryant (left) and Don Hutson

Hutson, but even that wasn't always enough.

On one of the most fascinating plays in NFL history, Hutson ran a deep post route toward the goal posts, then situated in the end zone. Followed closely by three of the Bears' best defenders, Harry Clark, Dante Magnani and George McAfee, Hutson raced toward one of the uprights, hooked his elbow around the post, stopped quickly enough to spin his body around to face the football and simply waited for the ball to land in his arms for an astonishing touchdown.

"I'll never forget that pass," Clark later said. "How could I? Halas was fit to be tied. He sent us in there, three of us, expressly to cover Hutson. That's all we had to do. Oh, were we sick."

Hutson soon made a habit of the play until the NFL moved the posts back a few feet and disallowed the use of the posts, but it didn't stop Hutson from becoming one of the NFL's all-time greats.

"There's no question in my mind he was the best receiver ever," said former Green Bay running back Chester "Swede" Johnston. "No one man could cover him. He always had the defensive backs running the wrong way. ... He was tough. He wasn't too big, weighed only about 180 pounds, but he could take a hit. He really was a good one."

With Hutson and passers Arnie Herber and Cecil Isbell teaming to form the NFL's best passing attack, the Packers won league championships in 1936, 1939 and 1944. The Packers also finished in the first division of the standings in all of Hutson's years with the team.

Hutson earned All-Pro honors nine times, led the NFL in touchdowns eight times and led the league in receptions eight times. He finished his career with 99 touchdown receptions, an astounding 62 touchdowns ahead of his closest competitor at the time.

Hutson also turned out to be an outstanding defender and kicker. Once he moved from defensive end (more of an outside linebacker at that time) to safety midway through the 1939 season, Hutson became one of the NFL's better defensive backs. In 1940, he led the league with 45 receptions and six interceptions. He finished with 23 interceptions in his final four seasons as a defensive back and also scored 193 career points as a place-kicker.

While Steve Largent and Jerry Rice went on to break most of his records, they also set their marks during the era of the 16-game schedule, while Hutson played 11 games per season. In his best season, 1942, Hutson caught 74 passes for 1,211 yards and 17 touchdowns, unheard of statistics at the time, and comparable to Babe Ruth's astonishing 60 home runs in 1927. He also intercepted seven passes, kicked 33 extra points and a field goal, and finished with 138 total points. While those numbers seem ordinary today, project them over a 16-game season and Hutson would have accumulated 108 receptions, 1,761 yards, and 25 touchdowns.

By the time Hutson retired he had 488 receptions and 7,991 yards, while the next best receiver had 190 catches and 3,309 yards. He scored 105 touchdowns in just 117 games, making 20 percent of all his receptions touchdowns. He held nearly every NFL receiving record, including most receptions in a game, season, and career; most reception yardage in a game, season and career, and most touchdown receptions in a game, a season, and a career. He was also the NFL's single-season and career scoring leader.

Following his retirement as a player, Hutson served as a Packers assistant coach under Lambeau for three seasons (1946-48). He then went on to become a successful businessman in Racine, Wisconsin, and eventually became a millionaire. During his business career he served on the Packers board of directors from 1952-80, when he was elected director emeritus.

Along the way, he became a member of the College Football Hall of Fame in 1951, a charter member of the Pro Football Hall of Fame in 1963, joined the Alabama Sports Hall of Fame in 1969 and entered the Packer Hall of Fame in 1972. He also earned spots on the NFL's all-50 year team and the league's 75th Anniversary Team. When the Packers built their $4.7 million indoor practice facility in 1994, they didn't have to go very far to find an appropriate name for the building now called the Don Hutson Center.

"I don't know if there is such a thing as royalty in professional football," Packers general manager Ron Wolf said as he stood next to Hutson at the dedication ceremony, "but this is the closest I've ever come to it. He most certainly was the greatest player in the history of this franchise. In the era he played, he was the dominant player in the game."

Hutson died three years later, on June 26, 1997, at age 84. At the time, he still held 10 NFL records and 18 team marks, but he lived long enough to witness dramatic change in the game and see many of his records fall.

"I love to see my records broken, I really do," he said in 1989. "You get a chance to relive a part of your life, the whole experience."

HARRY GILMER

HALFBACK 1944-1947

Tackle Charley Compton was a talented athlete and an intense football player but a rather flaky individual. He had been a decorated war hero in World War II, but he had no intention of getting on a plane to Boston when coach Frank Thomas decided Alabama would make it first team flight in late November 1946.

"He walked up to Coach Thomas—and nobody just walked up to Coach Thomas—and he said, 'Uh, Coach, I don't fly,'" Harry Gilmer recalls.

"Coach Thomas said, 'What do you mean you don't fly?' He said, 'I don't ride in airplanes.' Coach Thomas said, 'Well it's going to be the first time the team's ever had a chance to fly in an airplane.' He just said, 'I don't fly. You better let me get on the train Wednesday and I'll be there when y'all get there.'"

Thomas wasn't about to give in and let Compton travel by himself, and since Compton wasn't ready to give in, Thomas considered Compton's service record and suggested that Compton travel with a parachute.

"Coach Thomas said, 'You wouldn't hesitate to jump out would you?'" Gilmer says. "'We'll give you a parachute and you don't even have to wear it. You can slide it under your seat and put it on if there's trouble.'

"Compton said, 'Well, I don't know. ... No, I'm not going to do it.' "

By this time Compton had Thomas bewildered and befuddled.

"Coach Thomas said, 'I don't understand. You're brave enough and you can't handle flying with a parachute?'" Gilmer says. "Compton said, 'No, I know that as soon as this plane gets in some difficulty you would come running to me and say, 'Get that chute and give it Gilmer!'"

Such was Gilmer's worth to the Alabama football program from 1944-47. Despite his humble protest that "I'm not worth a chapter in any book," there's no way a book on Alabama football legends could be written without a section on Gilmer, an outstanding All-America halfback and defensive back that famed sportswriter Grantland Rice once called "the greatest college passer I ever saw."

It's startling to think that Rice's favorite greatest college passer almost didn't go to college. Gilmer spent his sophomore and junior seasons at Birmingham's Woodlawn High School as a sub behind older, more experienced players, including future Auburn star Travis Tidwell, so he had to wait until his senior season before he became a full-time player.

Gilmer never even threw a pass in a high school game until his senior year, but once he got his chance Gilmer didn't waste any time making a name for himself. That fall Zipp Newman of *The Birmingham News* wrote, "Harry is as fine a passer as there is in football. This goes for the pros." Naylor Stone of *The Birmingham Post* wrote, "The kid is just as fine a passer as [Georgia star Frank] Sinkwich."

Several college football teams also noticed, including Alabama. However, the coaches who came to visit Gilmer soon found he had no real interest in college. His father was a carpenter, and a good one, so Gilmer had just assumed he would follow in his father's footsteps.

"I just didn't grow up thinking about college," Gilmer said. "Going to college by playing ball never entered my mind. I never dreamed of that opportunity."

Thomas helped convince Gilmer to try college and football at Alabama by hiring Woodlawn coach Malcolm Laney, who remained on staff at Alabama until 1957, and

Gilmer showed up on campus in 1944 in time to become part of the University's first team after a one-year hiatus for World War II.

With most of the era's finest young men off to fight the war, the nucleus of Alabama's 1944 team was comprised of freshmen and 4-Fs. One of those was Gilmer, who arrived at Alabama weighing 155 pounds and carrying an ulcer in his gut. Doctors forbid him from eating meat and placed him on a strict diet of milk, cream, cereals and strained vegetables. The diet didn't exactly add any bulk to Gilmer's thin frame, but it didn't prevent him from making an immediate impact, either.

After waiting three years to play a major role for the varsity at Woodlawn, Gilmer suddenly found himself starting for the Crimson Tide as an 18-year-old freshman, playing left halfback in the Notre Dame box offense, the same position Dixie Howell had played at Alabama.

"There weren't any upperclassmen there to be ahead of me," Gilmer said. "We only had about 35 players on the whole squad. I didn't know any better. I was the one who was there to do that job and I worked at doing it. I liked it. I loved it, really. I really enjoyed playing football."

Gilmer not only started, he surprised Thomas, and even Laney, with his passing ability. During the final practice before the season opener at LSU, the players were supposed to be preparing for practice when Gilmer started throwing the ball as far as he could.

Laney saw Gilmer's display, ran toward him in a huff and yelled, "What in the name of Pete are you doing, Harry? Stop that before you hurt your arm."

Gilmer apologized and reported that his

arm didn't hurt, so Laney asked the players for the distance of Gilmer's passes. One player told him the throws went 69, 72 and 71 yards, all with pinpoint accuracy.

Laney couldn't help himself. He ran over to Thomas and said, "Frank, do you know how far that boy threw, and dead to his receivers? Tommy, hold your hair, because he got an average of better than 70 yards in three tries."

According to the legend surrounding the story, Thomas simply smiled, shook his head and said, "Well, make him come in and get that arm checked. Apparently that boy has a good one."

That was apparent from the start. With relatively few teams restarting football in 1944, Thomas's "War Babies" played an eight-game schedule and finished 5-2-2. That was good enough to earn an invitation to the Sugar Bowl to play against a veteran Duke team loaded with U.S. Navy trainees. Despite the age, experience and depth differences between the two teams, the Crimson Tide battled the Blue Devils for four quarters of a game that was not settled until the very end. Duke escaped with a 29-26 victory, but Alabama left New Orleans with a feeling of accomplishment and a new level of respect from their coach. Gilmer also came away from the game with a national reputation, thanks in part to Rice, who called him "the most amazing back that football can show today."

Duke star Tom Davis certainly agreed, telling Rice, "Gilmer? He is no 158-pounder. He must have nailed me 10 times today, and I thought he was going to tear me apart."

That momentum carried over to the 1945 season, with victories in all nine regular-season games and an invitation to the Rose Bowl.

Of course, as Gilmer was quick to admit, the Crimson Tide had a distinct advantage that year.

"It was a close-knit team because nearly everyone was in the same boat," Gilmer said. "Most of us were sophomores. A few guys had been in the service and were already out, and some were 4-F. And you have to keep in mind that most of the schools that had a team started back playing in 1945, and we had already played the year before. We were playing a lot of teams that were in the position we were in the year before. The times were not normal and we hit it just right and we had a good team."

Harry Gilmer's jump pass

Alabama's advantage and its success in five previous trips to the Rose Bowl obviously didn't impress one West Coast writer, who wrote, "You've won the Rose Bowl before, but Alabama, you haven't played Southern Cal yet." Gilmer erased any doubts by rushing for 116 yards and a touchdown on 16 carries and passing for another touchdown in a 34-14 victory over the Trojans. After earning All-America and SEC Player of the Year honors that season, Gilmer topped it off by being voted MVP of the Rose Bowl.

By the next fall, many football players had returned from the war to join their old college teams, so Alabama lost some of its earlier advantage. Even worse, Thomas's health had begun to deteriorate, and he spent most of the 1946 season either in bed or coaching from a special cart as the Tide slipped to 7-4.

"Other teams were catching up to us, and Coach Thomas wasn't with us much," Gilmer said. "We lost some of the unity that we had had before, and we lost all that Coach Thomas brought to the team. We knew how to work a team and how to make everyone feel like a team. When you have someone who is strong in a leadership role and then you lose him, it's hard to keep the parts running together smoothly."

By the end of the 1946 season, Thomas's health forced him to resign, and the players started over with a new, but familiar coach. Harold "Red" Drew, who had been an Alabama assistant from 1931-41 as well as the 1945 season, spent the 1946 season as the head coach at Ole Miss before returning to Tuscaloosa as the Crimson Tide's head coach in 1947.

The Tide only improved by one game in Drew's first year, going 8-3 and finishing with a 27-7 loss to Texas and Bobby Lane in the Sugar Bowl, but "We were on the way back in 1947," Gilmer says. "Under Drew we were able to gain a little better unity than we had had."

Gilmer finished his Alabama career with 3,108 passing yards and 32 touchdown passes and 25 more touchdown runs. He spent most of his college career leading the Tide in passing, rushing, punting, punt returns, kickoff returns and interceptions and catching the attention of professional football teams.

"Harry Gilmer was a real leader," said teammate Vaughn Mancha, Alabama's All-America center. "He wasn't a tremendously big guy, but he took a beating on offense and then he would punt and play defense or he would return a kick and play offense. Harry always had a smile on his face. I don't care if he was bleeding; he was just really a great leader and a guy that everyone admired. Harry was truly one of the greatest football players I have ever seen."

The next spring, Gilmer became the first Alabama player to be the No. 1 pick in the NFL draft and joined his new team, the Washington Redskins, as soon as Thomas helped him complete contract negotiations with Redskins owner George Preston Marshall.

Unfortunately for Gilmer, he suffered an injury in his first training camp and missed his entire rookie season. It could also be said that Gilmer was unlucky to spend most of his pro career backing up two future NFL Hall of Fame players, Washington's Sammy Baugh and Detroit's Lane, but Gilmer considers himself fortunate to have played with two of the game's all-time best. His status as a backup allowed him to move into a new role as a versatile player who could also play running back or defensive back.

"My strength as a pro was that I could help out as a utility player," Gilmer said. "I wasn't outstanding at any one thing, but I could do a lot of things well."

Gilmer managed to play in the NFL nine years and made the Pro Bowl twice before moving on to a coaching career that took him to the Pittsburgh Steelers and the Minnesota Vikings as an assistant. He then became the first former Alabama player to become a NFL head coach when Detroit hired him in 1965. His two years with the Lions were filled with losing and controversy, much of it supplied by meddling owners and recalcitrant players such as the talented-but-enigmatic Joe Don Looney. When Gilmer attempted to use Looney to carry a message into a game, Looney responded, "If you want a messenger boy, call Western Union."

When fans near the field pummeled Gilmer with snowballs after his final game, the affable Southern gentlemen quipped, "At least they didn't have rocks in them."

In truth, it was an awkward time to coach the Lions, and no coach since Buddy Parker in the early 1950s has experienced any significant level of sustained success with the misbegotten franchise. Gilmer simply says, "I wish I had done better," but at least the experience didn't hurt his career. He moved on to assistant coaching jobs with the St. Louis Cardinals and the Atlanta Falcons, and then returned to St. Louis, where he served as an assistant and then a scout until he retired in 1994.

"I enjoyed the scouting, but I enjoyed coaching, too," Gilmer said. "I coached offense and defense at different times. I've had a life most anyone would have loved."

After playing for nine years, coaching for 27 and scouting for 11, Gilmer has no real regrets about his professional career. At 78 years old, he lives on a small farm in O'Fallon, Missouri, a burgeoning St. Louis suburb. Wearing his ever-present cowboy hat, a habit ever since he bought a horse with his signing bonus, Gilmer continues to raise chickens, turkeys, guinea hens, peacocks, goats and horses. Local children have been known to knock on his door to ask for a chance to pet his farm animals, and it's obvious Gilmer takes joy in showing them around.

Through it all, Alabama has remained close to his heart. He didn't attend many Alabama games during his playing and coaching career simply because of his schedule, but he ran out the first game ball used in the Mike Shula era before the 2003 season opener.

"I try to go back now whenever I can," Gilmer said. "Alabama's still special to me."

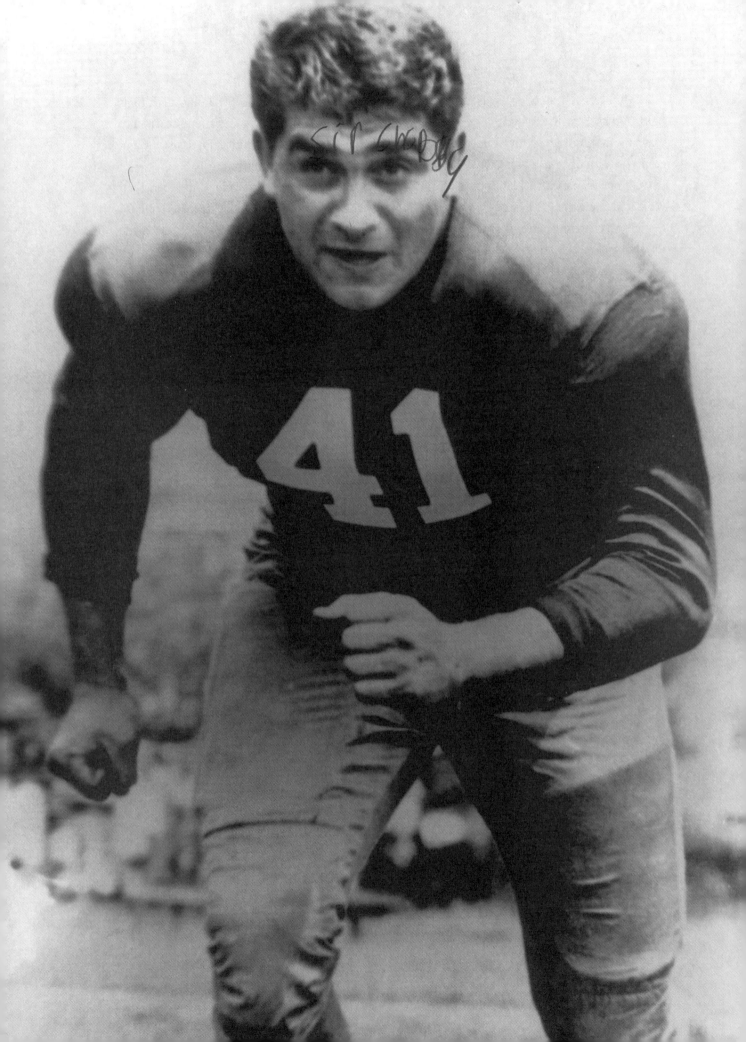

VAUGHN MANCHA

CENTER 1944-1947

Deion Sanders thought he was something special at Florida State in the late 1980s as a dangerous cornerback, an explosive punt returner and occasional receiver. But he also spent a considerable amount of time on the bench, taking a break, gulping down a cool drink and taking it easy, waiting for his time to return to the field.

When Florida State fans marveled about Sanders being a "two-way player," Dr. Vaughn Mancha would just laugh and shake his head. Mancha, who retired as FSU's athletic director in 1972 and taught Sanders in a communications class wasn't all that impressed. A two-way player? So what? Mancha was an every way player at Alabama.

"I see a lot of programs giving a deep snapper a scholarship just for snapping the ball back on punts and kicks," Mancha says. "Well, I was a deep snapper, too. I also snapped the ball on every offensive play back to the back-

field in a single wing offense, and I played linebacker and every special team. Those special teams really got me. I was on every one of them. Coach [Frank] Thomas always wanted to kick first, so I'd be running down the field on the first play getting knocked all over the place. You can get killed on those kickoffs.

"But I played 60 minutes all the time. And I didn't get any breaks or any water or Gatorade. It would be 150 degrees in August and Coach Thomas wouldn't give us water back then. He thought it would kill us."

Mancha not only survived a career as Alabama's 60-minute man, starting four years at center and linebacker for Alabama's post-World War II "War Babies," but he's also one of only 28 players and one of only seven players since 1945 to have played every snap in a Sugar Bowl game.

"If I could have just gone in on defense—boom, boom, boom—and then taken a little rest, drank a little water, I'd have been pretty good," the 83-year-old Mancha says with a laugh.

Pretty good? Mancha earned consensus All-America honors in 1945, as well as a spot on Alabama's Team of the Century and a place in both the College Football Hall of Fame and the Alabama Sports Hall of Fame.

"He was probably the truly great player that we had during that time," says Harry Gilmer, Alabama's All-America halfback and Mancha's teammate from 1944-47. "He had the size and so much more quickness than other people his size. He could really run. He was also one of those people who could hit you, and the lick would hurt you because he had that burst, that quick step and the punch right at the last second.

"It was almost hard to keep him in good running shape. At the end of each practice we would put the ball on the 20-yard line and snap it and run the play and sprint to the goal line. Mancha was so quick he could come out of his stance so quickly after snapping the ball that he would be so far ahead of everyone and he'd have to slow up and coast the last 10 yards so we could catch up and finish together. He was a very talented guy."

Gilmer has always been thankful he had Mancha as a teammate and not an opponent, with good reason.

"I made him great," Mancha says, laughing. "I protected him, knocked people off of him so he could get all the glory ... *on both sides of the ball.*"

Beneath his self-effacing humor lies the serious side of a man who learned to work hard, do the job right and not accept any excuses early on in his life, often through adversity.

Mancha was six years old and living in Sugar Valley, Georgia, when a child playing with a bow and arrow shot him directly in the middle of his left eye, leaving him with decent peripheral vision but blurred straight ahead vision. Mancha never made much of an issue on or off the football field and learned to make the best of his situation, especially when his family moved to Birmingham and he played for coach Cannonball White at Ramsay High School.

"Vaughn Mancha is a natural," wrote *Birmingham News* sportswriter Bill McArdle. "He could block and tackle with the best and was very quick for his size."

His vision didn't become an issue until he attempted to join the armed services. Mancha actually signed to play with Alabama after his senior season in 1941, but like most young American men of the time, Pearl Harbor changed his plans. While all of his other buddies were joining the war effort after graduating in the spring of 1942, Mancha found none of the four primary services willing to give him a chance, even in the reserves. Instead, he joined the Merchant Navy, moved to California and worked repairing destroyers for two years. Having already spent most of teenage years working his way through the depression as a boilermaker for Engel's Iron Works on the south side of Birmingham, Mancha was a good fit for his new job.

During his time in California a coach from UCLA attempted to recruit him, but Mancha wanted none of it. "All I could think of was wanting to get back to Alabama," Mancha says.

The U.S. Army finally inducted him in 1944 and placed him on hold in case he was needed. During a trip home to Birmingham he suddenly found himself being recruited by Auburn coaches, a move that caught Thomas's angry attention and led to an official protest and a hearing at the SEC office with commissioner Martin S. Conner. After hearing both sides, Conner finally asked Mancha where he wanted to play.

"If I'm going to play," Mancha says, "I'm going to play at Alabama."

Mancha headed for Tuscaloosa, but a possible call from the Army continued to hang over his head. The call never came and allowed Mancha to turn his attention to football, where he was older, bigger, stronger and more mature than the average freshmen that made up most of Alabama's first post-war team because of his time in the Merchant Navy.

"I was 240 [pounds] with good speed," Mancha says, "and that helped."

It also helped that Alabama was re-starting its football program in 1944, a year before most college programs returned to competition. After a 5-2-2 record and impressive performance in a dramatic 29-26 Sugar Bowl loss against a seasoned Duke team loaded with older, more experienced U.S. Navy trainees, Gilmer wasn't the only first-year Alabama player to capture the attention of legendary sportswriter Grantland Rice.

"Gilmer, it might be suggested, isn't the only football player Frank Thomas has on his squad," Rice wrote. "Mancha, one of the best centers in football, heads a strong, fast charging line."

Mancha and the line led the way in 1945 as Alabama won all nine regular-season games and an invitation to the Rose Bowl, where the Crimson Tide dominated Southern Cal for a 34-14 victory. Mancha's performance stood out, leading to praise and a prediction from

his coach. "Vaughn Mancha played his usual outstanding game at center. He is destined to become one of the greatest centers of collegiate football."

Despite an undefeated record and a Rose Bowl win over USC, the Tide failed to win the national championship. Army also finished without a loss, and in postwar America, it was difficult to be more popular than the Black Knights of the Hudson.

"They didn't have bowl alliances or weekly polls back then. At least they didn't publicize the polls," Mancha says. "You just played who you were supposed to play. I'm sure the coaches were upset that we didn't win the national championship, but we really didn't worry about it."

Unfortunately for Mancha and his teammates, they didn't get another shot at the national championship. With the uncertainty and lack of continuity caused by Thomas's ailing health, his resignation following the 1946 season and the hiring of former Alabama assistant Harold "Red" Drew as head coach in 1947, the Tide finished 7-4 and 8-3 over the next two seasons. The team also finished on a sour note, losing 27-7 to Texas in the 1948 Sugar Bowl. Still, Mancha looks back on his career with tremendous pride and satisfaction.

"I really wanted to play football at Alabama, and my time there was very special," he says. "I have a lot of great memories and thrills that I will never forget."

Mancha's professional career as a player was mostly forgettable, through no fault of his own. Mancha already owned a degree in industrial arts and 15 hours toward a masters when he became a first-round draft pick of the NFL's Boston Yanks in 1948. When a torn anterior cruciate knee ligament ended his career after two seasons, Mancha simply returned to Tuscaloosa to complete his master's degree in educational administration.

Mancha was sitting out on the porch, still wearing a cast on his leg, when Livingston State Teachers College president W.W. Hill

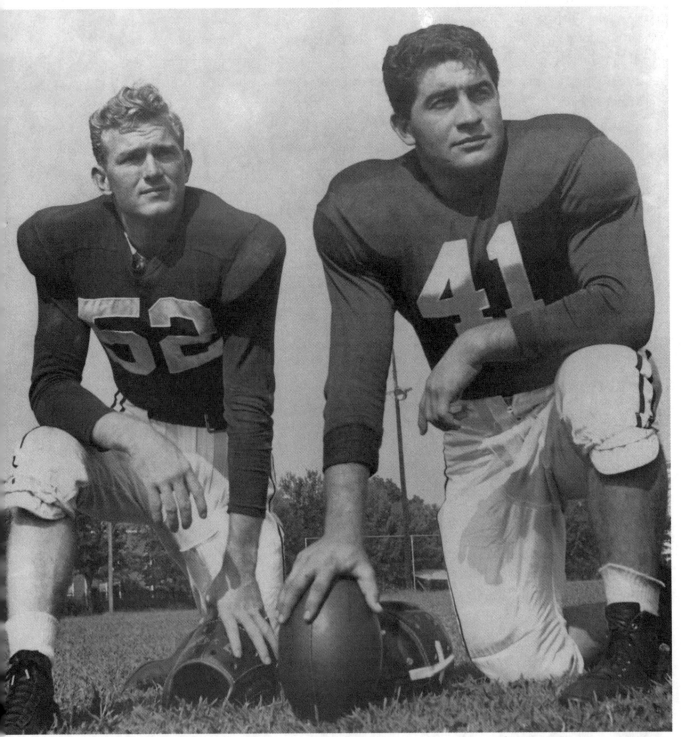

Harry Gilmer (left) and Vaughn Mancha

pulled up in front of his house and offered him the chance to be his head coach at his little school.

"I got up and ran across that porch," Mancha says, "even with my cast."

During his three-year stay at Livingston (now West Alabama), Mancha caught the eye of Florida State administrators when his Tigers beat the Seminoles. In 1952 he moved to FSU as coach Tom Nugent's defensive coordinator and also served as an assistant professor in the College of Education.

After coaching at FSU for six years Mancha moved on to Columbia University in urban New York, where he became a serious opera fan and found that his players, including future actor Brian Dennehy, often struggled to make sense of his Alabama accent.

When Paul "Bear" Bryant took over as Alabama's head coach in 1958, Mancha was a name several people in Tuscaloosa suggested Bryant contact about a position on his staff. Bryant called Mancha at Columbia to offer him a job, and Mancha even flew down to Tuscaloosa for a day to discuss the situation with Bryant. Mancha still has the Western Union telegram Bryant sent after offering him a job as an assistant coach, at the annual salary of $7,000, effective July 1, 1958. However, Mancha still needed more time that spring and summer to defend his dissertation for his doctorate in communications and asked for more time. Bryant wanted someone immediately, so it wasn't long before Bryant wired him to tell him he had completed his coaching staff.

Mancha didn't waste much time regretting his decision and it wasn't long before Florida State called and asked him to return as athletic director, a position he held for 15 years. During his tenure Mancha pushed the athletic department forward, mostly by making an annual habit of scheduling some of the South's best programs to build the program's budget and reputation. One of the highlights of Mancha's time at FSU was a dramatic 37-37 tie with Alabama at Legion Field in the Crimson Tide's 1967 season opener.

During his time at FSU, Mancha worked with or coached several famous people, including NFL head coaches Bill Parcells and Joe Gibbs, former University of Washington coach Don James, former Louisville and Indiana coach Lee Corso and a young assistant named Bobby Bowden, a Birmingham native who spent a little time as a player at Alabama before playing and coaching at Howard College (now Samford) and went on to lead FSU to national prominence as its head coach. Mancha also coached several future Hollywood actors, including Burt Reynolds, Robert Urich, Paul Gleason and Sonny Schroyer.

When Mancha retired as athletic director he was tempted to move back to Alabama, but his love for teaching at FSU made it difficult for him to leave.

"Our kids were born here, and our lives were here," Mancha says. "And I had a lot of fun in the classroom."

These days Mancha stays busy doing part-time graphic and photography work for *The Osceola*, an FSU fan magazine. The walls of his den are covered with photos of former teammates and famous stadiums where he played, including the Rose Bowl and the Sugar Bowl. Many of those teammates are dead now, but they live on in the photos, and in Mancha's heart and mind.

"I'm a Seminole, too," Mancha says, "but Alabama's still in my heart."

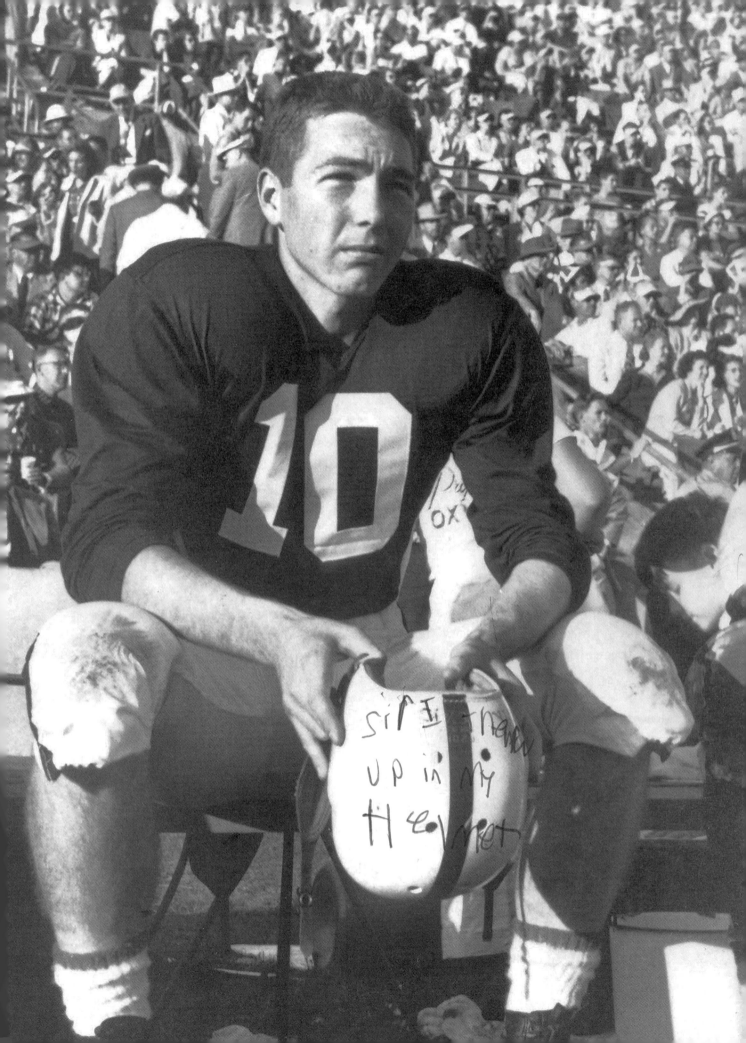

BART STARR

QUARTERBACK 1952-1955

Kentucky seemed like such a natural fit for young Bryan Bartlett Starr. Paul "Bear" Bryant was the head coach, Bryant had played at Alabama, and Starr's father was a big Alabama fan. Plus, Starr's coach at Montgomery's Sidney Lanier High, Bill Moseley, had played for Bryant. Then Moseley and Bryant arranged for Starr to travel to Lexington in the summer of 1951 and spend about a week working with Kentucky's star quarterback, Vito "Babe" Parilli.

"It was a fabulous experience," Starr says. "He taught me more about the position in just a few days than anyone ever had before because I had never been coached by a quarterback of that caliber. It was quite a thrill, so I was zeroed in on going to Kentucky."

Throughout his life, as a husband, father, quarterback, coach and businessman, Starr has made plenty of important decisions. Some of those choices involved split-second decisiveness and resolve. None have been more important than the decision he made in 1951.

"I had started dating a beautiful young lady in high school, and I think God gave me enough common sense to realize that if I went to the University of Kentucky in Lexington and she stayed in Alabama and went to Auburn University that I would lose her," Starr says.

Playing at Alabama, Starr realized, would please his father Benjamin Bryan Starr, a career U.S. Air Force master sergeant, and still keep him close to the apple of his young eye.

"So I made what I call the greatest audible of my life and decided to go to Alabama so I could chase her during the off season," Starr says. "It worked out well. We were married after my sophomore year in college and Cherry helped put me through school."

Bryant moved on to Texas A&M, so Starr

never got the chance to play for him anyway, but just in case anyone questioned the decision at the time, history has validated Starr's commitment time and time again.

"We just celebrated our 50th wedding anniversary," Starr says, "so that's the greatest decision I ever made."

History also validated Starr's entire football career. Despite a disappointing football career at the University of Alabama, Starr went on to become one of the most successful quarterbacks in the history of professional football, leading the Green Bay Packers to five championships under coach Vince Lombardi and becoming a member of the Pro Football Hall of Fame.

"Bart Starr stands for what the game of football stands for: courage, stamina and coordinated efficiency," Lombardi said. "You instill desire by creating a superlative example. The noblest form of leadership is by example and that is what Bart Starr is all about."

While no one who ever spent any significant time with Starr could come away questioning his character or heart, it would have been easy to question the direction of his football career after four years at Alabama.

Starr's college career actually began with considerable promise. He arrived at Alabama in the summer of 1952, at a time when the Crimson Tide was still a force to be reckoned with under coach Harold "Red" Drew. Starr even saw considerable playing time for a freshman and earned a letter as Alabama won 10 of 12 games. When the Crimson Tide crushed Syracuse 61-6 in the 1953 Orange Bowl, Starr came off the bench to throw a 22-yard touchdown pass to Joe Cummings,

giving the Crimson Tide the Orange Bowl scoring record.

Starr became a part-time starter and shared the quarterback and punting duties for most of his sophomore season, finishing second nationally with a 41.1-yard punting average as Alabama went 6-3-3 and played Rice in the Cotton Bowl. Just when it appeared he was ready to take over the starting job, he spent most of his junior season watching from the sidelines because of a back injury. A 4-5-2 finish that fall led to Drew's dismissal as head coach.

"It was very disappointing for me and for the team," Starr says. "As a team we were sliding, and when you combine the two, the physical problems and the way we were performing as a team, it was a disappointing season."

The situation didn't improve in 1955. The University brought in former Alabama player J.B. "Ears" Whitworth as the new head coach, and he had no real use for Drew's seniors. Between Whitworth's decision, a severe ankle sprain and a new offense that called for a more run-oriented quarterback, Starr found himself sitting the bench for an 0-10 team.

"I hadn't lost the desire for football, so it was a very disappointing season," Starr says. "At the same time, it was an internal strengthening time for many of us. You have to look at yourself and check your attitude, your courage, your discipline and commitment and see where you are, because you can let that sort of push you under, and that's something all of us had to fight."

Instead of giving up on football, Starr says his senior season, "reinforced my desire to at least have a chance to compete again and hopefully be drafted by someone."

Fortunately for Starr, he had two important people on his side. One was Johnny Dee, who coached the basketball team and assisted with the football team. When the athletic department wouldn't give Starr any footballs to work with, Dee provided him with three new balls. Dee also used his contacts with Jack Vainisi, the personnel director of the Packers, to get Starr a shot in the NFL.

"I didn't have any resume from my final two years of college," Starr says. "There was almost nothing there. I don't know how, to this day, I lettered as a senior. I don't think we played enough to even letter. I think it was just gratuitous.

"But because of Coach Dee, whom I had gotten to know well, he influenced the gentleman there in Green Bay to take me in the 17th round, and back in those days, they had I think 20 rounds. Otherwise, I probably wouldn't have been selected."

The other important person in Starr's life at the time was Cherry, who wouldn't let him give up on his dream.

"I really became pumped after the draft and I never worked harder in my life preparing for a season than I did before I went to Green Bay," Starr says. "I was literally throwing at a tire hung in an A-frame, and my wife would joke that those footballs looked more like soccer balls because of how many times they had hit the ground. They were pretty well worn by the time I left for Green Bay, but she'd help me by retrieving them every day. That's the type of lady she is, and she deserves a lot of credit."

The hiring of Lombardi as the Packers head coach and general manager in late 1959 brought another pivotal person into Starr's life. Starr shared the starting job for a 1-10-1

team in 1958, but Lombardi gave Starr and the Packers a new start.

"When we had our first meeting with Coach Lombardi he invited about 10 to 12 offensive players to what would be considered a mini-camp today, and he began the session by thanking the Packers for the opportunity they

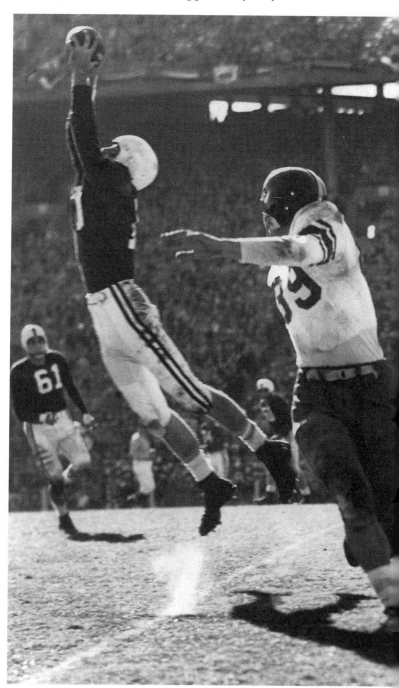

Bart Starr (left) intercepts a pass.

had given him to become their coach because of the rich tradition of the organization and his respect for what they had been able to accomplish over the years," Starr says. "Then he said we were going to relentlessly chase perfection knowing full well we're not going to catch it because perfection is not attainable, but we're still going to chase it because in the process we will catch excellence.

"Then he paused for a moment and looked directly at all of us, right in the eye, and said, 'I am not remotely interested in being just good.' We didn't even need chairs after that because we were so pumped."

When the meeting adjourned for a short break, Starr ran downstairs and immediately phoned his wife back in Birmingham.

"All I said was, 'Honey, we're going to begin to win,'" Starr says. "It was that obvious."

The Packers went on to win five NFL championships and six division titles from 1959-67, including three consecutive league championships from 1965-67 and the first two Super Bowls, and Starr went on to become one of the NFL's most accomplished quarterbacks. Starr not only proved to be an excellent fit for Lombardi's hard-nosed run-oriented offense because of his ability to make the right decisions in tune with Lombardi's coaching, he also proved himself as a passer, leading the NFL in passing percentage four times, earning Pro Bowl honors four times and receiving the league MVP award in 1966. Starr also won MVP honors in Super Bowls I and II, throwing for a combined 452 yards and three touchdowns against the Kansas City Chiefs and Oakland Raiders.

The Packers went 62-24-4 under Starr

and lost only one playoff game, the 1960 NFL Championship game against the Philadelphia Eagles. After that, the Packers went 9-0 in postseason play with Starr at quarterback.

Former Minnesota Vikings coach Norm Van Brocklin called Starr "the smartest quarterback in pro football," but Starr is quick to credit a cast of outstanding players and coaches for his success. Among those coaches and players, no one stood out more than Lombardi.

"He was an outstanding teacher and very committed to the coaching profession," Starr says. "He surrounded himself with quality coaches who were great coaches on and off the field. I've never been around someone who was more committed and disciplined in his approach. I used to love going to our meetings just to listen to him—even years later, after I heard the same things over and over and over. It was very inspiring.

"I also respected the quality of the man's life. He was rigidly prioritized: God, family, others. He never varied. He was in mass at 7 a.m. every morning for the nine years we knew him. When you're working with someone like that, it's contagious. When you have your priorities in order, it's amazing how you can keep your life balanced."

Starr always regretted not playing for Bryant, but always imagined it would be similar to playing for Lombardi. "He had the same impact on his people at the collegiate level," Starr says, "and the results are there."

Starr finally retired as a player in 1972 and spent a season coaching quarterbacks for the Packers before moving to the Birmingham area and becoming part owner of several car dealerships throughout the Southeast. He returned to Green Bay in December 1974 to become the team's head coach and general manager, only to find a franchise in the kind of disorder similar to what he had encountered as a player before Lombardi arrived. Starr's team experienced their share of ups and downs and made the playoffs in 1982, but he was finally dismissed after an 8-8 season in 1983.

Since then his life has presented a series of challenges and opportunities. In 1988 the Starrs lost their youngest son, Bret, at age 24. One year later they returned to Birmingham so they could be close to their older son, Bart Jr., and their grandchildren.

An attempt to help Phoenix land an expansion franchise and an attempt to buy the Tampa Bay Bucs as part of an investment group never materialized, but Starr has continued to experience business success as the chairman of a company that develops medical centers for groups of doctors. The Starrs also continue to support a home for wayward boys in Wisconsin called the Rawhide Foundation, and Starr himself remains in demand as a motivational speaker, with good reason.

"There's the good and the bad in life sometimes and we've experienced that," Starr says, "and that's a check-up time for you. You have to check yourself and find out a lot about yourselves."

One of the things Starr has learned is that he has a lot for which to be grateful. He remains close with several Alabama teammates who made a significant impact on his life, people such as Harry Lee, Hootie Ingram, Bill Oliver, Tommy Lewis, and Bobby Barnes. Despite the fact that he was not a major star at Alabama, he also remains a popular figure among Crimson Tide fans because of his quiet dignity and grace.

"It's an honor and a blessing," Starr says. "The University of Alabama has been blessed with a rich history of athletic success and also of academic excellence. The school is highly regarded in various areas, like the business school and the law school, and to have been part of the university was really a thrill and a blessing."

Then to add his days with the Packers, Starr can say he is truly one of the few athletes who can say they played for some of the nation's most devoted and passionate sports fans.

"I think the words honored and blessed are appropriate," Starr says. "It's hard to express how you feel about being part of both programs [Alabama and Green Bay]. We fell in love with the people in Green Bay and we lived there for 31 years. They don't come any better than those folks. We're thrilled that we're back in Birmingham and have been for the past 14 years and we've been able to get back to the college scene. It's been a tremendous experience for our family. Bart, Jr. went to the University of Alabama, and we have some wonderful ties there. It's been a joy, an honor and a blessing to have been part of two programs like that."

BILLY NEIGHBORS

TACKLE 1959-1961

Billy Neighbors knew from an early age that he wanted to play college football for Alabama. It took some tough lessons from coach Paul "Bear" Bryant to show him just how much playing for the Crimson Tide meant to him.

Neighbors was born in Taylorville, played his high school football at Tuscaloosa County in Northport, lived next door to former Crimson Tide star Harry Gilmer and even baby-sat Gilmer's daughters from time to time. In fact, it was Gilmer who bought Neighbors his first set of weights at age nine.

"I never planned on going anywhere else," Neighbors says.

Even the absence of a head coach at Alabama couldn't change that. When Neighbors signed his scholarship with Alabama assistant coach Hank Crisp at a Northport fruit stand the Crimson Tide was between coaches and

Neighbors had no idea the University was about to hire Bryant as its head coach.

"I'd never heard of him really," Neighbors says. "I don't even think we took the paper, so I didn't know anything about him."

It didn't take long for Bryant to make a strong first impression on Neighbors. When Neighbors's older brother Sid showed up three pounds overweight for preseason practice, the day before younger brother Billy arrived in Tuscaloosa, Bryant kicked Sid off the team right there and then.

"I was scared," Neighbors says. "When somebody runs your brother off for being three pounds overweight, what else are you going to think? Think about that. I knew he was serious. I came from within a hair of going to Florida State, and if I hadn't wanted to play for Alabama so bad I wouldn't have stayed there."

Instead, Neighbors stayed and listened

to what Bryant had to say when the new coach met with his first recruiting class. At that meeting, Bryant vowed that his freshmen would someday, "be undefeated and win the national championship before y'all leave here—if you'll do what I tell you to do."

Some players bought in. Some didn't know what to think. Neighbors was convinced of one thing.

"I thought he was crazy," Neighbors says.

Bryant turned out to be as crazy as a fox, and in 1961 his first freshman class became the first of his six national championship teams. It was a team loaded with tough, quick players who were willing to pay the price for success. Neighbors, who played both ways on the offensive and defensive lines and earned All-America honors in 1961, was a good fit for the team and the era.

"With the players on that team there was a familiar thread," says Alabama athletic director Mal Moore, who played at Alabama from 1958-62. "They were all great competitors and Billy was one of the greatest competitors around. He was very tough, very strong and quick and an aggressive player."

Part of Neighbors's success was his ability to remain strong and quick regardless of his weight. Those childhood weight-training sessions, thanks to Gilmer, turned Neighbors into a stocky, powerful package.

"All my buddies thought I was crazy," Neighbors says. "They were out shooting rabbits and squirrels and chasing girls, and I was lifting weights like a fool."

Neighbors had the last laugh during his football career, even though it took him a while to learn how to manage his weight and meet Bryant's expectations, both on and off the field.

"You know you hear a lot of talk now about education and players getting a degree. Buddy, let me tell you something: It was big to Coach Bryant back in 1958," Neighbors said in *Talk of the Tide*. "I wasn't doing too well in school my freshman year, and my second semester, matter of fact, I wasn't doing anything. I was cutting classes. So Coach Bryant asked me to eat lunch with him, and man, I was scared to death because I knew I had a problem, but I didn't know why he was mad. To tell you the truth, I didn't think he knew what kind of grades I was making!

"He had the dean of the school with him, and I went and sat down with them. He introduced me to the dean, and we started talking. He pulled out my IQ and pulled out how many classes I'd cut, and boy, I didn't look up—I just kept my head down. Coach Bryant said, 'Look up at me, boy, I'm talking to you!' So I looked up, and he said to the dean, 'Now this boy right here can help us win, but if he doesn't start getting better grades, he isn't going to be here!' The dean started talking about the classes I'd taken, what I should take, and all this stuff, and Coach Bryant said, 'Well, I'm going to give him one more semester. I'm going to move him into my house with me, and I'm going to do him like I do Paul, Jr., when he comes home with a C, I'll beat him with a damn dictionary!' So, I got straightened out real fast!"

Neighbors also arrived on campus with too much bulk on his frame until Bryant's demanding regime helped him play most of his career in the 240- to 250-pound range. Neighbors recalls Bryant insisting he report for his senior season at 225 pounds. Neighbors responded by arriving at a very lean 218. Bryant didn't weigh him again until the day before the

Sugar Bowl and Neighbors weighed in at 262, but still played both ways for the entire game.

"I was in good shape," Neighbors says, "because he'd run you until you couldn't walk, or he'd find someone else to take your place."

Bryant didn't need to find anyone else, because Neighbors brought a combination of strong intangibles and unique talents to the field.

"He was one of the quickest blockers, as far as his first three steps, and he could run and block a guy at the same height and level as his stance," says former linebacker Lee Roy Jordan, who played with Neighbors from 1959-61. "Most offensive linemen when they start to block someone, they raise up. Most big guys can't stay that low and you can get under them and get leverage on them. You couldn't do that with Billy. He came right out of his stance and stayed low and got up under you.

"Billy and John Hannah [an Alabama All-American in 1972] were the only two players I've ever known who could run almost full speed and hit you at the same level as their stance. Those two were probably the best two blockers I ever saw in my whole career."

Like many of his classmates, it took awhile for Neighbors to see just how good he and the Crimson Tide could be under Bryant. Most of the freshmen that came in 1958 were unable or unwilling to pay the price, but those who stayed were in for an amazing journey.

"We worked like hell for the first two years," Neighbors say. "I think there was something like 118 of us who came in as freshman, and eight of us left after four years. But by the time we were juniors he had us where he wanted us: he had us all well trained, and

we knew how to run his system and we could beat people in the fourth quarter by being in better shape than other teams. He taught us that if we were in better shape than the other team we would win sooner or later.

"And he had something special about him that got you fired up to get ready to play and got his coaches ready to coach, so you'd do anything he told you to do."

Neighbors admits he still thought Bryant might be a little "crazy," especially about all this championship talk, until the fifth game of his senior season.

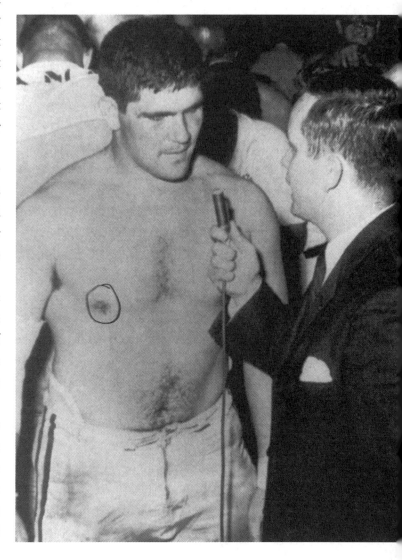

"We beat Tennessee 34-3 in Birmingham and after that game he came on the bus after the game and told us we had a great football team," Neighbors says. "Three or four weeks before he had told us we wouldn't win a game, that we were sorry as hell."

By the end of the regular season, the Crimson Tide was 10-0 and champions of the SEC and all of college football, since the polls did not wait for the bowls in those days. The Tide still entered the Sugar Bowl against Arkansas with a perfect record and a lot of pride on the line, and Neighbors did his part to turn Bryant's promise into reality.

"We went to Biloxi, Mississippi, to practice a week before the game and the whole team got the flu," Jordan says. "We were all drained of our strength, and by the third quarter of the Sugar Bowl we were all pooped out.

"But Billy Neighbors was probably the reason we won that game. He was exceptional both ways."

Alabama won 10-3, and Neighbors moved on to a professional career and a draft that produced offers from both the NFL's Washington Redskins and the fledgling AFL's Boston Patriots. The AFL was enticing players with better money in many cases and Neighbors went on to start with the Patriots as a rookie. In eight years with Buffalo and Miami he served as a captain and a player representative and earned All-Pro honors three times before retiring after the 1969 season.

"I'm not even six foot and I weighed about 260 pounds when I played, but I played eight years in the pros, and not many people can say that," Neighbors says. "Coach Bryant made a football player out of me. He pushed me to be disciplined and prepared to play. He taught

me how to work hard every time I played, and I learned to work hard in the off season, too."

Neighbors was also smart enough during his career to look toward the future and take a cue from Bryant. After watching Bryant carry around the *Wall Street Journal* and pay particular attention to the financial reports, Neighbors bought stock in Texaco during his college years and spent his off seasons in the pros investing his time and energy in the financial world and continues to work as a financial consultant.

"You know what the NFL stands for? Not For Long," Neighbors says. "It's a tough business, and those owners don't care about anyone but themselves. That's hard to handle when you're a young person. That's why so many players have a hard time when they get out. That's why I always worked as a broker in the off season so I'd be ready when my career ended."

It wasn't until his pro career ended that Neighbors entered into a new, and very different relationship with his old coach—a relationship he never thought possible. They almost ended up working together when Bryant came dangerously close to leaving Alabama to coach the Miami Dolphins in 1970. After Bryant initially agreed to an offer from Dolphins' coach Joe Robbie, he called Neighbors and wanted him to come out of retirement to serve as a player and coach. Before Neighbors could give it much serious thought, Bryant called him several hours later and told him he had changed his mind and decided to remain at Alabama.

It was just as well for Neighbors, because he was still intimidated by his old coach.

"I never had very much to do with him

except when he'd catch me at lunch in the dining hall or if he caught me walking down the street, because I always hid from him," Neighbors says. "If I saw him coming down the street, I would run to the other side or get the heck out of there. He'd ask about if you were going to class or not and if you lied to him, he knew it. ... I was horrified I was going to do something to upset him."

When Bryant called Neighbors twice during his pro football career and asked him why he hadn't written, called or stopped by, Neighbor admits, "I didn't tell him that I didn't want nothing to do with him. I was still scared of him."

It was Bryant who continued to pursue the relationship. In 1970, when Neighbors and former Tide teammate Benny Nelson were visiting campus to attend a basketball game, Bryant saw Neighbors, called him up to his office and asked him why he hadn't stopped in to see him.

"That's when I really became his friend," Neighbors says. "Before I was just a football player who was scared to death of him, but from then on we became buddies. He'd call me all the time and I'd call him. He'd always return a phone call."

Neighbors has remained close to the pro-gram over the years. His brother Bobby, who was born with spina bifida, received a golf cart as a gift from Bryant and rarely missed a game. Neighbors's sons, Wes and Keith, went on to play for Alabama. While Billy was part of Bryant's first recruiting class, Wes was part of Bryant's last signing group, and Keith was a member of the 1992 national championship team.

"I was proud of them, happy for them," Neighbors says. "There wasn't much you could do but sit and watch and hope for the best, but they both worked hard and became good, disciplined people."

The same can be said of Neighbors, who went to become a member of the College Football Hall of Fame 2003 and the Alabama Sports Hall of Fame in 1983 and is widely regarded as one of the two best blockers in Alabama history, along with Hannah.

"It was probably what I wanted to be when I was a kid and just didn't really understand it all," Neighbors says. "I didn't know you had to have the ability or be lucky enough to be around the right people or the right circum-stances to do that. I got lucky and got to play for Bear Bryant and that was the difference. Of course those first two years I didn't think I was too dang lucky, but after that I did."

PAT TRAMMELL

QUARTERBACK 1959-1961

It was coach Paul "Bear" Bryant's custom to wait until after he had watched game film on Sunday before publicly assessing the Saturday performance of his team. It took a rare player or a unique performance to move Bryant to immediate praise.

Such was the case with quarterback Pat Trammell's performance after the 1961 Tennessee game. After Trammell completed 13 of 19 passes for 156 yards in a 34-3 victory at Legion Field, Bryant's first win over Tennessee since his return to Alabama in 1958, Bryant actually used the word "great" to describe Trammell's afternoon.

"You can't really single out anyone until after you've looked at the films, but goodness, you had to notice Trammell," Bryant said.

Then, for good measure, Bryant yelled across the locker room, "Hey Trammell, I want you to get home early tonight, so you can get up tomorrow and work on your passing."

The postgame praise was an unusual exception by Bryant. Then again, Bryant made a lot of exceptions when it came to Trammell. That's because Trammell was special, distinctive, an exception not just to the norm, but even to the greatness that surrounded him on the Alabama football team from 1958-61.

Trammell, according to teammates and coaches, would argue with Bryant and get away with it. Trammell, they say, would reject plays sent in from the sidelines and call his own. Trammell, they also say, had a special relationship with Bryant that went beyond coach and player. Trammell, they insist, was Bryant's all-time favorite player and one of his all-time favorite people.

He wasn't just the exception. He was truly exceptional, and not because he had the talent of a Joe Namath or a Ken Stabler.

"As a quarterback, Pat had no ability," Bryan often said. "He was not a great runner, but he could score touchdowns. He didn't pass with great style, but he completed passes. All he could do was beat you."

A thorough examination of the Alabama record book doesn't reveal much about Trammell, a six-foot-two, 205-pound doctor's son who could run as well as pass. His name won't be found on pages 177-179 of the 2003 Alabama football media guide under the listings of Alabama's records for attempts, completions, yardage, touchdowns and completion percentage. In fact, his name doesn't appear among Alabama's long list of accomplished quarterbacks until the final column of stats on page 179, under two categories: lowest interception percentage and Alabama's winningest quarterbacks. In 1961, Trammell set the school record by throwing only two interceptions in 133 attempts (1.5 percent). From 1959-61, he set another record by throwing only four interceptions in 225 attempts (1.8 percent).

Most important, in his three seasons as a starter, the Crimson Tide finished 26-2-4, good for third on Alabama's all-time list behind Jay Barker (35-1-1 from 1991-94) and Harry Gilmer (30-9-2 from 1944-47, though technically not a quarterback, but the left halfback who did most of the passing in the Notre Dame box offense). In fact, Alabama lost only three games during those three years, and Trammell missed one of those games because of an injury.

It is Trammell's record as a winner that comes as close to any stat that could possibly define his Alabama career. In addition to his outstanding record as a starter, it was Trammell who led Bryant's first Alabama recruits to an 11-0 record and the national and SEC championships in 1961, their senior season.

"Pat was the perfect quarterback at that time," says Mal Moore, a backup quarterback from 1958-62, a longtime Alabama assistant coach and the university's current athletic director. "When Coach Bryant came to build the program he needed someone to lead the team and Pat was an outstanding leader. He was very smart, he was very tough, mentally and physically tough, and he was a great competitor. All of that together was what Coach Bryant was looking for and what was desperately needed from that position at that time, and Pat Trammell had it. He was the fit."

Perhaps Trammell knew that when he left his hometown of Scottsboro and arrived on campus in 1958 as part of Bryant's first recruiting class. Former Alabama defensive back and defensive coordinator Bill Oliver remembers how Trammell stepped up in the midst of several players talking about what positions they planned to play at Alabama and said, "Well y'all can just forget about quarterback. I'm going to be the quarterback."

Trammell won the job and won over Bryant with a combination of toughness and smarts. Teammates recall that Trammell had a knack for knowing what every player was supposed to do on every play and understood when teammates missed assignments. He also had no problem with jumping on a player for missing an assignment, for sending a teammate out of the huddle and off the field or using physical threats to take control in the huddle if players wasn't pulling their own weight. And, as former teammate Charley Pell once said, "Everybody knew he could back it up, too."

"It was attitude," says former Alabama linebacker Lee Roy Jordan, Trammell's teammate from 1959-61. "It was like Coach Bryant said, 'He didn't pass too good, he didn't run too good, all he did was win.' If we needed six yards, Pat would run for seven. If we needed eight yards, Pat would pass for nine. Whatever we needed, he got just a little more than we needed. He had that tough mental attitude that said we can do anything. He just wanted to win so bad and he was such a confident guy."

Billy Neighbors, Alabama's All-America tackle in 1961, insists, "Pat Trammell was the smartest and best football I ever played with, period—and I played with some great players, like Bob Griese and Babe Parelli. Pat Trammell was still the smartest football player I ever played with. It was just the way he ran the team, the offense."

From left: Coach Paul "Bear" Bryant, Pat Trammell and General Douglas MacArthur

On one particular occasion, against Auburn of all teams, Trammell defied one of Bryant's play calls by quick kicking on third down. When Bryant confronted Trammell as he came off the field, Trammell simply said, "Those guys weren't blocking anybody, so I thought we might as well see if they can play defense."

Bryant made a habit of having lunch with his quarterbacks during the week and before games to make sure his quarterbacks were on the same page with the game plan. Jack Rutledge, who played guard from 1959-61 and later ran the athletic dorm for Bryant, remembers one particular occasion when Bryant pulled out a pen and started drawing something, most likely a play, on a napkin.

"Trammell's just watching him, and Coach Bryant takes that play and slides it over in front of him and says 'Pat, what do you think of this play?'" Rutledge says. "Pat just says, 'I don't think that'll work worth a damn.' Coach Bryant just reached over and took that napkin and put it in his pocket."

Only Trammell could get away with that kind of behavior, and with good reason.

"They'd send in plays and he wouldn't run 'em because he knew more about what was going on than the dang coaches," Neighbors says. "And Coach Bryant never would say anything to him about it, because he knew Pat was right. Every time I can ever recall, he was right. I would think he was crazy, but he knew what he was doing."

Jordan recalls, "Pat didn't hesitate to tell Coach Bryant what he thought. The rest of would us would just say, 'Yes sir, Coach Bryant,' but not Pat. If he disagreed with Coach Bryant, he'd let him know. He was the only one. The coaches didn't do it, either. But he got away with it because he was brilliant—and he was usually right. He knew what all of our guys were doing on every play, he had a real handle on what the defenses were trying to do, and he knew how to take advantage of the situation."

In Bryant's opinion, those qualities suited Trammell better as a doctor than as a professional football quarterback. Trammell was a questionable professional prospect already, due to his relatively limited athletic ability, but his other qualities were even evident to strangers. One of those who met him and became immediately impressed was legendary Green Bay Packers coach Vince Lombardi, who met Trammell and Bryant at a MacArthur Bowl presentation in New York and soon asked Trammell is if he was interested in playing pro football for the Packers.

Trammell was interested, but Bryant jumped in quickly and said, "He's not going to play pro football. He's going to med school."

Lombardi countered with, "We have four boys who are playing for us and going to med school."

"He's going to med school," Bryant responded. "He's not good enough to play pro football."

Trammell committed himself to medical school and eventually became Dr. Trammell, a dermatology specialist in private practice in Birmingham. In a feature story for the 1968 Alabama-Auburn game program Trammell later confessed that it took him awhile to realize what Bryant was up to.

"Coach Bryant had several players playing

pro football but didn't have any of his players in med school then," Trammell said. "He needed somebody there for recruiting purposes."

Trammell and Bryant's relationship remained close throughout the next few years, but it took a deeper step in the summer of 1968 when Trammell learned he had a malignant tumor. The news of Trammell's diagnosis hit Bryant hard, and he responded by traveling to New York twice to visit Trammell at an experimental clinic. Trammell promised to fight cancer like he had fought on the football field, and his prognosis took a positive step when he went into remission that fall, but it wasn't long before the cancer returned to attack his body. At the time, he told then-assistant Gene Stallings, "Coach, don't feel too sorry for me. I have had a wonderful 29 years."

Trammell also did his best to put up a strong front with Bryant.

"I went up to Birmingham to see him about a week before he died," Bryant said years later. "When I walked in the room he looked at me and asked, 'What are you doing here? Why aren't you out recruiting?'"

For all of Trammell's tenacious spirit, it was obvious by the end of the season he was running out of time. After Alabama beat Auburn 24-16 on November 30, Trammell "was outside the dressing room after the game and you could tell," Moore says.

"We had won the game and it was, of course, a happy moment there, and then Pat came in the dressing room and [linebacker] Mike Hall presented him with the game ball. It was a very tearful, very sad time for all of us but it was a precious moment for all of us. Anybody who saw that would not forget it."

Just 10 days later, at the age of 28, Trammell passed away and left a powerful legacy for his family, friends, coaches, teammates, and future Alabama players. Bryant is said to have wept like a baby over the loss of a man he loved like a son, saying, "This is the saddest day of my life."

Over the years, Bryant poured his love and respect for Trammell into family. Trammell's son and daughter not only became the first to benefit from the visionary scholarship fund Bryant established with an initial gift of $1 million to send the children of any former Crimson Tide player under Bryant to the University, but he also became something of a surrogate grandfather, checking in with the family, calling on the children's birthdays, offering them advice and guidance and making sure their needs were met.

"It was one of the most remarkable things that I know a coach has done for his players," Moore says. "When Pat Trammell died, he wanted it done [for Pat, Jr]. He realized the need. From then on, there have been a little over 700 children of coach Bryant's players to go through the university on a scholarship."

Lee Roy Jordan and the silver dollar
from the 1963 Orange Bowl

LEE ROY JORDAN

LINEBACKER 1960-1962

When Lee Roy Jordan showed up in Tuscaloosa in the summer of 1959, it was quickly obvious he didn't just play football with aggression and toughness. He played like it was the most important thing he could ever do with his life.

"For Lee Roy Jordan, playing football was a joy," says Mal Moore, Jordan's teammate from 1959-62 and Alabama's current athletic director. "He loved it. He was a hitter and he was at the right position at linebacker to display his skills and his personality. And he was such a competitor. You could just see it in him from the time he arrived here."

The more coaches and teammates came to know Jordan, the more they came to realize why football was so special to him.

"I grew up pickin' cotton on my daddy's farm," Jordan says. "To me, football is like a day off."

Growing up on a family farm near the south Alabama town of Excel taught Jordan the reality of waking up early, working hard and staying late, regardless of the circumstances. He learned those lessons before he stepped foot on the University of Alabama campus and applied it on the football field throughout his college and professional football career with the Crimson Tide and the Dallas Cowboys.

Jordan won a national championship at Alabama and a Super Bowl with the Cowboys, earned All-America honors in college, was Alabama's defensive player of the decade for the 1960s, earned All-Pro honors in the NFL and spots in both the College Football Hall of Fame and the Dallas Cowboys' Ring of Honor, but he never left his Excel roots behind.

Jordan was "the finest player I ever coached," according to Bryant. "He's one of the finest football players the world has ever seen. He never had a bad day. He did everything an All-America football player should do, with class. He was a 100-percent performer in practice and a 110-percent performer in games."

Hard work was a way of life for Walter and Cleo Jordan, who farmed primarily cotton on their Monroe County farm but also grew corn and peanuts and raised their own cattle, hogs, chickens and turkeys.

"Most everything we ate was raised on our farm," Jordan says. "We basically bought flour, salt and pepper."

The Jordans also raised six children on that farm and lost another child, a two-year-old girl, to leukemia. Lee Roy, their fifth child and the last of four boys, saw his parents work hard to make the farm a feasible business, even if his mother had to take up some of the slack when his father fell ill.

"She was the workingest human being in the world," Jordan says. "My father had some health problems in his early 50s, but my mother worked like a farm hand all her life. Up until she was 75 years old, she was still farming her own garden. She had a garden that could feed the whole county that late in her life, because that was her love."

Cleo Jordan had to have been some kind of cook to feed four boys who played high school football. Her pecan pie must have been particularly good, because it sparked larceny in the heart of an otherwise honest young man.

"I went home with Lee Roy once and spent a weekend with his family, and his mother made the best pecan pies ever," Moore says. "Cotton Clark and I were roommates and Lee Roy and Richard Williamson were roommates, and Lee Roy had gone home for the weekend, and he came in from Excel about 8:30 or 9:00 and left a big slice of that pecan pie on his cabinet and went out on a date. I came in a little earlier than he did and walked through the bathroom we all shared into their

room and saw that big slice of pecan pie. I actually went over to a little cafeteria nearby and bought a pint of milk and I ate that pie and drank my milk.

"Lee Roy comes in about 12:30 after his date with a quart of milk and he's ready to eat that pie, but, of course, it's not there. He came over and asked me if I had seen anyone in his room and I said I hadn't, which was true. I did tell him 20 or 30 years later, when I didn't think he would care anymore, that I was the one who ate that pie, and he still got real upset over it."

It wasn't easy to make time for football and farm chores on the family farm, so Jordan was fortunate to have three older brothers who paved the way for him as a football player. By the time he reached high school, his parents allowed him to play both football and basketball at the only school in Excel.

"You went in first grade and you left after high school," Jordan says. "We must have had 15-18 classrooms. You started on one end and went out the other end."

None of his older brothers or sisters had attended college before him, but Jordan started giving thought to the possibility late in his junior season after a standout performance against one of the bigger areas schools, W.S. Neal High in Brewton.

"They had a big running back that Alabama was looking at recruiting, and I had a much bigger game than he did and we won the game," Jordan says. After the game, Alabama assistant coach Jerry Claiborne made it a point to talk to Excel coach W.C. Majors about Jordan, and it wasn't long before Alabama made a pitch for the rugged young linebacker.

Even though Auburn had just won the

national championship in 1957 and followed that season with a 9-0-1 mark in 1958, Jordan didn't have to think twice about playing football at Alabama, mostly because Auburn offered a scholarship and then withdrew the offer. Jordan was actually relieved at the time, "because I thought those guys at Auburn were too good for me, and I didn't think I'd ever play if I went to Auburn."

More importantly, Jordan had heard enough about the Crimson Tide's new coach to be encouraged about the future. Jordan

also heard Bryant, whose first Alabama team had shown some positive signs during a 5-4-1 season in 1958, had a penchant for players like Jordan: smaller, tougher kids who weren't afraid to work or hit.

"He was a great athlete and a tough player who would knock your dang brains out," says teammate Billy Neighbors.

"When he hit, it just sounded different," longtime assistant coach Clem Gryska said. "Some people just hit you, but he just hit through people."

Lee Roy Jordan (No. 54) in the 1963 Orange Bowl

That made Jordan a perfect fit for Bryant's methods. "I think you'll find there's a familiar thread with the players who were here at that time, and they were all great competitors, and Lee Roy was one of the greatest competitors around," Moore says. "He was very tough, very aggressive and he was here at the right time, because Coach Bryant was looking for players like Lee Roy."

Those qualities manifested themselves in All-America selections in both 1961 and 1962, two seasons in which the Crimson Tide allowed just 25 and 39 points respectively. During an era in which accurate tackling stats were not kept for most games, Jordan's production was probably best described when Bryant said, "If they stay inside the boundaries, Lee Roy will get 'em."

That was particularly true during Jordan's best collegiate game, the 1963 Orange Bowl against Oklahoma. The Crimson Tide didn't need any extra help that day, but it came anyway from President John F. Kennedy, who made the mistake of visiting the Oklahoma locker room before the game and sitting on the Oklahoma side of the stadium.

"Coach Bryant did mention that to us a little bit before the game," Jordan says with a wink.

Before the game Secret Service agents escorted Jordan and the Oklahoma captain up to Kennedy's seat in the stands. After the coin toss the captains posed for photos with the president.

"I still have that coin—it was a silver dollar," Jordan says. "For a kid from Excel to meet the president, that was a big deal."

During the game, Jordan proved to be the big deal for Alabama, with an extraordinary 31 tackles.

"I had no idea I had that many until someone told me," Jordan says. "After the game I felt like I had hit a lot of people, though. But to be honest, so many of my teammates had taken on blocks to give me and the other linebackers the chance to make tackles. That was our defensive scheme, and people like Billy Neighbors and Charley Pell and Jimmy Sharpe did their jobs really well, or we wouldn't have made so many tackles."

With the defensive front doing its job and Jordan plugging the gaps for tackles, Alabama shut down Oklahoma's star halfback, Joe Don Looney, and forced him to fumble twice. The Tide allowed 240-pound fullback Jim Grisham to rush for 107 yards, but the Alabama defense also kept him out of the end zone and forced him to fumble the ball away at the Alabama 7-yard line. Alabama went on to win the game 17-0.

"The president sure came by after the game," Jordan says, laughing.

The Tide finished 10-1 and finished fifth in the nation. Only a failed two-point attempt in a 7-6 loss to Georgia Tech prevented the Tide and Jordan from winning a second consecutive national championship, but Jordan left Alabama with the knowledge that he and his fellow seniors had done their part to restore the program's place on the national scene, having gone 29-2-2 in three years.

"Between our group and the group right before us," Jordan says, "we felt like we had done something pretty special."

Jordan's pro football career also turned out to be something special. From 1963-76, Jordan stood out as one of the NFL's best linebackers on one of the NFL's most successful teams. Jordan earned All-Pro honors twice, played in the Pro Bowl five times, set the Cowboys' team record with 1,236 career tackles and set another team record with 154 consecutive starts. Most importantly, he played on teams that won five conference championships and eight division titles and played in three Super Bowls, winning Super Bowl VI.

"The Cowboys were a great experience," Jordan says. "We were coming up at a time when the country was looking for a little something different, and Coach [Tom] Landry had an offense that would do anything, throw the ball anytime and put anybody anywhere to try to gain an advantage. Plus we were an exciting team. We could be down 21-0 and still come back and win, and people loved that kind of exciting football."

Jordan considers it an honor to have played for both Bryant and Landry, but says the two men approached the job with different mindsets. Landry's style was more intellectual, while Bryant brought more passion to the game.

Of Landry, Jordan says, "He was an engineer by education, and he knew all about angles and who had the best advantage to beat who. He was the smartest coach I ever met. He could have been one of the greatest defensive coaches ever or one of the greatest offensive coaches ever, if he had just focused on one side of the ball, but he coached both sides."

Of Bryant, Jordan says, "He was such a great person and motivator. He always made you feel like he was totally concerned with just you. ... He got a lot of us to probably overachieve with his nurturing and teaching us how to compete.

"If I hadn't called in a while Coach Bryant would call me every few months. He'd say,

'What are you doing? How's your family doing? Why haven't you called me lately? Why didn't you call?' And I'd promise to do better and try to call him in two or three weeks."

When Jordan retired, he remained in Dallas, where he and his wife, Biddie, have raised three sons. Jordan continues to own and operate several business interests, including the Lee Roy Jordan Redwood Lumber Company in Dallas, but the lessons he learned from Bryant are never far away.

"Those two words he taught us—never quit—have stuck with me," Jordan says. "They've stuck with me in business. I had a few times in business when I could have taken bankruptcy real easy, because it's tough to keep going. But somewhere down deep I said, 'That's not the way I'm going. That's not the way I was taught.'"

Of the two teams he played for during his college and pro careers, Jordan's Alabama experience continues to play the more significant role in his life. In 1999, he received the University of Alabama National Alumni Association Paul W. Bryant Alumni-Athlete Award, a fitting reward for his years of continued support for the University and the athletic program.

"In my four years at Alabama I was closer to the program than I ever was in 14 years with the Cowboys," Jordan says. "It was in those formative years at Alabama when I was growing up and maturing into the Lee Roy Jordan that I was with the Cowboys. By the time I got to the Cowboys I already had that work ethic and the want to win. The University made a great impact on me, and still means a lot to me now. It was a wonderful experience going there, and I love staying in touch."

JOE NAMATH

QUARTERBACK 1962-1964

Alabama coaches and players knew something was unusual about the new recruit from the moment coach Paul "Bear" Bryant summoned him to the top of his tower. No one climbed that tower overseeing the Crimson Tide practice fields without Bryant's permission, and suddenly Bryant was beckoning the visiting prospect to join him for a private chat.

"He goes up on that tower and we were all kind of watching out of the corner of our eyes," says Mal Moore, current Alabama athletic director and former Crimson Tide quarterback and assistant. "We knew for that to happen Coach Bryant must have thought he was pretty special."

It didn't take long for the coaches and players to understand the visitor's special treatment. As a member of the scout team offense in his first week of practice in 1961, the defensive coaches were frustrated with his quick release and passing. One month into his freshman season, he ignored a coach's call for a punt on third down and threw a 30-yard touchdown pass on the next play. Just one week into his first spring with the varsity in 1962 he became the starting quarterback.

"I was a backup quarterback to Pat Trammell until my senior year when I had a shot at being the quarterback," Moore says. "I was the starter ... for about week, until Joe Namath got the snap count down. There was no question he was going to be great."

Greatness has surrounded Namath like an aura throughout his football career and life, even transcending the mountains and valleys to became more than a superstar on a football stage. Instead, Namath rose to the status of cultural icon. Between his talent and skill, his good looks, his position, his success, his charisma, his gunslinger bearings, his national stage in New York, his infamous guarantee before Super Bowl III and his fortuitous timing as a media focal point during the peak of a social and political revolution in the late 1960s and early 1970s, Namath can be mentioned alongside names such as Babe Ruth, Joe DiMaggio, Muhammad Ali and Michael Jordan in the lexicon of American sports legends. Like The Babe, Joe D., The Greatest of All Time, and His Airness, the mere mention of "Broadway Joe" or "Joe Willie" is enough identification for most sports fans. Mention the most famous arms, personalities and knees in pro football history, and Namath's name will quickly join the discussion.

Whatever "it" is, Namath has it in abundance, even in his 60s as he raises two teenage daughters as a single father, serves as an active spokesman for arthritis sufferers, works toward his undergraduate degree and remains physically active on two artificial knees. Yet, for all of his larger-than-life persona and fame, Namath somehow remains firmly rooted and surprisingly humble for a man who has spent his life being placed on pedestals by fans and media.

"He's the real deal," says Lee Roy Jordan, a former Alabama teammate and longtime friend. "He was a true superstar, *the* star of the American Football League, and he was one of the biggest reasons the AFL was able to force a merger with the NFL. But when I think of Joe, I think of how he's handled himself through the years, how he's raising two daughters, and how he's trying so hard to be a terrific dad to his girls, even during the ups and downs in his life.

"And he's still so humble and he continues to impress me with his loyalty to the University and Coach Bryant and all the play-ers he played with—all of that still means so much to him. He wants to make sure that he doesn't put himself up there, though other people try to, but he doesn't think that he's better than anyone else. He's so humble, it's unbelievable.

"I'm really impressed by that and I tell him every time I see him, how much we appreciate, as alumni and players from the University, that he continues to support the University and all the endeavors we're involved in there. I don't know if there are a lot of guys who are still as loyal and supportive as Joe is to the University, and that's such a great asset to the University. That shows the real respect and love he has for the university."

Namath's love affair with the University started as a college romance, despite the disparate cultural differences between the University's Tuscaloosa campus and Namath's hometown of Beaver Falls in Western Pennsylvania. Considering the geographic and social distance between Namath's home and his first meeting with Bryant, it's a wonder he ever wound up at Alabama.

Born May 31, 1943, in Beaver Falls, a blue-collar steel mill town about 30 miles outside Pittsburgh, Namath was the youngest of five children from John and Rose Namath, who divorced when he was in the sixth grade. Namath grew up with his mother, but both parents and his older siblings played a part in convincing him to attend college instead of signing one of the many professional baseball offers that came his way.

It would be more dramatic to say Bryant simply out recruited the rest of college football for Namath, but it would also be fiction. Alabama was not among the many schools that originally recruited Namath in 1961, and he eventually settled on Maryland because "I actually thought it was down South, and I wanted to play in a better climate."

When Namath came up five points short on his college board exams of qualifying to attend Maryland, he turned his attention to Penn State. However, Penn State was on Maryland's schedule at the time, and Maryland coaches quickly steered him away from the

Nittany Lions. That's when a Maryland assistant called an old friend on the Alabama staff, Tide assistant Charley Bradshaw, and let him know Namath might be interested in Alabama. It helped that Namath's older brother Frank had been recruited by Bryant at Kentucky, and that another Western Pennsylvania quarterback, Vito "Babe" Parilli had played at Kentucky for Bryant.

"Coach Bryant's relationship with Babe was one of the major keys in building my relationship with [him]," Namath says. "When I was with the Jets and we traded with Boston to get Vito 'Babe' Parilli on our team, I couldn't believe it. His locker was right next to mine. I still get goosebumps just thinking about it.

"I used to walk from St. Mary's School up to the five and dime at lunch time to see my mother who was working there, and I'd always stop at the Army & Navy store because the store had this gold football helmet with Babe Parilli written on it. I'd just stare at it."

With opportunity knocking, Bryant sent offensive assistant Howard Schnellenberger to Beaver Falls to check out the situation, and Schnellenberger spent a week trying to out recruit several other schools, including Notre Dame, for Namath's talents.

"When Howard came to the house, my mother took a real liking to him, and my mother decided that's where I was going," says Namath, who admits he didn't know much about Bryant or the Crimson Tide at the time. "I had watched Alabama play in the Bluebonnet Bowl the year before, and I liked their headgear. I was just blessed and fortunate to be pointed in the right direction."

Schnellenberger eventually whisked Namath out of town for an official recruiting visit. It was on that trip that Namath ended up in Bryant's tower.

"I knew he was supposed to be a great coach, but he had a real Southern accent, of course, and he sort of talked real low, and I could barely understand him," Namath says. "I don't think I understood a word he said."

Namath immediately found himself wondering what he had gotten himself into, but before he could back out, he thought back to the advice of his mother and brothers. "Everything starts at home, and my family was determined that I go to college and improve myself through education," Namath says. "And Coach Bryant was very convincing."

On the field, Namath's transition was smooth and impressive. Off the field, he had a lot to learn about the segregated South of the early 1960s. Namath made the adjustment and even answered to "Joe Willie," but it took some time and effort on his part as well as his teammates and coaches.

"If not for the camaraderie of the football players and the coaching staff, it would have been very difficult for me," Namath says. "It was perplexing at times, the different social structure and different beliefs, but that's where I learned and came to believe that we're influenced tremendously by our environment growing up. I knew the coaches and players better than anyone else, and I knew they were righteous, good people, but I didn't agree with the thought process and the social structure.

"I remember sharing a lot of conversations with my roommate, Butch Henry, and people like Lee Roy Jordan and Butch Wilson and Gaylon McCullough and a bunch of guys who were willing to take the time and share with me, and it helped me understand the social structure. It was a tremendous education."

Those friendships are still important to Namath, who is careful not to upstage former teammates and coaches when he returns to Tuscaloosa to help promote the University's fund-raising efforts. Moore knows he can pick up the phone and call on Namath anytime, and if Namath's still-busy schedule allows it, Namath will be there to lend a hand, raise some money and hang out with old friends.

"Mal was one of my best friends there, but you know what? We were all friends," Namath says. "We really developed a closeness there. We were all interested in the same thing: winning. We had so many good players there, and I was fortunate to be part of that."

Namath did more than just play a part in Alabama's success from 1962-64. Namath stepped into Trammell's large and uncompromising shoes in 1962, and even though Alabama's passing game barely compared to today's wide-open offenses, Namath still elevated the Crimson Tide with his passing skills, setting new school records for completions (76) and passing yards (1,192) and tying Harry Gilmer's single-season school record for touchdown passes (13). One year after winning the national championship, the Tide went 10-1 and came within one play, a failed two-point attempt in a 7-6 loss to Georgia Tech, of playing for the national title again. In the 1963 Orange Bowl, after Bryant accidentally referred to Namath as "Babe" (as in Parilli) during his pregame locker-room speech, Namath got the Tide started with a 25-yard touchdown pass to Richard Williamson for a

7-0 first-quarter lead, and Alabama went on to win 17-0.

Namath's junior year is remembered more for what happened off the field. The Tide won nine games that season but also lost two games by a total of six points (10-6 to Florida and 10-8 to Auburn), falling agonizingly short of playing for the national championship. Even if the Tide had played for the title, Namath would have been on the bench after Bryant suspended him for the final two games of the season.

Nine days after the Auburn game Bryant announced Namath had been suspended, forcing him to miss the Miami game (moved from November 23 to December 14 due to the death of President John F. Kennedy) and the Sugar Bowl game against Ole Miss. Immediately the rumors flew about Namath's rebellious behavior, but the truth came down to one simple mistake: Namath and several teammates had been out drinking one night, and Namath was the only one recognized by a witness who informed Bryant. Bryant asked if the story was true, and Namath forthrightly admitted it was. Bryant suspended him on the spot, and despite experiencing second thoughts in a later meeting with his assistant coaches, he stood by the suspension. Namath was forced to move out of the dorm for the time being and would not return until the spring.

"In the long run, it made a very positive impact on me," Namath says. "Rules are rules, and they're not made to be broken. I have two daughters, 18 and 13, and I'm trying to teach them that, too. Like it or not, we need to understand that, and to understand that life's not always fair. Coach Bryant did the right thing, and I had to accept it and learn from it and move on."

Moving on also meant learning to play with knee injuries that diminished what had been a talented all-around athlete who could tuck the ball and run. Namath ran and passed his way to a strong start as a senior before he suffered a knee injury in the fourth game of the season against NC State.

The injury limited him throughout the season, and he was forced to share the starting job with Steve Sloan, but Alabama still managed to go 10-0 and win the national championship before accepting an invitation to play Texas in the 1965 Orange Bowl. Namath came off the bench in the Orange Bowl to throw for 255 yards and two touchdowns and may have crossed the goal line late in the game on

From left: Joe Namath, Jonny Musso, and coach Paul "Bear" Bryant

a fourth-and-goal quarterback sneak. While he did emerge from the pileup with goal-line chalk across his chest, certain he had scored, the officials ruled Namath had had come up short, and Texas won 21-17.

Bryant called Namath "the greatest athlete I've ever coached," but Namath's knees would never be the same. After multiple injuries and surgeries, his knees were finally replaced by artificial implants in 1992.

"The good Lord did a great job with these bodies of ours, but He didn't design them for football," Namath says. "There are too many sudden stops to play football. But if you want to succeed at football, or anything else, you have to have a passion and a desire, so I was willing to play through the injuries."

Even with his knees crumbling underneath him, Namath remained a gifted passer with a confident approach to the game that many confused for arrogance.

"I don't know if I ever felt that way, but I did have a desire to do well and a desire to win," Namath says. "With three older brothers and an older sister, I was never treated special, and Coach Bryant and the coaches I was around wouldn't let people get caught up in their own ego.

"Believe me, I had a lot of confidence as a player, but I made a lot of mistakes at every level, from high school to the pros. I made mistakes that would just gnaw at me, just eat me up. I never played a game the way I wanted to play it, never had anything close to a perfect game.

"But those same coaches taught me how to learn from mistakes. No matter how good you are, or how good you think you are, you make mistakes, and you'd better learn from them instead of running from them."

Those lessons proved to be valuable assets during the early stages of Namath's pro football career. In 1965 Namath turned down the established NFL and the St. Louis Cardinals for a record-breaking deal with the AFL's New York Jets. With guidance from Bryant and the vision and legal skills of Birmingham attorney Mike Bite, Namath signed a contract that included a $427,000 salary, a significant signing bonus and jobs for two of Namath's brothers, making him the first genuine "bonus baby" in sports. Namath's first few seasons with the Jets were marked with more losing than winning, more interceptions than touchdowns, and more questions than answers, many involving Namath's stylishly long hair, his sideburns and Fu Manchu mustache, his trendy clothes and his proclivity for women and New York's nightlife.

"I wasn't accepted as a professional football player by a lot of people early on, but I was accepted by my peers and coaches because I had played for Coach Bryant," Namath says. "Those were my credentials when I became a pro. A lot of veterans didn't like the idea of a rookie making so much money, but they knew I had played for Coach Bryant, and that was my ace in the hole."

Namath and the Jets eventually became winners and carved out their permanent place in pro football history during the 1968 season. With the AFL breathing down the NFL's neck, Namath became the first quarterback to pass for more than 4,000 yards and earned AFL Player of the Year honors. Then he shocked the sports world by guaranteeing victory over the NFL's Baltimore Colts in Super Bowl III, and the underdog Jets followed through by winning 16-7, giving the AFL its first Super

Bowl win and Namath a monumental chapter in sports annals.

In the process, Namath helped raise football's television ratings, attendance and salaries. He also finished with 27,663 passing yards and 173 touchdowns and earned all-league honors four times in 13 pro seasons before his ailing knees finally put him on the sidelines for good.

Namath was far from finished, however, and remained a celebrity through his performances in commercials, movies and stage plays. More than 25 years after his final NFL season, Namath remains in the public eye. Unfortunately for Namath, he was inebriated when he appeared on live television in late 2003 for a controversial sideline interview during a Jets-Patriots game. In true Namath style, he quickly apologized for his behavior and sought professional help for a drinking problem.

"I remember Coach Bryant telling us when we were freshman that we'd probably remember the bad times more than the good, the bad games and the losses more than the good games and the wins—and he was right," Namath says. "Sure I remember the good things, but you really learn from the tough times. We're survivors. You can wallow in the pain and the bad memories, or you can reflect on them and say, 'Okay, let's deal with that.'

"In everything I do, I'm trying to help my children to learn. We need to lead the way as parents, whether it's teaching kids to wear a helmet when they ride a bicycle or whatever. I wear a helmet when I ride my bicycle, and I expect them to do the same. I don't want them to say, 'Well, daddy you don't wear a helmet,' or 'Daddy, you didn't finish college.'

"I also want them to know it's important to always keep growing and learning. It's like the incident I had a while back with drinking. I realized I had to do something about it. So, I got an education and I don't drink anymore, and if people want to talk about that, yeah, I'll share that. I'm one of those people who can't drink, and it took me a while to learn that.

"We all make mistakes, and boy I sure have, but you have to recognize your mistakes, own up to them and learn from them. The only thing that's constant in life is change, and you can't sit still. You either fall behind or move ahead, and I'd like to think I'm trying to improve each day."

That's one of the primary reasons why Namath is back in school, working toward his degree in humanities at the University of Alabama. He's met his requirements by traveling back and forth between Florida and Tuscaloosa, meeting with professors and academic advisors on campus and doing most of his work at home. As of June 2004, Namath only needed one major writing assignment and a senior project to become the first person in his family to graduate with a college diploma.

"I had always planned on doing that, and I had told my mother I would do that many years ago," Namath says. "Procrastination is one of the things I'm still dealing with in life, and I'm trying to get better at not putting things off, but I was at home a while back with my daughters when Jessica [the oldest] said something about being the first one to finish college in our family. My immediate reaction was, 'You wanna bet?' I didn't like the way she said that, you see, and that was the trigger, the thing that pushed my button and got me more determined than ever to finish my degree."

"When I went to register, it was interesting because naturally I looked around the room and felt a little bit strange because I was the oldest student in there. But then I got tickled because I had five times the hours anyone else in there had. I left Alabama with 115 hours or so, and I only need 15 hours or so to finish. Well, things have changed since I left, of course, and I need a few more hours than what I needed when I first left, but that doesn't bother me because I'm learning, and I like what I'm doing, and the time will come, God willing, when I finish."

The awkwardness Namath originally experienced when he returned to the University to register for classes was soon replaced by the acknowledgment of several young students who actually recognized the old guy in their midst. Even to a new generation of Alabama fans, Namath remains somebody special. As special as Namath is to Alabama fans, it's possible that Alabama fans and supporters—especially his coaches and teammates—mean even more to Namath.

"To be considered a legend by Alabama people ... I think, first of all, that I'm not worthy," Namath says. "Second, I think it's mainly because of my association with Coach Bryant and some great coaches and teammates. I gladly accept that love because I love life and people, but I know it's not just Joe. I know I reflect Coach Bryant and the people I've been around, and I think that's basically why people care about me.

"Winning championships and being part of a championship, even when I was a freshman in 1961, that's special, but when I think of what Alabama means to me, Coach Bryant comes first, and then the people and friends I met at Alabama. That's been lasting. That's part of me. It's always been with me, and it's still with me today."

KEN STABLER

QUARTERBACK 1965-1967

Ken Stabler was supposed to be taking a break from football to rest his injured knee in the spring of 1967, but coach Paul "Bear" Bryant never said anything about letting his left-handed senior quarterback take a break from reality.

After quarterbacking Alabama to an 11-0 record in 1966, Stabler needed a little time off to recover from some torn cartilage early in spring practice. Stabler wanted to practice, and if he couldn't do that, he wanted to be with his girlfriend in Mobile at every opportunity, even if it meant skipping study hall, classes and sleep.

"I'd drive four hours down there, hang out for four hours and get back in the car and drive four hours back to try to get back in time for a seven o'clock class," Stabler says. "I didn't make many of those."

Eventually it all caught up with Stabler, who finally received a telegram at his parents' house in Foley. The telegram read: "You have been indefinitely suspended. —Coach Paul W. Bryant."

The next day, Stabler received a telegram from a teammate that read: "He means it. —Joe Namath."

Like Namath, Stabler had to learn the hard way that when Bryant said something, he meant it. That meant Stabler had to return to Alabama for five hours of summer school and a daunting visit to Bryant's office to beg for another chance.

"I went in there and said, 'Coach I've done everything necessary to become eligible, and I want to come back out for the team,'" Stabler says. "He looked me in the eye and said, 'You don't deserve to be on this team. Get your ass out of here.'"

Stabler somehow found himself summoning up the courage to respond, "Well, I'm going to come back out anyway." Bryant simply said, "We'll see."

Two days later assistant coaches Jimmy Sharpe and Pat Dye told Stabler he could return, but Stabler soon realized he had to start over at the bottom of Bryant's barrel.

"The uniform dictated the team you were on: red jersey, first team; white jersey, second team; blue jersey, third team; orange jersey, fourth team; green jersey, fifth team," Stabler says. "And if you were out of favor with him he'd call you a turd. Well, I came back out after being All-SEC and the MVP of the Sugar Bowl and I get my basket, and it had a brown jersey in it."

Bryant made Stabler work his way back during preseason practices, but Stabler eventually came to see it was for his own good. Nearly 40 years later, Stabler can't imagine how his life would have turned out without Bryant.

"My whole life would be different," Stabler says. "I was very capable of throwing it all away. I was young and dumb and making bad decisions and not doing what I needed to be doing, but Coach Bryant saw something worth saving and let me know all that I was throwing away. Without Coach Bryant, who knows where I'd be."

Sports helped put Stabler on the path to success during his childhood.

His father, Leroy "Slim" Stabler, had been an outstanding athlete in his own right before he lost his father and gave up sports to help raise his younger siblings. Slim pushed his son toward sports at a young age in a small town where sports kept a lot of active young men on the right track.

"I played all the sports, no matter what the season was, so I kept pretty busy," Stabler says. "I can remember growing up, the only thing I wanted to do, the only thing I ever wanted

to be was a professional athlete, whether it was pitching baseball or playing football. I just loved doing it, and I wanted to do it all the time and do it for as long as I could. My high school football coach, Denzel Hollis, was a terrific coach, and we were two-time state champions in high school, so I was blessed to play in a really successful program with a lot of support from the city. I played with a lot of great athletes, which has been a thread throughout my entire career."

Along the way, Stabler also picked up an infamous nickname. He was running with the football, weaving in and out of traffic and cutting across the field when Hollis supposedly yelled, "That boy runs like a snake." Thus, Stabler was tagged with a moniker that follows him still today. Even his grandchildren call him "Papa Snake."

In addition to his numerous football exploits, Stabler also became an outstanding pitcher and first baseman who caught the attention of pro baseball scouts. The New York Yankees offered Stabler an impressive bonus of $20,000 and a college education to sign a professional baseball contract.

"Financially, $20,000 could have helped my family an awful lot," Stabler says. "I loved playing baseball, and you thought of the Yankees in the same context as the University of Alabama when it came to winning.

"But Coach Bryant wanted me to play football at Alabama, and Alabama was dominating the SEC at that time and winning national championships. I wanted to go and see if we could carry on that legacy."

Stabler also jumped headfirst into the quarterback legacy looming over the program, stepping into the immediate path paved by Namath, Pat Trammell, and Steve Sloan.

Stabler even wore the same No. 12 jersey worn by Namath and Trammell. If Stabler was scared, he never showed it.

"It was a motivating factor for me—that's the reason you go there, because you want to quarterback that team and be part of that winning thing," Stabler says. "You hear all the talk and the lore, about Trammell and the national championship in 1961, and then when I got there as a freshman, Alabama won another championship in 1964 with Namath, and then Alabama won it again in 1965, and I was Sloan's backup. I wanted to get my time in so I could continue to do that. That's what drives you, so you can be mentioned in the same breath with those great quarterbacks."

Before Stabler could get his chance to make a name for himself as a starter, he had to overcome a memorable mistake in a big game. Alabama was driving in the final minutes of a 7-7 game against Tennessee in 1965 when Sloan left the field with an injury. Stabler replaced him and drove the Tide to the 2-yard line, then he purposefully threw the ball directly out of bounds in an attempt to stop the clock and set up for a potential game-winning field goal. Unfortunately for Stabler and the Crimson Tide, his throw away came on fourth down, and Alabama had to settle for a tie.

"We got the ball inside the 10, then we had a sack for a loss, then I ran an option for 10, 11 yards inside the 10, and I thought it was a first down, and I looked up at the field marker and it said one down," Stabler says, "and the scoreboard said another down.

"When you look back on it, we probably shouldn't have been in that situation anyway. We were a heavy favorite to win the game and the SEC and we didn't play very well, but you make a wrong decision and you have to live with it."

Bouncing back from adversity was not an issue for Stabler after the Tennessee game, nor was it ever much of an issue for a quarterback who never seemed to fear anxious situations throughout his career.

"He had a real quarterback's mentality when it came to handling pressure," says Mal Moore, a former Alabama quarterback and assistant coach and the University's current athletic director. "He always knew how to handle himself when things got tough. A quarterback's got to be able to forget about a mistake or an interception and put it behind him, and he could always do that and move on without getting bogged down in what hap-

pened. Ken just had that kind of personality."

That quality helped prepare Stabler for the starting quarterback job in 1966, despite Bryant's assertion that "You can never trust left-handed crapshooters and left-handed quarterbacks." Alabama's defense was dominating, allowing only 44 points for the entire season. The Crimson Tide also scored 301 points, and Stabler did his part by leading the team in both passing and rushing. In his finest hour of the season, Stabler rallied the Crimson Tide from a 10-0 fourth-quarter deficit to an 11-10 victory over Tennessee in the only close game of the season.

That team combined for an 11-0 record, a 34-7 victory over Nebraska in the Sugar Bowl and what appeared to be outstanding prospects for a third consecutive national championship. After the victory over Nebraska, Bryant called his 1966 squad, "The greatest football team I've ever been associated with. It's the greatest football team I ever saw."

Unfortunately for the Crimson Tide, Bryant's declaration and Alabama's one-sided win over the Cornhuskers came too late to convince the poll voters. Notre Dame and Michigan State had already finished first and second in the national polls, even though the Fighting Irish and the Spartans both finished 9-0-1 after playing to a 10-10 tie on November 19.

Despite a perfect record and two previous national championships in 1964 and 1965, the Crimson Tide finished third in the polls and considered themselves the "uncrowned champions" of college football. It was, and still is, one of the most disappointing and frustrating turn of events in the history of Alabama football.

"Coach Bryant went through the roof," Stabler says. "We were a good football team, but most of the votes came out of the East back then. The worst thing about it was that Notre Dame played for a tie and Coach Bryant always said a tie was like kissing your sister. It was a tie because Notre Dame wanted it to be and we beat Nebraska 34-7 in the Sugar Bowl. It was frustrating, really frustrating, because we knew what it was like to win the national championship and wear the ring."

The Tide opened Stabler's senior season in 1967 with a surprising 37-37 tie with Florida State in Birmingham. Stabler also threw a school-record five interceptions in Alabama's only regular-season loss, a 24-13 loss to Tennessee at Legion Field in the third week of October, but he found his redemption in the worst possible conditions in the season's final regular-season game.

In weather Bryant called "the worst conditions I've ever seen a football game played in," Alabama played Auburn in a swamp of pouring rain, standing water and thick mud at Legion Field on December 2, 1967. In the fourth quarter, with Auburn holding onto a 3-0 lead, both teams struggling to move the ball and Bryant frequently kicking on third down in an attempt to bury Auburn and force a turnover, Alabama had the ball on the Auburn 47-yard line when Stabler took off on an option run to the right. With effective blocks from Dennis Dixon, Bruce Stephens, John Reitz and David Chatwood, Stabler snaked his way around a decisive cutback block by split end Dennis Homan and headed for the sidelines and some semblance of grass. Stabler outraced Auburn defenders to the 5-yard line and pulled away from Auburn safety Jimmy Carter on his way into the end zone for a touchdown and a 7-3 win.

"It was a driving rainstorm, ankle deep in mud, the wind was turning umbrellas inside-

out. The winds must have 40-50 miles an hour," Stabler says. "Auburn pushed us around most of the day, but prior to the game Coach Bryant had told us we weren't going to do much on offense, so were going to play defense and special teams and Auburn would do something to screw up the kicking game. Sure enough, they snapped the ball over the punter's head once, and I think they fumbled a punt snap once and another field goal attempt, and one of their mistakes gave us the ball on the 47. I got some great blocks, and I sloshed down the sideline until I hit that chain-link fence."

Stabler's NFL career, particularly his prime years with the Oakland Raiders, proved to be just as memorable as his college days. The Raiders won Super Bowl XI, and Stabler earned numerous individual honors, including NFL Player of the Year in 1976 and AFC Player of the Year in 1974 and 1976. He was selected to the Pro Bowl in 1973, 1974 and 1976, won more games than any quarterback in Raider history (71) and left the Raiders in 1979 as the team's all-time leading passer in attempts, completions, completion percentage, yardage and touchdowns. By the time he retired in 1984, having spent his remaining pro seasons with the Houston Oilers and the New Orleans Saints, Stabler was widely regarded as one of the most successful quarterbacks of his era.

For better or worse, Stabler also became known as something of a rebel during his career. Even his 1986 autobiography *Snake* bears the subtitle: "The Candid Autobiography of Football's Most Outrageous Renegade." With his long hair and beard and a reputation for enjoying the nightlife in the Bay Area and the "Redneck Riviera" along Alabama's Gulf Coast, Stabler proved to be a good fit for the rambunctious Raiders of the 1970s.

"I've always enjoyed having a good time and always enjoyed people and tried to live life to the fullest," Stabler says. "I always admired athletes like that, too. ... At that point in time it was glamorous to go out and have a good time and maybe break curfew every now and again. I don't know if that's as cool as it used to be.

"It's really hard to say how much of [my reputation] is true and how much of it has been blown out of proportion because there's been so much written and an awful lot said. I'm not sure how accurate it all is, because I've never paid much attention to all that. Some of it may be, some of it isn't."

Stabler says with some disappointment that he actually hears more questions about his individual plays and his life off the field rather than his team accomplishments. A more appropriate lasting image of Stabler's career might be his resilience under pressure. Stabler always seemed to be at his best waiting until the last second or moving around the pocket to buy some time and squeezing a perfect spiral into a tight space between defenders for the winning touchdown in the waning moments of a big game.

"If you're marked by one play or one thing, whoever does the marking is kind of narrow-minded when you go out and do the things we did," Stabler says. "We were 28-3-2 with two SEC championships and a national championship when I was at Alabama and won the Sugar Bowl and the Orange Bowl and I was the Sugar Bowl MVP. At Oakland, we played in five consecutive AFC championship games and won Super Bowl XI. Along the way I made a lot of plays, some of them good, some of them bad, but I still made a lot of plays.

"The big thing here is that I was blessed with great players around me, so I had a lot of opportunities to make plays. Most great plays are the result of some other great plays being made around you, whether it's a great block or a great route or a great catch. The players I played with gave me the chance to play in big, exciting games, like bowls, playoff games, Super Bowls, and big rivalry games, where you get the chance to make those plays in front of a lot of people.

"That's been a constant thread throughout my entire career. I had a lot of great players around me in high school. We were 29-1 and you don't do that by yourself. A lot of players never get to play with Hall of Fame players, but we had four off our starting offense at Oakland: Fred Biletnikoff, Dave Casper, Gene Upshaw and Art Shell. On the [defensive] side we had Hall of Famers Ted Hendricks and Willie Brown plus Ray Guy, who should be a Hall of Famer.

"I also played for some great, great coaches, people you really love to play for, someone you want to please, from my high school coaches, to Coach Bryant, John Madden and Bum Phillips. Wherever I was, I was surrounded by great players, great coaches, great teams."

For all that greatness, there is one symbol of achievement that continues to elude Stabler. Despite the membership of six Oakland teammates and so many quarterbacks with comparable numbers and accomplishments, the Pro Football Hall of Fame has yet to call his name.

"I don't know what the criteria is. I don't know how much your image, hearsay, reputation and innuendo have to do with it, combined with what you do on the field," Stabler says. "I don't know what all that has to do with wins, awards, numbers and things of that nature. Do you combine that with the things that happened off the field? I don't know. It's kind of a complicated thing. Every year when the Hall of Fame announcements come around in January, ESPN always comes out with a story about the best players not in the Hall of Fame, and I'm listed right there at the top."

As much as Stabler would like to be in the Hall of Fame, he's not exactly wasting his life away worrying about it. Instead, he's keeping busy with a number of business interests in Mobile and along the Alabama coast, as well as his work as the color commentator for Alabama football radio broadcasts. He tries to see daughter, Kendra, and her twin boys in Arizona whenever possible, and most of his

family time is spent raising his teenage daughters. "I've got little Snakes coming to the door these days," Stabler says, "and I'm chasing them out of the yard."

More than anything, Stabler still enjoys life on his own terms, even if the pace is a bit slower than his days with the Raiders.

"This is a really good time for me to be connected with the University of Alabama," says Stabler, a member of Alabama's Team of the Century, as well as the Alabama Sports Hall of Fame and the Bay Area Hall of Fame. "It keeps me connected with Alabama football, keeps me close to the school I love, and now my children are headed there."

Ken Stabler's run in the mud against Auburn, 1967

JOHNNY MUSSO

HALFBACK 1969-1971

Here it was, one of the most important games in the history of Alabama football, a game coach Paul "Bear" Bryant had already signified as a turnaround game for his program after two disappointing six-win seasons, and one of the key players in Alabama's new wishbone attack was on the bench.

While his Crimson Tide teammates battled Southern Cal in the first half of the 1971 season opener, Johnny Musso sat on the sidelines with an injury. What did the senior halfback think he was doing?

"I'm not even sure how it happened, if I fell, got hit or whatever, but I knew I had hurt my hand. At first it was no big deal, but when I took the next hand off I was holding the ball in my left hand, and when I tried to squeeze my fingers over the top of the ball that pinky bone would go straight down and come out of joint," Musso says. "It really hurt, so I pulled it back out and as long as I kept the finger

straight it was fine. But as soon as I tried to grip with it again, it would pop out and it was hard to hold the ball."

What was he supposed to do? Get it fixed, right?

"I took myself out and went over to our trainer, Jim Goosetree, and he was putting some tape on it when [running backs] Coach [John David] Crow pushed his way over to where we were and said 'What's the matter?'" Musso said, "And Goosetree said, 'Johnny hurt his little finger.'"

The sarcastic tone in Goosetree's voice was already enough to embarrass Musso, but the situation took a turn for the worse when Crow, whose face had been paralyzed at birth into something of a grimace, put in his two cents.

"Coach Crow looked at me with that look of his, with that scowl, and looked at me like he was saying, 'You sissy!'" Musso says. "He just couldn't believe it."

Things got worse before they got better. Of all people, Coach Bryant himself came over to check on Musso, and Goosetree gave him the same witty explanation for the halfback's absence.

"Coach Bryant looked at me like I had lost it and he just walked off," says Musso, whose finger is still crooked. "I was only out two or three plays, but it was awfully embarrassing at the time."

Musso can laugh about it now, because he knows he did his part to help Alabama win a key game. Musso not only carried 16 times for 85 yards in Alabama's wishbone debut, but he also scored both touchdowns in a 17-10 victory that put Alabama back on the national map and triggered a decade that would produce 103 wins, eight SEC championships and three national titles.

While the story of his broken pinky finger might have been a little embarrassing at the time, it also says a lot about the qualities that made Musso special as a player. He went on to become Alabama's career leading rusher with 2,741 yards from 1969-71 (a record since eclipsed by Bobby Humphrey and then Shaun Alexander) by doing it the hard way, using his five-foot-eleven, 200-pound body to push, shove and power his way through defenders for 4.77 yards per carry.

When Musso was honored as a member of Alabama's Team of the Century, he joked that after watching highlight runs of dramatic long runs by Bobby Marlow and Humphrey someone obviously must have lost the tapes of his long runs. Instead, most of his highlight carries showed him carrying defenders for carries of seven or eight yards, burrowing his way for first downs and touchdowns.

"He was one of my heroes," says former All-America guard John Hannah, who blocked for Musso in 1970-71. "When you look at the way Johnny played football, he could gain more yardage on one leg than most people could on two, because he'd hit, jump, struggle and fight for every yard. He was just so tenacious, I can't see why anybody wouldn't want to emulate the way he played the game.

"Seeing him inspired me to play like him, with his determination, because he sure had it. I don't think I've ever been around a player who had more determination than Johnny Musso."

Fortunately for the Crimson Tide, that determination became a cornerstone of Alabama's 1971 success when it could have ended up at Auburn, teaming up with his friend and fellow Birmingham prep star, John Carroll High School's Pat Sullivan. Musso grew up in Birmingham as something of an Alabama fan, but mostly because his oldest sister, Mary Jo, was an Auburn student, and young Johnny and his brothers wanted to get under her skin.

Musso actually started out with little preference between the two schools, but by the time he reached Banks High he had immersed himself in Alabama football. "I was born in 1950, so I remember Coach Bryant's teams in 1961 and 1962. My first college football game was Alabama-Auburn in 1961. My cousins and I snuck into the stadium. We didn't have tickets, but they had done this before. We caught a bus to the game, snuck in and sat on the 50-yard line in the middle of the aisle and watched Alabama win. If there was any doubt, that made me an Alabama fan."

Still, Musso had nothing against Auburn, and he also found himself fascinated with two Tiger stars, Tucker Frederickson and Banks graduate Jimmy Sidle, both of whom played at Auburn from 1962-64. "I pulled for them, too, but Alabama just had a certain magic to it," Musso says.

When it came down to decision time, Musso found himself torn between the two schools. Sullivan was already committed to Auburn, and Musso enjoyed his visit to The Plains. In the end, Musso calls it "the hardest decision I ever made in my life. At the end of the day, when it was all said and done, I decided to follow my heart."

His heart led him to Alabama and was almost immediately tested by difficult circumstances. Musso sat out as a freshman in 1968 and became an immediate starter as a sophomore but suffered through two seasons (6-5 in 1969, 6-5-1 in 1970) that had Alabama fans grumbling and wondering if the game had passed Bryant by.

"If you win six games at Alabama, that's bad," Musso says. "At least it was back then."

It was a time of tremendous change at Alabama, and throughout college football and American society in general. Bryant had been forced to abandon a long-held successful strategy of winning with smaller, faster, tougher two-way players who could outlast opponents in the fourth quarter to bigger, stronger one-way players and a different game.

The mass arrival of African-American athletes also brought an advantage to college football that did not reach Alabama until the 1971 season. The absence of black football players at Alabama had more to do with southern segregation than Bryant himself, but it still hurt his football program. A 42-21 loss in 1970 to Southern Cal and star Sam "Bam" Cunningham, a black tailback, didn't make the situation any easier for Bryant.

Add to those factors the social and political unrest on college campuses regarding Civil Rights and the Vietnam War, and the transition was taking its toll on Bryant's program. Bryant was already in the process of making some of the necessary adjustments, but it wasn't showing on the field, and many Alabama fans were losing patience.

"We didn't have great teams, and that was frustrating and hard," Musso says. "Coach Bryant was able to reach within himself and change what he was doing without changing who he was. He adjusted, he adapted and I got to see that, but in the meantime it was frustrating. Teams that had been beaten by Alabama for years licked their chops when they saw that our talent wasn't as good as it had been. In those two years I don't think we had better talent than maybe one or two teams we faced, and we got beat up. And they weren't letting up in the fourth quarter. They were still trying to score. Nobody gave us any quarter."

To his credit, Musso did his job and did it well, rushing for 516 yards and 10 touchdowns on 157 carries as a sophomore, and rushing for 1,137 yards and eight touchdowns on 226 carries as a junior, earning All-America honors in 1970. On a passing team with a professional-style attack, Musso was an outstanding fit.

"He was a complete player," says former assistant Mal Moore, now Alabama's athletic director. "He was a tremendous pass protector, an excellent blocker, very tough, had exceptionally good technique. He could catch the ball out of the backfield, and he was a real competitor running with the ball. He fought for every yard he could get. And, he was a very smart football player, really understood the game."

Musso also understood that if he got the ball enough times as a senior, he could possibly emerge as a serious Heisman Trophy candidate. In an offense such as Ohio State's, where Archie Griffin got the ball 30 or more times a game on his way to the Heisman in 1974 and 1975, Musso could have led the nation in rushing in 1971. Instead, Bryant took a long, hard look at Alabama's personnel and decided quarterback Terry Davis would be a much better fit for a triple-option attack such as the wishbone. Bryant made the commitment to the wishbone over the summer and spent time, along with his offensive assistants, studying Texas's wishbone with Texas head coach Darrel Royal and assistant Emory Ballard.

When Bryant gathered his team together to spring the surprise in August 1971, it would have been understandable if Musso had balked at the change. The wishbone, theoretically, could have cut his carries in half, or worse, if teams schemed to stop the halfback in the triple option. Instead, Musso looked at Bryant's reasoning, particularly the use of Davis as an option runner, and quickly sensed the change could reap huge benefits for the Crimson Tide.

"I was not disappointed that we switched offenses, because it was obvious we didn't have a true drop-back passer and we were adjusting to what Terry could do," Musso says. "Plus we had Jim Rosser, John Hannah and Buddy Brown, three All-Americans on the offensive line. Going to the wishbone made perfect sense."

Even more important, "Coach Bryant told us we could win seven or eight games in our old offense, or we could have a great team in the wishbone."

That's all Musso needed to hear. Southern Cal wasn't prepared for the wishbone when Musso, lining up at left halfback, took the first carry on an option pitch from Davis and ran for seven yards. He closed out the drive by taking another pitch for a 13-yard touchdown and a 7-0 lead. He later completed Alabama's scoring with an eight-yard touchdown run. Southern Cal coach John McKay later called Musso, "the best we played against" in 1971.

Musso went on to finish that season with 1,088 yards and 16 touchdowns on 191 carries, earning 28 individual awards as a senior and leading Alabama to an 11-1 record, the SEC championship and a trip to the Orange Bowl. He also finished his career with three touchdown passes. Bryant, who coached John David Crow when he won the Heisman at Texas A&M, saw enough that season to call Musso, "the finest running back I've ever coached. I doubted that anybody could ... run any better than John David, but Johnny does it every bit as well, and he's a better passer."

Musso's success also went a long way toward perpetuating a nickname he never really wanted. When it became obvious that Musso would start at running back as a sophomore, longtime sports information director Charley Thornton decided Musso needed a flashy nickname for publicity's sake. "He asked me, 'What's your nickname?' I said I didn't have one. He asked, 'What do people call you?' I said, 'Johnny,'" Musso says. "That summer he tried several different things, and they went from bad to worse. They were all bad, but the one I really remember was Johnny 'GoGo' Musso."

Musso thought Thornton had given up by the time the team arrived in Blacksburg, Virginia, for the 1969 season opener against Virginia Tech. On the way to the pregame meal that morning Musso found himself more nervous than ever and had not slept much the night before.

"When I walked in the door, people immediately started laughing at me and making horse noises," Musso says. "I didn't know what they were talking about until someone threw me a paper, and the headline on the local paper said, 'Alabama to Unleash the Italian Stallion.' From then on, it stuck. The nickname really embarrassed me for a long time."

In later years Musso came to appreciate the nickname more, simply because of the opportunities it brought his way. He was invited to speak to various Italian-American groups in New York, New Jersey and Pennsylvania and saw countless Italians treat the nickname with pride. Musso says he still hears the nickname, but remembers with genuine fondness how surprised people would be when he opened his mouth to speak.

"I guess they just assumed I was from up North and went to Alabama," Musso says, "so when I'd start to speak with a Southern accent their mouths would literally drop open. They'd never heard such a thing."

Ironically, Musso later played professional football in Canada with a linebacker named Carl Weathers, who used to tease him about his nickname. Weathers later played the part of boxer Apollo Creed in the *Rocky* movies featuring Sylvester Stallone. Stallone's character, Rocky Balboa, went by the nickname "Italian Stallion," so, naturally, Musso always wondered if Weathers had planted the seeds for the movie version of the nickname.

For all the attention focused on his running and his nickname during his college career, history should recognize Musso for his academic honors and his blocking as well. Those aspects of college football aren't very tantalizing, but Musso was an outstanding student who earned Academic All-America honors and an NCAA postgraduate scholarship, as well as a dangerous lead blocker in the wishbone.

"Johnny is a great football player, and the thing that doesn't show up in his statistics is the way he blocks," Bryant said. "He simply wipes people out."

Instead of pointing to his own team-oriented approach, Musso prefers to praise the attitude of split end David Bailey. "He was a wonderful receiver, and he sacrificed a great deal for the team," Musso says. "He was asked to become more of a blocker, and he did that and never complained. He never showed any signs of selfishness. He's the guy who gave up the most to be a team player."

Like Bailey, winning was more important to Musso. Even though the Crimson Tide didn't win a national championship in 1971, losing 28-6 to national champion Nebraska in the Orange Bowl, Musso and his fellow seniors always felt like they paved the way for the 1973 national championship and Alabama's success throughout the 1970s.

"I wish we had had more than one great season, but it was worth the struggle," Musso says. "I still feel a lot of gratification that our senior class hung true, and at the end of the day we were the guys that helped turn it around."

The Chicago Bears liked Musso enough to select him in the third round of the 1972 NFL draft, but it took a long time before Musso would like the Bears enough to play for them. At the time the Bears were floundering on the field and in the box office under aging owner George Halas, and Halas was unwilling to pay what other teams were paying. Musso had no desire to follow his winning senior season with the drudgery of playing for one of the NFL's worst teams, so he spent the next three years playing for the Canadian Football League's British Columbia Lions.

"I missed three miserable years in Chicago and had three wonderful years in Vancouver," Musso says. "It was a great experience."

The Lions agreed to let him go in the wake of a knee injury, allowing him to return home and play for the World Football League's Birmingham Vulcans for one season. Despite being less than 100 percent Musso still rushed for 681 yards and four touchdowns and enjoyed the time he spent playing before hometown fans before the league folded.

When the Bears called him back to reclaim their original draft rights, Musso wasn't interested until he found that Halas had turned over control of the club to Jim Finks, the new general manager. Finks, who also went on to build successful teams in Minnesota and New Orleans, was in the beginning stages of reconstructing the Bears and wanted Musso's veteran presence on the team, even if he was still less than 100 percent.

"Jim said, 'This kid we've got at running back is really talented, but emotionally he's all over the board. He's always up and down so if you can give us some stability at that position it would really help,'" Musso says. "That young kid was Walter Payton. I'd never heard of him, but he definitely lengthened my career by a couple of years."

By the time he retired in 1978, Musso was ready to move on to his new career in the financial world. After years of trading stocks on the Chicago Board of Trade, he opened his own business, the Schreiner-Musso Trading Company. Musso, who resides in Hinsdale, Illinois, and his wife Tanner have five children, including three who played college football, two at Northwestern. He's also involved with an inner-city youth ministry as well as his own home church, so it's been difficult to uproot his family from the Chicago area.

"To me home is still Birmingham, and home for my wife is still Columbus, Mississippi," Musso says, "but to our kids this is home. We've been here 28 years and our oldest is 30, so they've lived most of their lives here. Two of them went to Alabama, but they moved back here, and we never wanted to uproot them. But home to me is still in the South, and I wouldn't be surprised if we spend more time there in the future."

Wherever he is, his career at Alabama will always be close by.

"I've never regretted my association with Alabama, I've always been proud to be from the state and the University," Musso says, "When you talk about people who love and appreciate the game, there's no place like it. When you've gone other places, you realize how wonderfully unique it is to play at Alabama."

Johnny Musso (left) and coach Paul "Bear" Bryant

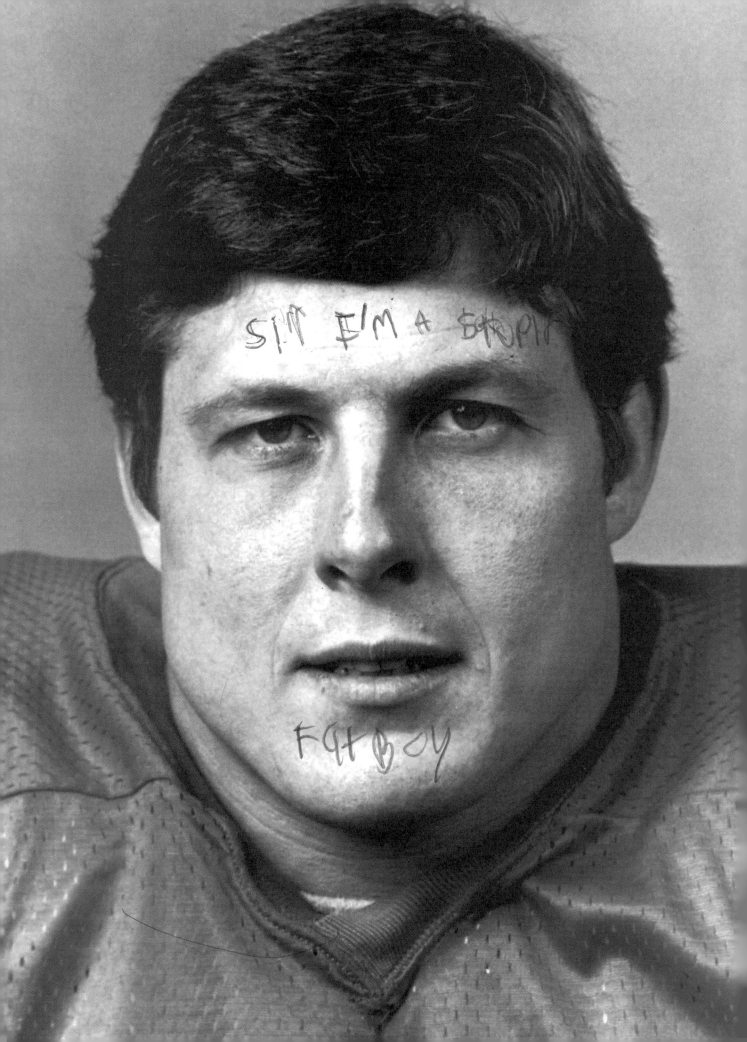

JOHN HANNAH

OFFENSIVE GUARD 1970-1972

Major Luke Worsham would be proud. So would Paul "Bear" Bryant. They'd be pleased to see John Hannah pouring his heart, soul and sweat into a group of young high school football players. They'd be grateful for the chance to stand on the sidelines at one of his practices, watching Hannah giving his players the kind of coaching and guidance that helped make Hannah one of the best football players in the history of the game. They'd be satisfied to know he wasn't doing it for the money or the glory, but for the same reasons they coached him when he was growing up.

It was Worsham, the legendary Tennessee high school coach, who coached Hannah and his brothers David and Charles at The Baylor School in Chattanooga. It was Worsham who Hannah honored when he was inducted into the Pro Football Hall of Fame in 1991, saying, "[It's] people like Luke Worsham, my high school coach, who taught and revealed to me what love truly means. He was a man who always helped me shoulder my problems, who never lost hope in who I could be or what I could do."

It was Bryant who signed Hannah out of high school and pushed him toward an All-America career at the University of Alabama. It was Bryant who later called Hannah "the best offensive lineman I ever coached." It was Bryant who "taught us how to win when I was at Alabama," Hannah says. "He inspired you to give your maximum effort on every play. He told us that usually a game is decided by only four or five plays. You never know when those plays are coming so you have to be ready on every play."

And now it's Hannah doing the coaching at Somerville (Massachusetts) High School, trying to make a difference in the lives of young men who will most likely never follow in his massive footsteps but can still learn a lot from the steps he has taken.

"I had done okay in the financial service business, working with pension funds, and then I was doing the retail side of the business and I was doing okay, but I wasn't doing great," says Hannah, who came to the Boston area in 1972 as a first-round draft choice of the New England Patriots and has lived there ever since. "I don't want to deceive anyone and make them think I was making millions of dollars, but I was holding on. Then I sold my company and I had some free time and I had re-married and my stepdaughter had started going to this private school, the Governor Dummer Academy, and they asked me if I would work with the football team up there on a volunteer basis. I did that for three years and really enjoyed it and got a lot out of working with the guys, and I felt like I was making a difference.

"I came to the realization that the monetary rewards might not be as great as some of the satisfaction of doing something more important. When I talked to my wife, Elise, about it, she pointed out that when I worked in the financial services business I had one look in my face and when I coached football I had another, and it really seemed to float my boat to work with those kids. She said go ahead and do it and she was willing to make the financial sacrifices to change our lifestyle and expectations."

Doing the right thing for the right reasons has always been important for Hannah, whose father, Herb, played at Alabama from 1948-50 and raised his boys in his own hometown of Albertville in northeast Alabama. Hannah gave careful consideration to playing at Southern California and Georgia as a high

school senior, but in the end, "Alabama was an obvious choice, because that was my school and the team I had rooted for all my life. That was 95 percent of it."

The advice of his father and his Uncle Bill, who also played at Alabama from 1957-59, couldn't adequately prepare Hannah for the demands of playing football at Alabama. When he arrived in Tuscaloosa, he quickly learned his status as a big-time recruit didn't mean a thing. His combination of size, strength and quickness wouldn't help him if he wasn't willing to do something with his gifts.

"It's something I can tell my kids about even now: you can be an All-Star in Pop Warner, but it's different in junior high and high school, and there's a weeding-out process, and some of those guys aren't going to make it because there are fewer teams," Hannah says.

"Then some of those who do make it in high school don't make it in college. Then even fewer make it to the pros. At every step you're eliminating people, so what happens is that people with relatively equal talent come together and compete, and success is no longer a matter of talent but work ethic. Those people who rely on talent and ability alone usually get weeded out, and the people who rise to the top are the ones with the talent and the ability and add to it with work ethic and discipline.

"Every step requires more and more work ethic and discipline to make the most of their abilities. That's why a lot of people with lesser talent can make it over players with more talent."

Fortunately for Hannah, he was willing to pay that price, especially when it came to absorbing teaching and coaching regarding fundamentals, techniques and strategies. His

physical gifts, especially his combination of power and quickness, were obvious in the way he fired low out of his stance and pummeled defenders without rising up and losing his leverage. In that way, former Alabama and Dallas Cowboys linebacker Lee Roy Jordan said Hannah was a lot like former Alabama All-American Billy Neighbors.

Hannah's self-motivation to improve, learn and work at his position became more and more obvious with time. Even though Hannah was an undeveloped talent when he arrived at Alabama, he put his heart and soul into learning the more detailed nuances of the offensive line and applying them throughout his career.

"When he came to Alabama you could tell he was going to be special because he just had so much raw ability," says Mal Moore, an offensive assistant under Bryant from 1964-82 and Alabama's current athletic director. "He had these huge thighs, the biggest thighs I had ever seen, and he was just so powerful. This was before linemen could block with their hands, and he was just so good at using his lower-body strength and staying low and just blocking right through people. And then as he got more experienced, he really worked hard at learning his position and becoming more of a technician."

After a freshman season spent mostly as a blocking dummy for the varsity, Hannah started the first four games of his varsity career until he blew some assignments in a 48-23 loss to Ole Miss. After that, senior Billy Strickland would start and play the first series or two before Hannah would come in and play most of the rest of the game.

"I think it was a great lesson, because it gave me a little time to stop and watch and learn some things," Hannah says. "And to be quite honest with you, it also made me realize that my coach hadn't prepared me for every situation and taught me all the things I needed to know about things like blitz pickups, so I not only had to learn what I was being told, but I also had to learn to question more and force the coaches to teach me everything I needed to know instead of waiting for them to tell me."

After the Crimson Tide endured two disappointing seasons in 1969-70, going 12-10-1 overall, Hannah's junior and senior seasons restored Alabama to its winning ways. He was a cornerstone of the new wishbone offense installed just before the 1971 season and one of the keys to Alabama's momentum victory over Southern Cal in the 1971 opener, as well as the Crimson Tide's 21-3 record and two SEC championships in 1971 and 1972.

"There wasn't a whole lot of discussion about the wishbone," Hannah says. "Back then players were taught not to question coaches so much. We trusted in our leaders and they sold the concept to us. They came in and said, 'Here's what we're going to do and why,' and we bought in and said 'We're going to make it work,' and then we just went out and made it work."

Hannah still has sour memories of the 38-6 loss to Nebraska in the 1972 Orange Bowl game and a 17-16 loss to Auburn in the "Punt Bama Punt" 1972 game, and still looks back with some regret about not winning a national championship, but he can also look back and see that his senior class helped pave the way for the 1973 national championship team.

"I take a lot of pride in the fact that we

are that group that began the turnaround," Hannah says. "I believe we're the ones who put them back on the right path."

Hannah's All-America success at Alabama put him in a position to be selected by the New England Patriots in the first round of the 1973 draft. Hannah became an immediate starter at guard for the Patriots and a consensus choice on the NFL's all-rookie team, but the NFL experience wasn't everything he imagined it would be. "It was really a step down from Alabama," Hannah says. "Football was kind of an unwanted stepchild in New England at the time and the facilities were substandard. I remember one of the newspaper guys asking what it was going to feel like playing in front of national TV and 55,000, and I looked at him and said, 'It won't be too disappointing.' He looked at me like I was crazy and I said, 'You've got to remember, I've been playing in front of 80,000 people for the last three years.'"

Hannah, who played most of his pro career at six foot three, 265 pounds and earned the nickname "Hog," witnessed a wide variety of highs and lows in his 13 seasons in New England. The Patriots made the playoffs five times during Hannah's career and finally advanced to Super Bowl XX at the end of the 1985 season. Hannah, by now trying to play through torn rotator cuffs in both shoulders and a constant knee problem, calls the Patriots' 46-10 loss to the Chicago Bears "my biggest disappointment of my career, because I never got the ring."

By the time Hannah retired after the 1985 season, he had amassed a multitude of honors, making the AFC Pro Bowl team 10 consecutive times starting in 1976 and winning the NFL Players Association's Offensive Lineman of the Year award four straight seasons from 1978 to 1981.

During that same period, Sports Illustrated put him on the cover of its magazine under the headline, "The Best Offensive Lineman of All Time." While the magazine paid Hannah an awesome compliment with its story, Hannah has always regarded the honor with a degree of humility and skepticism, saying, "Beauty is in the eye of the beholder."

More seriously, Hannah admits, "It was special. It was quite an honor. But when you're playing, if you don't feel like you're better than most, I don't think you've got the right attitude."

Hannah's success continued to reap praise beyond his success, including a spot on the AFL-NFL team for the 1960-1984 period and Sports Illustrated's All-Century college football team. In 1991, he became the first Patriot to be elected to the Pro Football Hall of Fame. At the time he also was one of only two Hall of Fame inductees, along with Gene Upshaw, to play his entire NFL career at guard. At a position where few players stand out in the public eye, Hannah emerged as one of the most recognized players of any position in his era.

"When I look back at my career and assess myself, I can't really say I had any more talent than most players, but I think I had a lot better technique and worked a lot harder than most people," Hannah says. "And I know I out-hit most of them. I usually boiled football down to one key principle: I'm hitting you, you're hitting me, we both hurt, and eventually one of us is going to give up and it's not going to be me."

OZZIE NEWSOME

SPLIT END/TIGHT END 1974-1977

On the night Ozzie Newsome joined the Alabama Sports Hall of Fame in 1992, he made it clear where he stood among the Hall's members.

"I can't imagine being in the Hall of Fame with Coach Bryant," Newsome said. "There ought to be two Hall of Fames, one for Coach Bryant and one for everybody else. I don't deserve to be in the same one he's in."

Newsome meant it when he said it in 1992, and he isn't backing off that statement more than a decade later. Still, this is a man who has since joined both the College Football Hall of Fame and the Pro Football Hall of Fame, and even the most humble of men must admit there's something special about being members of such exclusive clubs.

"It is truly something to be proud of," Newsome says. "It's nice to have the recognition, but life is all about what's next. Don't ever take the opportunity to live off what

you've done, and always continue to strive. There's got to be something else. Right now, all that's good, but winning another Super Bowl is the most important thing for me. That's the priority for me right now, not looking back on what I accomplished."

"The Wizard of Oz" certainly has a lot to be proud of when he looks back on a career that includes success at every level, from his days at Colbert County High School to his All-America career at Alabama and his All-Pro career with the NFL's Cleveland Browns.

It is a career that is marked by numerous awards and honors, including a spot on the All-NFL team of the 1980s, the Walter Camp Football Foundation's "Man of the Year" award in 2004 and his status as the NFL's first African-American general manager.

In fact, the only thing his playing career lacked is a national championship or world championship ring. The Crimson Tide went

42-6 during Newsome's college career (1974-77) and won three SEC championships, but no national titles.

It's not like Newsome didn't do his part to create championship opportunities for his teams. To this day the 1977 team still believes, with good reason, that it was robbed of the national championship. The Tide entered the bowl season ranked third behind Ohio State and dominated the Buckeyes 35-6 in the Sugar Bowl. Meanwhile, Notre Dame came in ranked fifth and beat top-ranked Texas 38-10 in the Cotton Bowl. Yet, somehow the Fighting Irish jumped over Alabama in the final poll to claim a national championship that arguably belonged to the Crimson Tide.

"He's the greatest end in Alabama history, and that includes Don Hutson," Alabama coach Paul "Bear" Bryant said. "He's the best athlete we've had at Alabama since Joe Namath. Ozzie is the best end I've ever coached, because not only is he a great receiver, but he is also a total team player, meaning that he is a real fine blocker and an outstanding leader. He has everything it takes to be great as a receiver—concentration, speed, hands."

In his pro career, Newsome's Browns advanced to the AFC championship three times, only to fall frustratingly short of the Super Bowl each time.

"That may be the biggest disappointment of my career," Newsome says. "That would be one minus in a lot of plusses in my career."

That career full of positives almost didn't happen because a young Newsome was a lot more excited about baseball growing up in Leighton, Alabama, when he finally went out for football in eighth grade. The day he first stepped on a football field he showed up late,

didn't know what he was doing and had no idea what position he wanted to play.

"The first position I got to play was receiver," Newsome says, "and that's where I stayed."

He didn't understand the fundamentals or techniques of his position, let alone the assignments, but it didn't take long for him to show he could handle at least one job.

"All I knew is that when they threw it," Newsome says, "I would catch it."

After two years of middle school football, Newsome moved on to high school ball and soon learned the demands and expectations were much higher at the next level. After the team left town for a preseason of grueling two-a-days, an experience Newsome calls, "the toughest thing I'd ever been through in my life," Newsome decided he would play out the schedule and quit after the season so he could dedicate himself to baseball and basketball.

That changed in the first game of his varsity career. "I caught a touchdown on the very first pass in the very first game I played," Newsome says. "[And] the story begins."

Newsome played on a team that also included quarterback Phil Gargis and receiver Thad Flanigan, both one year ahead of Newsome, so it didn't take long for college recruiters to notice him. After Colbert County won the 1972 state championship game at the end of Newsome's junior season, Alabama assistant Jack Rutledge approached Newsome and told him he would have a scholarship waiting for him at Alabama.

Even though Gargis signed with Auburn and Flanigan signed with Alabama, giving Alabama one more receiver in a wishbone offense that featured only one split end,

Newsome was drawn to coach Paul "Bear" Bryant and Alabama's success.

"People said, 'You're going to have to go compete with Thad. Are you crazy?'" Newsome says. "But Alabama was just a better decision for me. I think it was the atmosphere of winning that did it for me. On the visit I took to Alabama, from the cooks at Bryant Hall to the players, everybody was about winning SEC and national championships. You knew you were going to be on national TV. You knew you were going to be in major bowl games. But it was all about winning—every-

thing they talked about was winning national championships, and that's what attracted me."

It also helped that the starting Alabama end from the previous season, Wayne Wheeler, had just graduated and left an opening. By the time Newsome arrived on campus for pre-season practice, he already had a friend and roommate in fullback Johnny Davis, whom he had come to know during summer orientation and a summer all-star game. Newsome also quickly discovered that he was already listed as the third-team split end. Newsome likes to joke that "They didn't have a lot of receiv-

ers," but it was obvious the coaches had high expectations for his freshman season.

It didn't take long for Newsome to start meeting some of those expectations. Newsome had never returned punts in high school, but when Coach Bryant told him to go catch punts, he didn't think twice. On one punt that fell far short of its destination, Newsome raced up about 25 yards to catch the ball, and Bryant noticed from his tower, praising him and calling him by his first name.

"That was the first pat on the back that I ever got from him," Newsome says.

Newsome figured at that point he might be fortunate enough to earn a spot on the traveling squad. Instead, he started the 1974 season opener against Maryland and caught a pass in his first game. He also showed a willingness to block defenders and stretch his six-foot-four, 220-pound frame out to haul in passes.

Four weeks later against Florida State, Newsome caught a key pass late in the game that put Alabama in the position for a game-winning field goal and an 8-7 victory.

"That kind of put me on the map," Newsome says. "The headline in *The Tuscaloosa News* said, 'Freshman Saves the Day.'"

If Newsome had been tempted to get a big head over his sudden success, veterans such as Sylvester Croom, Mike Washington, Willie Shelby and Leroy Cook would have been there to bring him down to earth. He also had Flanigan and basketball star Leon Douglas from Leighton looking out for him. Those players helped him understand where he stood in the big picture.

"I was raised by those guys," Newsome

says. "There were no stars on those teams. Coach Bryant was the only star."

Still, Newsome became an undeniable star in his own right. Newsome lacks the self-serving arrogance of many of today's players, but he admits his confidence reached a new level before his senior season when some of his teammates went to the NFL and earned roster spots.

"I had competed against those guys, and those guys had made it into the NFL," Newsome says, "so I felt like if they were good enough to play, I was good enough to play."

By the time his Alabama career was over, Newsome had started in 48 consecutive games and caught 102 passes for 2,070 yards and 16 touchdowns. That was enough to earn a spot on the Alabama Team of the Century and special distinction as the Tide's player of the decade for the 1970s, but those awards didn't mean nearly as much to Newsome as the life lessons he gained during his college career.

"Coach Bryant taught me about initiative," Newsome says. "A lot of people need to be pushed to be as good as they can be, but he wanted you to have your own initiative to do that. He taught us that the team was more important than any one individual, that you should be able to depend on each other.

"Then he taught us that you can push yourself a lot further than you think you can. That's what the fourth quarter was all about. There was a certain point in every game where Alabama football players would rise above everybody else, because we knew we could do it. He had pushed us to that limit so that we knew we still had something left."

Those lessons carried over to his professional career, where he made an immediate impact as a rookie, moved to tight end, adjusted to playing in cold weather and spent 13 seasons starting 176 of 182 games for the Browns and finishing with 662 receptions for 7,980 yards and 47 touchdowns. He also became the all-time leading receiver in franchise history, the all-time receiver among tight ends in the NFL and finished his career ranked fourth among receivers in NFL history with 662 catches.

Newsome is proud of his achievements, but he's also pleased about the fact that of all the touchdowns he caught in his pro career, he only spiked the ball once. In his mind, he was following Bryant's command to "Act like you've been there before" after a touchdown.

"From having been at Alabama, I didn't need an assistant coach or a strength coach to tell how me how to prepare," Newsome says. "I knew how to get ready to play. I didn't need a coach to look at film and tell me whether or not I played good or not. I had already set a high standard for myself. I knew whether I played good or not."

After 12 seasons in the NFL Newsome received an offer to join then-Alabama head coach Gene Stallings's coaching staff as an assistant. As much as he wanted to accept the offer, the timing wasn't right because Newsome still wanted to play at least one more season and his family had just finished building a new house in the Cleveland area. The media and Alabama fans often mention his name as a possible Alabama athletic director candidate when current athletic director Mal Moore retires.

Upon his retirement as a player, Newsome went to work with the Browns in an administrative position. He followed the franchise when it relocated to Baltimore and became the Ravens, where he became vice-president of player personnel and then vice-president of football operations. In 2000, Newsome was chosen NFL Executive of the Year. In 2001, the Ravens team he helped build beat the New York Giants to win Super Bowl XXXV. In 2002, he broke new ground by becoming the Ravens' GM and executive vice president.

"From a historical standpoint, this is very significant," Newsome said at the time. "I'm the only black general manager in the National Football League. Growing up in the South, there were a lot of times when I was one of the first. I was one of the first blacks to play little league baseball. Sometimes it's all about the right timing."

Ravens owner Art Modell added, "He was the architect of our Super Bowl team of two years ago, and he's the mastermind behind the transition we are undergoing right now."

Newsome says he still talks to someone associated with Alabama nearly every day and insists the foundation that supports that architecture was poured during his years at Alabama, saying, "What Coach Bryant taught me is what I use today in assembling a football team for the Ravens. When you're around good people, as you move forward in your life you know how to identify good people to work with and you can build a good foundation."

MARTY LYONS

DEFENSIVE TACKLE 1974-1977

Facing fourth down and about 10 inches away from the Alabama goal line in the fourth quarter of the 1979 Sugar Bowl, Penn State quarterback Chuck Fusina and Alabama defensive tackle Marty Lyons found themselves standing near the ball and wondering what move the Penn State coaches would make next.

The Nittany Lions, trailing 14-7 in a game that would determine the national championship, could attempt to run the ball again, as they had on first and third down on their way inside the 1-yard line. Or they could pass the ball, as they had attempted on second down, only to have Alabama cornerback Don McNeal stuff the play at the 1-yard line. Or, they could always kick a field goal and hope for another opportunity in the final minutes.

Fusina, looking toward Lyons, wondered aloud, "What do you think?"

Lyons, without blinking, simply replied, "You should throw the ball."

It would be easy to confuse Lyons's statement as cocky or brash, but it wouldn't be accurate. Instead, his words simply reflected the confidence of four years of working and preparing for moments such as these. Even as the Crimson Tide defense lined up for the play, the players yelled "gut check," a favorite rallying point for coach Paul "Bear" Bryant.

"It started with the way Coach Bryant and his assistants prepared us and coached us, the way they handled themselves and handled us," Lyons says. "And we also had a special relationship as teammates. After my freshman year I never went back home in the summer. I stayed on campus, and there were so many of us who did that.

"There was such a closeness and we weren't going to disappoint not just Coach Bryant or the University, but we weren't going to disappoint ourselves. We really played as a unit. We treated each other like family. We didn't have one star on the team—there were many, and we proved that by winning the national championship in our senior year on the goal-line stand against Penn State."

When Penn State coach Joe Paterno called for a running play and Fusina handed the ball to running back Mike Guman, the entire Alabama defense surged to the point of attack, collectively and individually. Linebacker Barry Krauss would get the public credit for the tackle, and Lyons would go down in history for his famous advice to Fusina, but as Lyons knows so well, it took more than one or two Crimson Tiders to get the job done.

"If you look at the play from the reverse angle or the side angle, you'll see all the defensive linemen were already one or two yards deep in the backfield," Lyons says. "That's the technique our defensive line coach, Coach [Ken] Donahue taught us. It's the scoop: get down low and come back up. If you look at Guman's legs, David Hannah was already knocking them out, and Guman was already falling forward when Barry Krauss hit him. The defensive line maybe didn't get the credit, but we got all the credit we needed when they crowned us national champions. That's what mattered to us.

"On that play, David hit the guy low, Barry made the stop, Rich Wingo came in, Murray Legg came in. It was a group of guys who played hard together and played well together because we liked each other and cared about each other. If you look at the guys we had on the offensive and defensive side of the ball, we always watched out for each other. There was a true friendship there and nobody was bigger than the team. We had that mentality for the whole four years, not just one."

That goal-line stand, perhaps the most popular and famous series of plays in Alabama

football history, provided just the kind of monumental test Lyons had hoped to experience when he left St. Petersburg, Florida, for Alabama in 1975.

As the fifth of Leo and Thelma Lyons's seven children and the fourth of five boys, Lyons was already well known by coaches, teachers, administrators and students the day he entered Catholic High. The expectations established by his brothers and sisters were high, and Lyons knew he would be challenged to meet them and surpass them. Lyons welcomed that challenge, and after a successful football prep career under coach George O'Brien he entered the recruiting process looking for a similar experience in college.

The letters, calls and offers came from throughout the Southeast, but Alabama quickly rose to the top of Lyons's list.

"Number one, it was the tradition, what Coach Bryant had built there, what it meant to the players," Lyons says. "All Alabama did was win. When you're being recruited by a lot of different schools, everybody tells you what they believe you want to hear. They tell you if you come here, you can start, you can do this, you can do this. Coach Bryant didn't do that. He was very honest. He just said, 'Son, if you're good enough to play, the opportunity will be here.'

"Second of all, it was far enough from home that it was going to be a challenge for me. If I didn't make it there, I knew if I left, it was going to be because I quit. I could have gone to any of the Florida schools where I knew if times got tough I could always go back home and be the big fish in the small pond again and have a built-in excuse.

"By going to [Alabama] I knew there was a lot expected out of me, and I knew that once

I got dropped off and I didn't have a car that if I left, it was over, I was quitting. And I wasn't about to quit."

Lyons's first two years at Alabama put his will to the test. Even Bryant's first meeting with the new freshman class made Lyons wonder if he had made a mistake.

"I remember going to my first meeting with Coach Bryant. We were all in there and he said, 'There are four things I want you to do while you're here,'" Lyons says. "He said, 'Number one, always be proud of your family. Number two, always be proud of your religion. Number three, get an education. Number four, if we have time, let's try to win some football games.'

"I sat there after the meeting scratching my head wondering if I had chosen the right place, if the head coach had his priorities in what I thought at the time were the right order. But I eventually found out that if you keep those priorities in that order and you work hard and work together, good things happen.

"We won three SEC championships, one national title and lost only six games. I'm 47 years old now, and I still try to keep those priorities in mind. Besides what I learned from my parents, Coach Bryant set a strong foundation for me."

Lyons spent his first two years at Alabama learning those lessons the hard way. First of all, he was certain graduate assistant coaches Mike DuBose and Wayne Hall were trying to kill the freshmen, or at least run them all off. Lyons dressed for most of the games, including six road games, but didn't play and spent most of his time going back and forth between the freshman team and the varsity.

Lyons spent his sophomore season playing a limited role behind established standout Bob

Baumhower, making 24 tackles and absorbing some valuable lessons from his roommate.

"I learned a lot from Bob," Lyons says. "We're still good friends. He's a tremendous, giving person and a gifted athlete. He brought me through the process, helping me understand how things worked on and off the field. He didn't treat me like he was a senior and I was a sophomore trying to take his job. He knew that wasn't going to happen, so there was sort of a comfort zone between us, and I knew I could learn a lot from him."

While Baumhower showed him the ropes, it was Bryant who showed Lyons the light when Lyons attempted to challenge his coach over a difference of opinion and vision.

"When they gave out the letters after my sophomore year I didn't get one, and I was mad because I had gone to every game and played in most of them, and I thought in my

own mind I had earned one," Lyons says. "Now, I had gone to the University with the understanding from Coach Bryant that I could play baseball my sophomore year. So when I didn't letter, I went in to talk to Coach Bryant about why I didn't.

"He was sitting at his desk and he gestured for me to sit on the couch. He had this massive desk and this huge couch that sort of sank when you sat on it, and when I sat down I must have sank about 12 inches. So right away, I've got a big lump in my throat because I knew there had been a lot of butts in that seat before mine. Instead of looking eye to eye with Coach Bryant, I was actually looking up.

"I remember him looking up over his half-glasses, smoking a cigarette and I said, 'Coach, why didn't I letter?' I anticipated he would say something about not playing hard enough or not playing enough plays, but instead he just looked at me and said, 'I don't think that letter means anything to you.'

"Then I got the courage to ask if I could ask another question. I said, 'Coach when I came here, you said I could play baseball in my sophomore year, and I'd like to miss spring practice to play baseball.' In my mind, that was the only way I was going to get back at him. He looked over at me again, looked down over his glasses and said, 'Marty, you have my permission to play baseball, but can I give you a little advice? Before you try to be good at two sports, try to be good at one, and make sure it's the one you're on scholarship for.'

"That was the end of my baseball career."

After Bryant got his attention, Lyons focused on living up to his football potential, earning All-SEC honors as a junior in 1977 and consensus All-America honors as a senior captain in 1978. He also earned a spot on Alabama's Team of the Century, as well as

a place in the Alabama Sports Hall of Fame in 2000. Lyons insists those honors wouldn't have come his way without Bryant's persistent push, and their relationship continued to grow during Lyons's standout 12-year professional career with the New York Jets.

"He was unique in that he was able to create different visions for different players," Lyons says. "He knew in his own mind what a player needed, whether it was a pat on the back or a kick in the backside. He was fair to everybody, but he still treated each person differently according to what they needed.

"Our relationship wasn't just a coach-player thing, but it was more like a father-son, friend-to-friend relationship and that was special for me. I can remember early in my NFL career before the start of every season getting a telegram from him, saying 'Show your class, stay healthy, best of luck in your upcoming season. —Coach Bryant.' Not everybody got one of those, so I count myself fortunate that I was able to be part of that relationship and take the teachings that he taught me on the field and off the field and implement them in my life."

Those lessons were evident on and off the field during Lyons's career. After the Jets selected him in the first round of the 1979 NFL draft, Lyons earned All-Pro honors twice, even though he was more of a solid, consistent blue-collar player who labored in the shadow of two more famous teammates, Mark Gastineau and Joe Klecko, as part of the Jets' New York Sack Exchange defensive line.

His impact off the field proved to be even more significant. Lyons was selected the NFL Man of the Year in 1984 for his regular contributions of time, effort and money to the United Way, the Special Olympics and United Cerebral Palsy, as well as his work against child abuse, alcohol abuse and drug abuse.

"I was well prepared for the NFL because of the techniques Coach Donahue taught us. I came in at 247 pounds so I was really undersized but my technique allowed me to play at that size as a rookie," Lyons says. "But I was also prepared because of the way we were taught to handle ourselves and handle the media. Off the field, I always remembered the words Coach Bryant told me when I went to thank him after I got done playing for him. He told me plain and simple, 'You're very fortunate; you'll be able to play a game you love and make a living at it and build security for your family. But remember this: The winner in the game of life is the person who gives of themselves so others can grow.'"

Lyons put those lessons to work in a profound way when joy and tragedy hit head on in his life. Four days after the 1982 birth of his first child, Rocky, Lyons lost his father to a chronic heart condition. The condition had prevented Leo from traveling to his son's games throughout his college and pro career, but Leo's influence over his son remained positive, powerful and lasting. "My dad set the standard for a parent," Lyons says. "He challenged me to become the best I could be in all endeavors. He inspired me with his spirit and, as it worked out, with his will to live."

Just as Lyons started coming to grips with the blessings of fatherhood and the loss of his own father, heartbreak struck again two days later with the death of a young friend named Keith, a leukemia patient Lyons had befriended through the Big Brother program.

"In six days, you go from the ultimate high to the ultimate low and you ask yourself 'Why?'" Lyons says. "Then six months later I woke up and said, 'Wow, I don't like the reflection I see in the mirror and there's only

two things I can do. I can either stay bitter or do something about it.' That's when those words of Coach Bryant really hit home. I decided to do something about it."

Lyons turned his grieving into meaningful action by establishing the Marty Lyons Foundation, a nonprofit charity that fulfills wishes of terminally ill children. The foundation started with six people and the original funds came from Lyons's speaking engagements in the New York area. Today, there are 14 chapters in 10 states ranging from Massachusetts to Michigan to Florida, and it has served more than 3,000 children.

"It's mind boggling how many kids are sick," Lyons says. "It's really a tragedy, and what these families go through every day is beyond belief. We're just trying to make a difference, and you don't have to be a football player to make a difference. All you have to do is care. When you take the time to look at your own life from the outside in, you realize how fortunate you are, and that's when you can give back something.

"But this isn't me doing this. We have a great supporting cast at the Foundation and throughout the country. Once again, it's the team concept at work, working together to make a difference."

Between his professional career in Long Island, New York, his Foundation, his work as a television football commentator for Hofstra University and his family, wife Chris and children Rocky, Jesse, Megan and Luke, Lyons has plenty to keep him busy. He also has enough Alabama running through his veins to keep him closely connected to his alma mater.

"I was an outsider from Florida, and I was accepted into the Alabama family," Lyons says. "I'm proud of that."

BARRY KRAUSS

LINEBACKER 1976-1978

There he is, right there in the middle of the story. In the photo. In the painting. Smack-dab in the middle of history, his crimson No. 77 jersey standing tall as the center of attention, his back arched in defiance against a Penn State ball carrier who never reached his destination.

People still ask Barry Krauss about the play all the time. They send him photos and paintings to be autographed and ask him what it was like to make the tackle on perhaps the most famous play in Alabama football history, the legendary goal-line stand against Penn State in the 1979 Sugar Bowl that gave the Crimson Tide a national championship.

The play has been immortalized by photographs in national magazines and newspapers as well as a popular painting by artist Daniel A. Moore. No matter what else he does, Krauss will always be No. 77 in the middle of the story.

"To think I made an impact or was part of an incredible moment in the history of Alabama, it's just fantastic," says Krauss, who owns his own copy of the painting. "To be able to play four years at the University of Alabama and know that our purpose was to win a national championship and then to win that championship, and to think that that game, that play, is still so important to Alabama fans, that's really special.

"Did it come down to that one play? Obviously there were a lot of big plays, but that play does seem to stand out the most, and to be a part of it is a thrill. It lives in my heart."

Krauss, who played linebacker for the Crimson Tide from 1975-78, will be the first to admit he wasn't alone on that play. He's quick to point out the Alabama defensive linemen and blitzing cornerbacks who forced Penn State running back Mike Guman to start his leap for the end zone too soon. Then he'll tell you after he met Guman at the top of the heap that he had plenty of help from teammates who rushed in to finish the play and keep Guman away from the goal line.

"That play is all about teamwork, about everyone working together, everyone have an opportunity and reaching a pinnacle together and taking advantage of that opportunity," Krauss says. "It represents everything Coach Bryant stood for. Besides, offense always gets all the glory, so it's great to see the defense stepping up and making things happen and being remembered for it."

It took a while for a younger Krauss to understand all the lessons Bryant and his staff taught at Alabama, even though Alabama seemed like a natural for fit for him during his childhood in Pompano Beach, Florida.

"When I was a kid, I used to go to the beach and play with a friend of mine, Eddie Blankenship," Krauss says, "and we used to run the wishbone against the waves down on Pompano Beach."

By the time he was a junior, Krauss was being heavily recruited by Florida, Florida State, Miami, Georgia Tech and several SEC schools, including Auburn. Late in the fall of his senior year he attended the Alabama-Miami game in Miami and found himself talking to an Alabama assistant coach about the possibility of making an official recruiting visit to Tuscaloosa. Krauss jumped at the chance, and it didn't take long for him to figure out where he wanted to go.

"When I walked through the locker room and saw the jerseys and helmets of guys like Woodrow Lowe, I thought, 'This is so cool,'" Krauss says. "I didn't know if I was good enough to play there, but I said all I wanted was the opportunity."

That opportunity didn't come quickly or easily for Krauss, who spent his first season at Alabama on the freshman team serving as scout-team fodder for the varsity. The freshmen made a regular habit of coming out to practice before the varsity and completing practice after the varsity. In between, the intensity of the drills and the demands were way beyond anything Krauss and most of his fellow freshmen expected.

"Coach Bryant wanted to test you to see if you would quit," Krauss says. "A lot of guys quit, but I think I was too dumb to even think about quitting. I didn't have anything else. I didn't want to go back to Pompano Beach."

The adjustment both on and off the field to college life wasn't an easy one for Krauss. In addition to the practices and the academic demands, college also offered the possibilities of late nights, parties, bars, and, of course, girls.

"I was 18 years old and away from home for the first time, and I wasn't the greatest student or the most focused person," Krauss says. "It was tough for me, because I didn't make a very good adjustment at first. I came from a very structured home life and had to be in by 11 o'clock and had never drunk beer or anything like that. ... I had a lot of fun—too much fun—and got distracted."

It took a missed curfew in his sophomore season, 1976, and a meeting with Bryant to put Krauss back on the right track. After an early season victory, Bryant surprised his players by jumping on them pretty hard and calling for an early curfew. Krauss, by then growing frustrated with his lack of playing time, hit the town with his roommate, stayed out too late and missed curfew.

The next morning, however, the players

learned they had a scrimmage that day, and Krauss found out he was in trouble for missing curfew. One of the coaches recommended he go to Bryant's office and beg for forgiveness. After a restless night, Krauss showed up on Monday at 5:30 a.m. and waited for Bryant.

"I said, 'Coach Bryant may I speak with you?' And he looked at me with disgust, so I just followed him into his office and he sat down," Krauss says. "Now, he sat down at his table and I had to sit down on that dang sofa, the one everyone sank down in. So I jumped right up and I was standing there in front of Coach Bryant and I said, 'Coach, I just want to say I'm sorry for missing curfew, and I just feel like I wanted an opportunity to play for you and you're not giving it to me.'

"Coach Bryant just had his head down and he wouldn't even look at me. So I said, 'Coach Bryant, I said I'm sorry.' That wasn't getting

Coach Paul "Bear" Bryant (left) and Barry Krauss

it done, so the next thing I know I'm crying, saying, 'Coach Bryant I'm sorry, I didn't mean to miss curfew, I'm sorry,' and looking at him with one eye open, but he still wasn't looking at me.

"Athletes like to talk about taking it to the next level, well, I took crying to the next level. I started crying even harder and I'm still apologizing and I'm telling him if I lose my scholarship and get kicked out of the dorm, my mom's going to kill me.

"Coach Bryant finally looked up at me and mumbled something about straightening up. I promised I would and took off as fast as I could and later on I found out that my roommate did not go to see Coach Bryant, and he got kicked out of the dorm and lost his scholarship. I got that second chance and made the most of it."

Krauss's playing time increased steadily over the next few weeks, but his big breakthrough came in a nationally televised game at Notre Dame on November 13. After Krauss came off the bench and played well in the first half, Bryant announced a lineup change at halftime. "He said, 'I want Krauss in there because he wants to hit somebody,'" Krauss says. "That was the defining moment of my career. I was just flying around hitting people and I don't think he ever regretted it."

After making 18 tackles against Notre Dame, Krauss led the team in tackles in a 38-7 victory over Auburn and then he earned the Liberty Bowl MVP award with a 44-yard interception return for Alabama's first touchdown in a 36-6 win over UCLA.

"When I look back, I can see that I played my best games in the big games," Krauss.

None were bigger than the 1979 Sugar Bowl game. After finishing 11-1 in 1977 and missing out on the national championship when poll voters leapfrogged Notre Dame from No. 5 to No. 1, Crimson Tide players were determined to do whatever it took to take the 1978 title out of the hands of the voters. Alabama entered the game ranked second and led top-ranked Penn State 14-7 late in the fourth quarter when the Nittany Lions recovered a fumble at the Crimson Tide 19-yard line with 7:57 left in the game.

Penn State earned a first down that put the ball at the eight-yard line, and two runs and a pass put the Nittany Lions inside the one-yard line for fourth down. It was, as Krauss has said many times over the years, a "gut check."

"We had stopped them on first down and then they tried the pass on second down and we stopped the run on third down," Krauss says. "Then Penn State called a timeout and Coach [Joe] Paterno decided he didn't want to settle for a field goal. He figured if we can't get one yard we don't deserve to be national championships, and I really respected that. He put it all on the line and we did, too. That's what champions are made of."

On the snap, Penn State quarterback Chuck Fusina handed off to Guman and both sides collided, with Alabama's line winning the battle up front. When Guman attempted to leap over the top of the pile, Krauss met him head-first, stopped his forward motion and then held on as his teammates, led by safety Murray Legg, rushed in to finish off the most memorable defensive stop in Alabama history.

"I actually broke my helmet, and I had a pinched nerve, so when I hit him, my whole left side was paralyzed. I had repeated problems with it, but it went totally numb and I was in excruciating pain," Krauss says. "When I hit him, it took everything out of me."

After the play Krauss just laid on the turf until teammate Marty Lyons picked him up and gave him the news that Alabama had stopped Penn State at the goal. Krauss didn't know it until Lyons told him, but he wasn't surprised.

"Murray Legg said it best: Coach Bryant had a great way of making us feel like we were a great team and a great bunch of football players, but we really weren't," Krauss says. "We were good football players who played well together because he made us feel like we were great football players. That play was the culmination of four years of hard work and believing in our coaches and ourselves."

The defense held one more time late in the game, but that one play still stirs Alabama fans.

"I think a lot of guys were sort of elevated by what happened on that play," says Krauss, who earned MVP honors in the Sugar Bowl says. "I'm not sure if I would have been a No. 1 draft pick without that play."

Krauss became a No. 1 pick with the Baltimore Colts the next spring, but his career with the Colts proved to test everything he'd come to value during his career at Alabama. The owner, Bob Irsay, cared more about money than winning and made a litany of questionable decisions, including uprooting the team in the middle of the night and moving it to Indianapolis. Six different head coaches came and went, none with any real success. A lack of team unity and racial strife just added to the turmoil surrounding the team. Krauss tried to stay positive, productive and loyal to the Colts, but it wasn't easy.

"I lost five games in three years at Alabama, won two Southeastern Conference championships, won a national championship, and I walked in there and we lost 11-12 games," Krauss said. "And what upset me the most was that nobody cared. Losing can be just as contagious as winning, and we had a lot of bad attitudes on our team."

After a severe knee injury, a fourth knee surgery and a brief training camp stint with the Cleveland Browns, Krauss was ready to give up until he received a phone call from a dream pro coach and his ideal pro team.

"I was a Miami Dolphin fan and a big Don Shula fan growing up," Krauss says. "I thought it was a prank at first, but it was really Coach Shula, and he wanted me to come down there and play."

Krauss played three rewarding and productive years before his career came to an end, but those three years helped erase a lot of the regrets from his years with the Colts.

"I fulfilled a childhood dream," Krauss says. "I got to play for the greatest college coach of all time and the greatest pro coach of all time."

Krauss continues to stay busy in Indianapolis as a motivational speaker, as a broadcaster for the Colts and the local Arena Football team and as the head coach and president of a successful minor-league football team, the Indiana Tornados. No matter where he goes, the goal-line stand against Penn State is never far behind, and his years at Alabama remain an important part of his message to his audiences and players.

"Alabama always has been and always will be home for me," Krauss says. "When I speak I always tell people that each and every one of us has moments and opportunities and the chance of a lifetime to make something great happen in our lives. The question I ask is: Are you ready?"

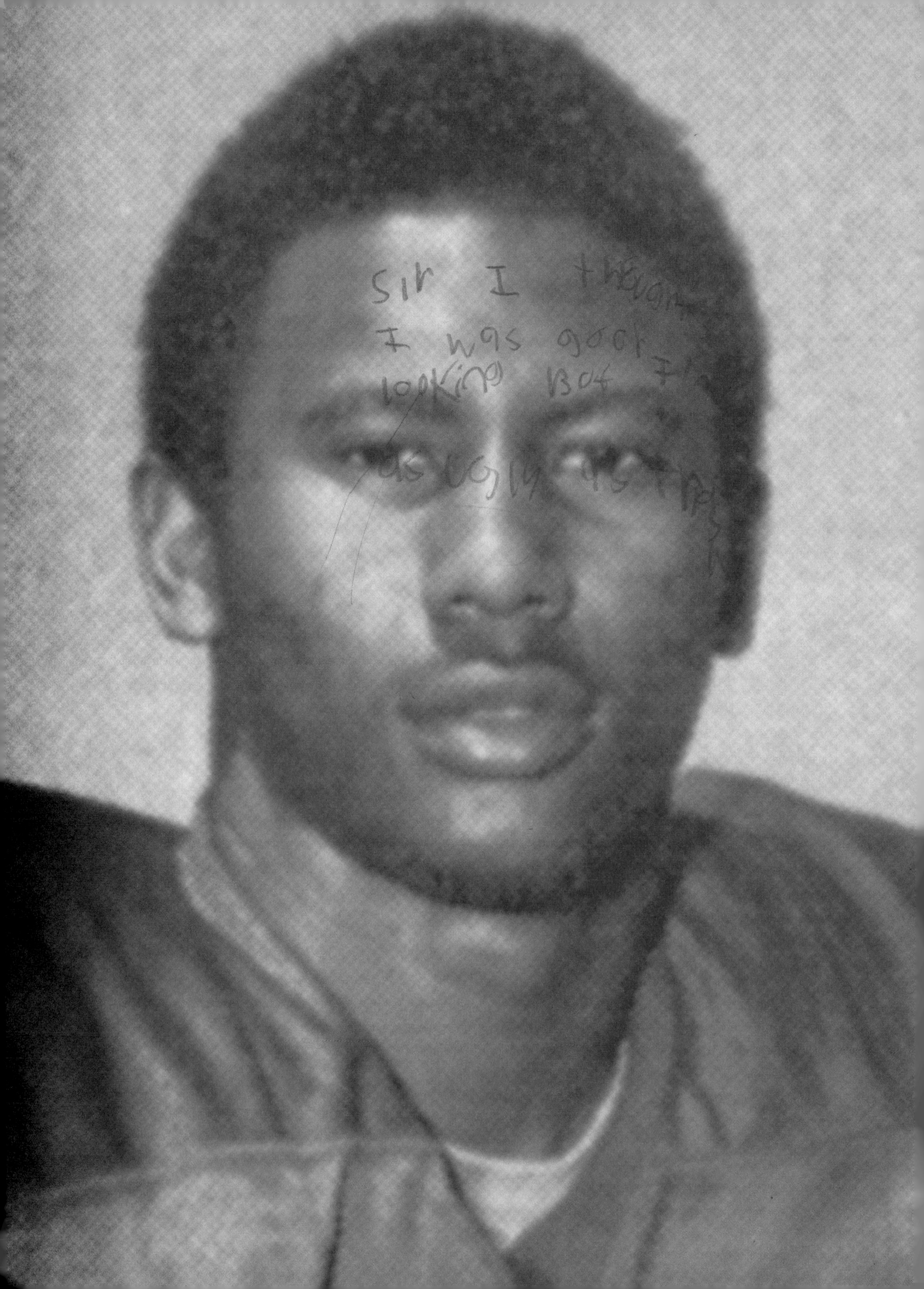
Sir I thought
I was good
looking But I
was ugly as

DON McNEAL

DEFENSIVE BACK 1977-1979

Don McNeal thought Miss Biggs was mean. He didn't like third grade, didn't want to do the work and wanted to be the class clown, so she made him sit up front, with his desk right next to hers. She also read the same poem everyday, so often that McNeal decided he didn't want to hear "that stupid poem" anymore.

"When your work has just begun, never leave it until it's done.

"Do your work, great or small. Do it well or not at all."

McNeal has no idea where Miss Biggs is today, but he can repeat the poem from memory because it remains in his heart as a testimony to the lessons that formed his life. Just like all those lessons from his parents, his brothers and sisters, his coaches and teammates. McNeal won't take the credit for his own success, as a football player, as a youth minister, as a husband or father. Instead, he insists the praise and recognition must go to all those people who cared enough to teach him how to live and work.

"All those people helped me make all those plays and do all those things," McNeal says. "They may not know it, but they did. To have the opportunity to go to a major university and play football and be a first-round draft choice in the NFL and play 10 years is truly special. I didn't do any of this alone. You can't make it by yourself. Can you imagine where I'd be without all those people in my life?"

It's hard to imagine McNeal being part of two national championship teams in 1978 and 1979, earning All-America honors as a corner-back in 1979, making Alabama's Team of the Century, playing 10 seasons of pro football with the Miami Dolphins or living such a rich, meaningful life today without the love and guidance of so many special people.

McNeal's youth presented countless opportunities to take another path, starting with the death of his mother Willie Mae when McNeal was six years old. Her loss left 10 children and her husband Henry to fend for themselves on four acres outside McCullough, a tiny town 13 miles from Atmore near the Florida state line.

"People say you don't remember at that age, but I remember my mother," McNeal

says. "She would do so many nice things, and she was always there for us. She could really sing. I remember that clearly, that she could really sing.

"It was tough to lose her, but at the same time, I had six sisters and three other brothers who made the difference. Without them and my belief in Jesus Christ, I don't know where I'd be today."

That family bond would not have survived if McNeal's father had not refused to let Willie Mae's death tear the family apart.

"After the funeral, some of our aunts and uncles told him, 'Henry, we'll all take some of the kids with us and take care of them.' They were trying to help us," McNeal says, "but my father made a great statement: 'Together we'll stand, but divided we'll fall away.' One of the greatest things my father ever did was keep us all together."

It took a long time for McNeal to realize the significance of his father's parenting and the challenge Henry accepted when Willie Mae died.

"As I was coming up I thought my dad was the meanest person in the world," McNeal says. "He used to whip my butt almost everyday, probably because I was kind of a bad boy. He was strict and had to raise us all by himself. He never got remarried and he did the best he could to raise us like he knew how to do it.

"I didn't realize it back them, but now I realize it every day, that my father was the greatest person in the world. In this day and time, when people don't talk about how important fathers are, my father is my role model. You can talk about role models like Michael Jordan and all these football players, and I'm sure some of them are good in their own right, but my father was my role model."

Henry McNeal worked hard to make the most of his farm, growing soybeans, peas and cucumbers and raising hogs. He built a three-bedroom house one room at a time with wood from two barns he tore down. When McNeal was still just a boy, his father and mother slept in one room while the girls slept in another bedroom and the boys slept in another.

"We went to bed all covered up and we had so many covers on our bed that it was tough to get up in the morning," McNeal says. "We didn't have indoor plumbing. I grew up without warm running water, and it was cold in the winter and hot in the summer. We didn't have any insulation. We cooked on a wood stove and had to get up in the morning to make a fire for the wood stove and another one in the fireplace because we only had one room that was warm."

The kids did their part to help out by chopping cotton and picking peas for local farmers, but when the girls got older they moved to Detroit one by one for jobs in the automobile industry and sent money when they could.

Henry McNeal's farming methods were simple and demanding, but effective. Instead of a tractor he had a 1950-something GMC truck and Kate, a mule he bought for $75. Kate had been a rodeo star in her younger days and knew how to work, so Henry took good care of her. The same, however, could not be said of young Don.

"I hated Kate," McNeal says. "Kate worked us to death. I even tried to kill Kate. All my brothers had gone, and I was the last one left and I got so tired of plowing this mule that

I tried to starve the mule to death, tried not giving her any water, tried giving her too much water so she'd have heat stroke or something, but none of it worked."

After plowing in the rain one day McNeal loaded Kate in the back of the truck, climbed in behind the wheel and came up with a plan to get rid of Kate once and for all.

"I knew I had a 60-degree turn coming up and a 90-degree turn coming up," McNeal says, "and if the first one didn't get her the second would."

McNeal raced through the first turn and cut the wheel hard, despite his father's warnings, but when he looked back Kate was still in place. McNeal then figured he'd have to try harder, so he swerved to throw Kate off balance as he tore into the second turn. This time, the ol' gal flew out of the back of the truck and down an embankment.

"I stopped the truck and my dad ran down the hill to look for that old mule and back in the truck I was celebrating. I knew she was done," McNeal says. "I had to pull myself together and follow my dad and act concerned about this mule. When I got down the hill, it was raining cats and dogs and that old mule, to my surprise, was standing up. She turned around and looked right at me like she was saying, 'Don McNeal, don't you ever try that again. I'm going to be with you forever.'"

You'd think a farm kid would appreciate any chance to escape the farm for sports, but getting McNeal to play football was about as easy as getting him to plow. McNeal was participating in physical education class at Atmore High when coach Glen Latham asked him to give football a try. Except for P.E. football, McNeal had never been exposed to the

game, and he knew his dad wasn't going to let him play. "I told him I had too many chores to do in the evening time," McNeal says, "and really and truly, I didn't want to play."

Latham made a deal with McNeal: if he would just go home and ask his dad, and if his dad allowed him to play, he had to come out for the team. McNeal agreed, knowing his dad would reject the idea. McNeal was right initially when his dad refused, and he was relieved until his dad returned to his room later that night with a change of heart. McNeal recalls, "He said, 'You're growing up and you're the last boy at home, so you can do it if you'll come home and do your chores in the evening and double up on the weekend.'"

McNeal, being a man of his word, showed up for football as he had promised and encountered challenges he'd never faced before. First, he was late for practice because he couldn't figure out how to put on his football equipment, including pants and shoes that were too big for his scrawny body. "I looked like a clown," McNeal says. When he finally reached the field he found he liked the tackling just fine, but he didn't think much of being tackled. On one hit, he found his head turned one way, and his helmet facing the other. Soon his ears started to bleed and when he complained, one of the coaches found that McNeal had thrown away the ear pads from his helmet because he didn't think he needed them.

Once he learned the game, McNeal proved to be a natural. It wasn't long before college coaches started noticing, and Alabama assistant Hayden Riley insisted that secondary coach Bill Oliver come down with him and see this skinny kid playing receiver and defensive back for Atmore High.

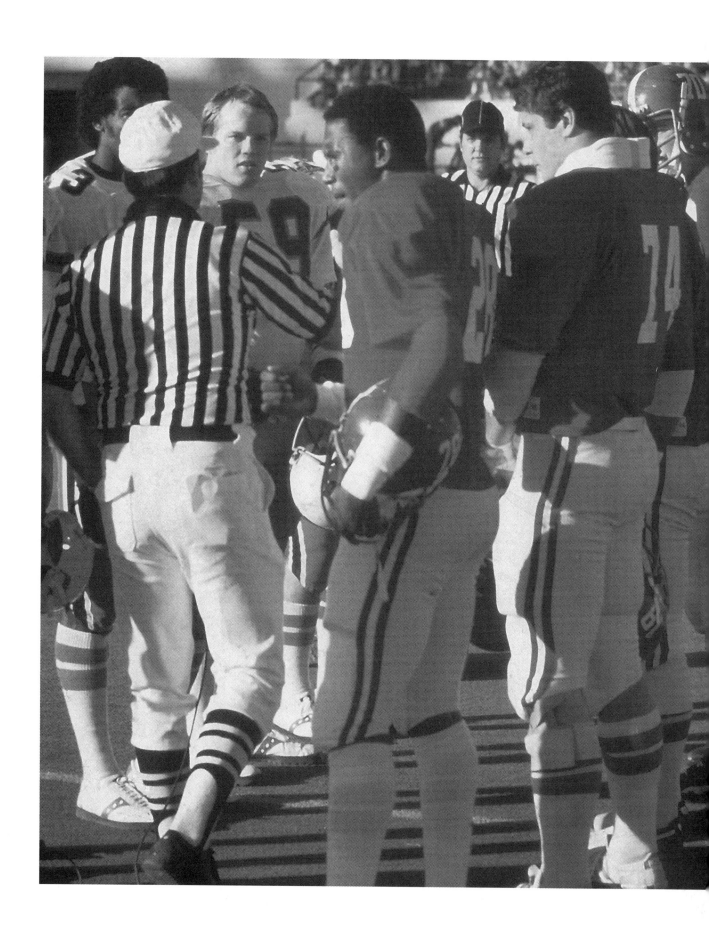

"We didn't get there until the middle of the first quarter, and when we walked to the fence around the field the first thing I noticed was that the grass was extremely high," Oliver says. "Then we noticed that Don had been moved to halfback in the wishbone. They ran a counter play right off tackle and I reckon he ran about 65, 70 yards just like you snapped your finger, even in that tall grass. I looked at Hayden and said, 'You're right. He's special.'"

The only person who didn't seem to understand that McNeal was special was McNeal himself. Choosing Alabama was the easy part for McNeal, the only member of his family to attend college, but staying at Alabama wasn't so easy. In addition to being homesick and overwhelmed by the University campus, he was convinced Oliver hated him because he was so tough on him. McNeal also had no desire to play defensive back, so he started doing all he could to get beat on defense and force the coaches to move him to receiver. The ploy might have worked if McNeal had not drawn the ire of the head coach up in the tower.

"I was wide open and dropped the ball, right in front of Coach Bryant," McNeal says. "He said, 'Don McNeal, go back down there and play defensive back.'"

McNeal kept trying to sabotage the move until Bryant confronted him. "He said, 'I know what you're doing, and if you don't go back down there and play defensive back the way I know you can play defensive back, I'm going to send you back to that farm and you're going to plow that mule again.' That's all it took. On the next play, a running play, I took on the lead blocker, put him on the ground and made the tackle. Coach Bryant almost jumped out of the tower, and from that day on I was a defensive back."

And an excellent defensive back at that. "He was such a student of the game and such an outstanding young man," Oliver says. "You never had to worry about him going to class or being where he was supposed to be. He always made good marks and he was very conscientious. He was a perfectionist, always trying to be the best student and player he could. He never had a bad day on the practice field. He was such a pleasure to coach."

McNeal produced a history of outstanding plays and winning performances during his three years with the varsity (1977-79), and he developed a habit of making his biggest plays in the biggest games. He was at his best on one of the biggest plays in Alabama history as the Crimson Tide won the 1978 national championship by stopping the Penn State Nittany Lions on the goal line late in the fourth quarter of the 1979 Sugar Bowl.

While the most memorable play in the famous goal-line stand came when linebacker Barry Krauss and a swarm of Crimson teammates stopped Penn State running back Mike Guman on fourth down at the Alabama one-foot line, Penn State players are quick to credit McNeal with making the game's decisive play on second down.

"He made a better play than Krauss," Guman says. "Krauss got the credit, but McNeal made the play."

Oliver recalls that "Penn State took Scott Fitzkee from the wide position and put him at tight end, so that gave them a two-tight end look, and Fitzkee was lined up to the flanker side and the flanker side was the wide side of the field. We were in a man to man with the flanker on Don's side, which put Don man to man with the outside receiver and Murray Legg man to man with Fitzkee.

"As the play unfolded, they ran the sprint draw and faked the handoff to the play-action pass. As Fitzkee started penetrating toward the goal line and to the flat, Murray Legg slipped. Don had the receiver who was running parallel to the back of the end zone, but athletes like Don have the presence of mind to overcome their coaching, as Coach Bryant used to say, and this was an example. He's covering his man, sees Fitzkee open and all the quarterback had to do was deliver the ball to the guy who's open."

Penn State quarterback Chuck Fusina completed the pass to Fitzkee, but before Fitzkee could turn toward the goal line, McNeal seemed to come from out of nowhere to make the hit, driving him out of bounds at the 1-yard line.

"The tackle he made was devastating," Oliver says. "It was just unbelievable. The distance McNeal covered from the back end line to come up and make the tackle at the one-foot line is just mind-boggling. A lot of times a guy in the secondary might come that far, but the ball carrier will still fall into the end zone and score, but not with Don. And if you go back and look at the film from his career, you can't find any missed tackles."

Ask McNeal about the play, and he'll insist he was just playing on instinct, just doing his job in the heat of the moment, just responding to what Oliver had prepared him to do.

"He'll tell you he just did it, because of the coaching, because he was conditioned to do it," Krauss says. "He'll say, 'I really wasn't thinking about it, I just did it.' We're in the right coverage, he's covering his man, he turns, he sees the guy make the catch just short of the goal line and makes a great hit and does a great job of driving him out.

"He'll just tell you he was doing his job, but there's more to it than that. He was a great player and a great person. Coach Bryant recruited a lot of guys with character who knew how to win as a team, and Don was one of those guys. He was a guy you could always rely on. You always knew he was in the right place at the right time, doing his job."

Those qualities helped convince the Miami Dolphins to select McNeal in the first round of the 1980 NFL draft, and McNeal went on to play 10 years in the NFL, participating in two Super Bowls, winning Dolphin Player of the Year honors twice and earning a place on the Dolphins' 25th Anniversary Silver Anniversary Team. Despite those accolades and his college success, he is not a member of the Alabama Sports Hall of Fame.

Injuries prevented his career from being everything McNeal wanted it to be, but "so many people have touched my life that my pro career has given me a chance to make an impact."

McNeal remains active in a number of positive causes in the Miami area, most notably through his works as the children's pastor at New Testament Baptist Church. He also travels the country speaking to young people through Sportsworld, an Indiana-based group that sends pro athletes out to bring a message of hope and encouragement to students.

Between his ministry work and life with his family, wife, Rhonda, and teenage daughter Jessica, McNeal insists, "I have been blessed in so many ways. I pinch myself sometimes. I'm so grateful, but I know I didn't do any of this by myself. It all goes back to people like Miss Biggs, my father, my brothers and sisters, my Sunday school teachers, my coaches, my teammates. All those people have a part in who I am today, so I've got to go out and make an impact on somebody else's life."

DWIGHT STEPHENSON

CENTER 1977-1979

It might be difficult to believe now, but Dwight Stephenson was once the kind of scrawny little boy neighborhood kids used to pick on. Not just any kids, either.

"In my elementary school days, sometimes it was tough for me to go to school," Stephenson says. "There were these girls, Sadie Garrison and her friends, who used to rough me up pretty good. She'd sit behind me in school and just make my day miserable. She'd pluck me in the head; hit me upside the head, whatever she felt like doing. If she didn't come to school that day, that meant I got a day off."

No one, even Stephenson himself, could ever picture him being the kind of kid who one day would push people around for a living and earn a college education and a considerable paycheck doing it.

"I was the kid you would never, ever have figured would be playing at the University of Alabama," Stephenson says, "let alone be an offensive lineman."

Those kids didn't understand where Stephenson came from or where he was going. If they had taken a closer look at his parents Eugene and Mable Louise and their determined will to make a better life for their children, perhaps they would have understood that Stephenson wasn't going to allow himself to fail.

They didn't see that Stephenson would grow, thanks to a combination of good genetics, hard work and the job he got at a local grocery story when he was 14 years old. Stephenson didn't make a lot of money because he ate most of his paycheck and fed a growth spurt that would turn him into muscular young man. It wasn't long before he was big enough to attract the attention of his high school football coaches.

Stephenson never played organized football until his junior year in high school, but by the time he retired from football in 1987, Stephenson had established himself as one of the top centers in both college and professional football history, earning a spot on Alabama's Team of the Century, the Alabama Sports Hall of Fame in 1994, and the Pro Football Hall of Fame in 1998.

"Dwight Stephenson was the best center I ever coached," Alabama coach Paul "Bear" Bryant said. "He was a man among children."

Stephenson would be the first to admit that wouldn't have been possible without the example of his parents. Dwight, the second of seven children, was five years old when his father made the decision to leave the family farm in Murfreesboro, North Carolina, and move to Hampton, Virginia, for a job in the shipyards.

"He's the guy I try to model myself after," Stephenson says. "For 30 years he'd work two jobs, weekends, overtime to keep the family going. He didn't just move a couple of miles from home. He made a decision early on as a young man to move off the farm and work in the shipyard and make a better opportunity and a better life for his family."

Stephenson's mother also did her part "raising seven children and working in the school cafeteria," Stephenson says. "She worked hard. They both worked hard. I just remember them both working day after day and they never complained or stayed home sick with anything. When my mother finally retired from her job she had something like 200-300 sick days she never used. They had the attitude where they got up each day and went to work no matter what."

Stephenson also had an older sister who did her part to raise the expectations for the Stephenson children. Before she died of breast cancer in 1997, Joyce was the first child in the family to graduate from high school, attend college, graduate college and make her own way in the world.

"She set the pattern for us," Stephenson says. "She set the standard. She was the leader among the kids."

Stephenson was happy to be a stocky six-foot-three basketball player until the coaches at Hampton High noticed him and convinced him to play football. Hampton High had a reputation for winning and sending players to college, and Stephenson proved to be a natural candidate for both measures of success. The Crabbers played in the state championship game during Stephenson's junior season and won the state championship as seniors, with Stephenson earning all-state honors at center and defensive end. At the time Stephenson and two of his teammates made a deal that they would stay together and attend the same college. When all three decided to sign with Alabama, Stephenson figured the plan was set in stone.

"It seemed like an awful long way for me, that's for sure," Stephenson says, "but I thought it was an opportunity that was worth it. Of all the schools that recruited me, Alabama was no question the biggest program, and I thought the best program. I was learning a lot about coach Paul "Bear" Bryant at the time, and I was really excited about playing for him.

"A week or so after that, the Alabama coaches came to town to sign us. The coaches caught me at school and I said I wasn't ready to sign yet, [and to] meet me at home later. I went home and then coach Ken Donahue and coach John Mitchell and I got in the car and drove to the other guy's houses and they had [already] signed with NC State. When I got home the Alabama coaches were all excited, telling me how much I'm gonna love playing for Coach Bryant and all that. And I'm thinking, 'I'm going to school 12 hours from home by myself.'

"As soon as I got home I went into the kitchen to see my mama. Now she had tried to stay out of it because she wanted me to make my own decision. I told her, 'Mama, I'm going to NC State.' At that point, my mama said, 'You aren't gonna follow anybody anywhere. You're going to the University of Alabama!'"

Stephenson walked back in the living room, signed with Alabama and never wavered from his commitment, even though he arrived in Tuscaloosa with plenty of doubts and concerns.

"I'm not going to say I wasn't scared playing for Coach Bryant, because I was," Stephenson says, "and I didn't know if I was good enough. I didn't know what to expect. You hear a lot of things and sometimes you get out there and get to hurting a little bit, and you think you made the wrong decision."

When Stephenson confronted his initial doubts, he made two conscious decisions about his Alabama career. The first one was to honor his family and his upbringing in everything he did.

"It made me think about everything going on back home," Stephenson says. "I had already decided that if I went back home I would do what my daddy did. If my daddy could do it, I could do it. But the more I thought about that,

the more I realized what a great opportunity I had there at the University of Alabama and if I could do well there, a lot of good things could happen for me and my whole family. That was part of my motivation. Thank God [my daddy] made those things possible for me there at Alabama."

His second decision involved learning all he could about his position as well as the commitment required to be a successful player for the Crimson Tide. Stephenson arrived at a time when success for Alabama meant contending for and winning national and conference championships, and soon realized Bryant's best players were more than willing to pay the price for the prize.

"When I first got to the University of Alabama, one of the first things I did was start looking around and paying attention to what made the great players so special," Stephenson says. "Guys like Gus White, Ozzie Newsome, Terry Jones, Bob Baumhower, Johnny Davis, Jeff Rutledge and some of those other guys—I wanted to know what made those players All-SEC and All-America. I learned they were smart guys who worked hard and they believed in themselves. And they were all team players.

"It was a great experience for me as a young player to get in there and see those guys work and learn from them and someday maybe get a chance to play and do what they did."

After sitting out the 1976 season as a freshman defensive end and center, competing each day in practice against the best linemen on Alabama's varsity, Stephenson made an immediate impact in his first spring. When the coaches decided to move Jones to nose guard that spring, Stephenson took over as the starting center.

"I remember coming home in the summer and me and my high school buddies would go to the drugstore and read all the college football magazines," Stephenson says. "I came home that summer after my freshman year and they asked me how it went, and I told them at the end of spring ball I was the starting center for the University of Alabama, like it was no big deal, and I don't think anybody believed me.

"When I went to Alabama the first time, everybody was thinking, 'This guy won't cut it down there. He'll go down there for a few days and come back.' One of my high school coaches, just before I was getting ready to go, he asked me when I was going to Alabama. I said I was leaving on Sunday and he said, 'You'll be back by Wednesday.' He said that joking, but I'm sure in his mind he wasn't sure if I could make it down there.

"A lot of people didn't think I could make it at Alabama, and they were surprised when I did."

His teammates and coaches were not shocked when Stephenson spent the rest of his Alabama career playing a key role on two national championship teams and earning All-America and All-SEC honors in 1979, as well as the Jacobs Trophy for the SEC's best blocker.

"Dwight cannot stand to get beat," assistant coach Jack Rutledge told *Bama Magazine* in November 1979. "He wants to win every battle, even at practice. He goes full speed on every play, always trying to help the team. There is no doubt about it. Dwight is the best center we've ever had at Alabama.

"We've had great centers, I know, but Dwight is the best of the bunch. He has done more than just live up to the standards set by those who played before him. He has improved a tradition. He blends quickness, strength, learning ability and burning desire into one package. He is a well-rounded, complete football player."

Even today, the status accorded by Bryant and Rutledge is somewhat difficult for Stephenson to digest, simply because he held previous Alabama centers in such high regard. Stephenson reels off the names of some of Alabama's best centers and wonders how anybody could be better than the players he saw on tape during his individual film study.

"That means so much to me, but I also know that I didn't get there by myself. I had so many great teammates to play with. I'm talking about guys like Vince Boothe, Jim Bunch, Buddy Aydelette and Mike Brock. I played with those guys, and they were great players, tough blockers, as tough as they come.

"All the individual stuff means a lot, but it meant a lot more to me to play with those guys and go the University of Alabama and play for Coach Bryant and his coaches and win national championship rings and win so many games."

Stephenson's Alabama success provided a strong foundation for his professional career, even if it took him a few days to convince the Miami Dolphins they had made the right choice with their second pick of the 1980 draft. At first, the coaches were concerned about his quiet, steady manner and wondered if they had made a mistake. Stephenson changed their minds early in training camp with a crushing block on cornerback Don McNeal, his former Alabama teammate.

"I looked away from the play, but then I heard the loudest collision I ever heard," Dolphins coach Don Shula said. "I rushed over to the sidelines and Dwight had bur-

ied McNeal, who was our No. 1 draft choice. Dwight is a very intense player. He never thought it was only a scrimmage or that he was hitting McNeal. We knew then that with time, Dwight would develop into a fine center."

Stephenson won the starting job late in his rookie season and went on to earn the NFL Players Association Lineman of the Year award, as well as All-Pro and All-AFC honors, five consecutive times from 1983-87. He started in Super Bowls XVII and XIX and was selected to the All-NFL team of the 1980s. He also played in 107 consecutive games from 1980 until the 1987 players' strike ended his streak, establishing himself as one of the best centers in pro football history and one of the best overall players of his era with his combination of quickness, toughness, intelligence and hard work.

"If I could tell a young player to learn from one of my veterans, to follow around and copy one player, that player would always be Dwight," Shula once said.

"Dwight Stephenson was a bear," said Baumhower, who also played nose tackle for Miami. "He was the toughest guy I ever played against, and that made it so much easier for me on game day."

"He makes it look so easy," said running back Tony Nathan, who also played for both the Crimson Tide and the Dolphins. "Sometimes you forget about Dwight during a game. Then on film day you remember. You watch him manhandle a player, and you can't believe he's the same size as Dwight."

Stephenson was still performing at his peak when he suffered a devastating knee injury on December 7, 1987. During a fumble return, New York Jets defensive lineman Marty Lyons, another former Alabama teammate, hit Stephenson with a legal block and Stephenson fell awkwardly, suffering torn anterior cruciate and lateral collateral ligaments in his left knee. Stephenson had played his way through injuries before and worked hard to rehabilitate the knee throughout the off season, but he was forced to retire the next summer after just eight seasons in the NFL.

Lyons has apologized repeatedly for his hit, but Stephenson continues to insist the incident and any hard feelings toward Lyons are buried in his past. When told Lyons still feels bad about what happened, Stephenson says he hopes Lyons will someday be able to let it go as well.

"I know Marty didn't mean to hurt me. I knew one day my football career would come to an end," Stephenson says. "If it had been God's will for me, I would have played again, so I don't hold any malice toward Marty. I see Marty all the time, and I don't want him to feel terrible about what happened. You've got to play hard and sometimes things just happen that you can't control."

Those eight seasons turned out to be enough to put Stephenson in the Pro Football Hall of Fame in 1998. He also earned a spot on the Dolphins' Silver Anniversary All-Time Team and place on the Dolphin Honor Roll at Joe Robbie Stadium.

Instead of spending all of his time collecting awards, Stephenson and his wife, Dinah, have been busy raising three children, Marshea, Dwight Jr. (a sophomore linebacker at Notre Dame) and Dwayne, and playing an active charitable role in the Miami area. Stephenson, who received the NFL's 1985 Man of the Year award honoring the NFL player who combines outstanding community service and playing excellence, serves on the board of United Cerebral Palsy and the Boys and Girls Club and oversees Dwight's Computers For

Kids, a program that provides computers for deserving students. He also runs his own commercial construction company.

"We need to get together with the University of Alabama and build one of their buildings," Stephenson says. "That's one of my goals."

That goal says a lot more about Stephenson as an alumnus than about his business ambitions.

"Alabama influences everything I do everyday," Stephenson says. "The construction business isn't an easy business. It's a rewarding business, but it's lot of hard work, and things don't always go well. Like Coach Bryant said, the ones who win are the ones who push through the tough times and move past those obstacles. Those are the people who are successful. Those lessons and the lessons I learned from my parents keep me going today."

Dwight Stephenson (No. 57)

JEREMIAH CASTILLE

DEFENSIVE BACK 1979-1982

Jeremiah Castille wasn't the kind of guy to do a lot of talking back in those days, especially in front of a lot of people. This was different. The time and the situation demanded that someone step up and say what needed to be said, and Castille was the right man for the job.

In Alabama's Liberty Bowl locker room, just minutes before the Crimson Tide would take the field against Illinois for the final game of coach Paul "Bear" Bryant's legendary career; Castille stood up and said what needed to be said.

"I had probably said four words my whole four years there, but we were sitting there getting ready before the game and the Lord just prompted me to let Coach Bryant know how much he had done for me, how much he meant to me," Castille says. "I can tell you I was fired up. I said 'I came here an 18-year-old boy, and I'm leaving as a 22-year-old man, and he had a lot to do with that. This is my last game, this is Coach Bryant's last game, and we're going

out a winner. There's no way we're going to lose this.'"

Castille did his part that night to ensure Bryant would go out a winner on December 29, 1982, intercepting three passes in a 21-15 victory. After the game, as Bryant was accepting the trophy, he pointed to Castille and said, "My career has been great because of men like this guy right here."

Twenty-eight days later, Bryant passed away at Druid City Hospital in Tuscaloosa. Two days later, Castille served as one of Bryant's pallbearers, at the request of Bryant's widow, Mary Harmon Bryant, as his coach was laid to rest in Birmingham's Elmwood Cemetery. On that day, Castille found himself thinking about all the other players who could have been chosen to be one of Bryant's pallbearers. He recalls being awestruck at the sight of thousands of mourners lined up to pay their respects along the 55 miles of Interstate 59 between Tuscaloosa and the cemetery. Castille remembers how all the cars and trucks pulled off along the side of the road, watching the hearse and the procession pass by. He recalls wondering how many lives Bryant had touched. He also found himself remembering his own relationship with his coach, and how Bryant had touched his own life in so many ways.

"I was a freshman and I had just arrived when Coach Bryant called me into his office and had me sit down so we could talk," Castille says. "He told me, 'I believe in you. I believe you can play.' Now when you hear that as a freshman from Coach Bryant, that's it. After that, I believed. I walked out of his office saying, 'Man, Coach Bryant believes I can play.'

"How many coaches have that kind of insight, especially with freshmen? A lot of them are nervous, scared, unsure, and don't have any confidence. For him to share those words with me also showed me he cared about me as a person."

When it comes to Castille, former teammates and coaches insist the person is as special as the player. Castille was successful enough as a player to start three years for Alabama, earn All-America honors in 1982 and a place on the Tide's Team of the Century and play six years in the NFL. As a person, he was the kind of guy who always seemed to have his priorities in order. Even today he heads his own ministry, serving the needs of University of Alabama students and athletes as a spiritual mentor, similar to his former role as a local director for the Fellowship of Christian Athletes.

"He had a lot of physical, God-given talent; he could run, change direction, cover people," says Louis Campbell, Alabama's secondary coach from 1980-84. "He would hit you, too.

He wasn't a little cover corner. He was a tough guy. He had the ability to play on Sunday, he was productive, he made plays, and you could count on him.

"But the thing that always stood out to me is what a humble, great person he really was. You could tell, through his upbringing, that he had some self-confidence as a player and a person, but he always kept his self-worth in balance. Sometimes it's hard to find a talented player who's still humble, but that was Jeremiah. You knew right from the start that he had a spiritual basis in his life and that set the tone for those qualities."

Those qualities were forged in the fire of a challenging childhood in Phenix City, Alabama, in a family Castille calls "dysfunctional."

"I had a mom and a dad, but I grew up in an alcoholic family, " Castille says. "I was number eight of nine kids, and I grew up around domestic violence. My mom and dad fought multiple times. It's the kind of home life most people don't make it out of. You hear people say they become a victim of their environment, and I almost became a victim if it weren't for God.

"When I was growing up I got suspended and expelled for fighting before I could get through junior high. I was a bad kid, and I was just doing what I had learned at home. The last time I had to tell my mom, and when I told her all she said was, 'Boy, I'm real disappointed in you.' I still remember those words penetrating my heart."

That summer, Castille found himself looking for answers when he attended a revival at a Baptist church down the street, heard the message there and made a dramatic turn. "The Lord saved me that summer, and I committed to a personal relationship with Jesus Christ," Castille says. "My life changed from that point on. I had real purpose and I dedicated myself to it and I didn't quit. Growing up in Phenix City, with all the temptations around to go off on the wrong road and all the people I saw throw their lives away, it was that dream of making life count for something that saved me."

Castille's brother Joseph wasn't so fortunate. He died at age 43 when he was fatally stabbed in an Alabama prison during an argument with another prisoner. Castille's mother, however, is now sober. When the Tampa Bay Buccaneers drafted Castille in 1983, he moved his mother to a different area of Phenix City and placed her in a rehab program. Through the program, she gained her sobriety and has been sober for more than 20 years.

"To me, that's what life is all about," Castille says. "It's all about winning those battles."

Castille's desire to win fueled his decision to sign with Alabama out of Phenix City's Central High in 1979. "I had several choices, but Alabama was one of the premier teams in the country, and some guys from my high school had played at Alabama, like Woodrow Lowe and Billy Jackson," Castille says, "so I grew up hearing Coach Bryant call Woodrow and Billy's name on his TV show. In fact, the first recruiting letter I got was from Alabama. I was still just a junior, and they won the national championship that year, and that pretty much did it for me. It was a done deal after that."

Castille made an immediate impression on his coaches and teammates and played as a true freshman, backing up All-American Don McNeal at one of the cornerback spots for the

1979 national champions. Castille recorded an interception that season, but it was a tackle on a kickoff return by Auburn's James Brooks that convinced him he could play big-time college football.

"It was a defining moment for me, a play that showed me, 'I can do this,'" Castille says.

When McNeal moved on to the NFL, Castille was ready for the starting job.

"He was the kind of player Coach Bryant loved because he was first class," McNeal says. "When he came in my last year and backed me up I knew he was going to take over for me and the position was going to be in great hands. He was a real competitor and wouldn't give anyone an inch, and that's how you have to be to win."

Castille started throughout the rest of his time at Alabama, improving each season and setting the school record at the time with 16 career interceptions in regular-season games and helping the Tide give Bryant his 315th victory, making him the winningest coach in college football.

Alabama continued to win a lot more games than it lost during this period, but the program also showed signs of decline in 1982, when injuries, suspensions and offensive struggles led to close losses and an 8-4 record. Late in the season, following a 38-29 loss to Southern Miss in Tuscaloosa, Bryant decided it was time to retire. Three weeks later, and two weeks after Alabama lost to an Auburn team coached by former Bryant assistant Pat Dye, Bryant made a formal announcement that shocked Castille and immediately made him think of his younger teammates and future Alabama players.

"I started thinking about the guys who wouldn't get to play for him or the guys who wouldn't get a chance to finish up their careers under Coach Bryant," Castille says. "I knew no other coach could ever replace him and do what he had done. I had grown into a young man, and I had come to a place where I could

truly appreciate what he had done for me and I knew those other guys wouldn't be able to go through the same experience with Coach Bryant."

After his three interceptions in the Liberty Bowl gave him 10 for the season, Castille turned his attention toward a professional career. Tampa Bay used a third-round pick to select Castille, and he spent four years with the Bucs before they released him. He spent the next two seasons with the Denver Broncos and played an important role in one of the most memorable plays in NFL history.

In the 1987 AFC Championship game between the Cleveland Browns and the Broncos at Denver's Mile High Stadium, Cleveland trailed 38-31 late in the fourth quarter but owned all of the momentum as quarterback Bernie Kosar and tailback Earnest Byner drove the Browns down the field and into scoring position.

The Browns reached the eight-yard line when Castille stepped into place in NFL history. Castille had been burned two times on Cleveland's previous possession, so he had backed off several yards on Browns receiver Webster Slaughter to prevent the deep pass and get a better look. When the Browns gave the ball to Byner on a draw play, Castille made his move.

"By backing off and getting six or seven yards, I could see the draw play happen," Castille says. "This let me beat the receiver and not give him a chance to block me. Byner had been running all over our defense in the second half. As I was running up on the play I'm thinking, 'This guy is so much bigger than me that he'll just run over me and carry me into the end zone if I don't do something.' I figured the best way for me to tackle him was to try and strip the ball."

Castille poked the ball loose near the two-yard line and recovered the fumble, securing a victory that sent the Broncos to the Super Bowl and a distinctive place in NFL history. He remains something of a hero in Denver and a villain in Cleveland, all for that one play.

Castille spent one year as an assistant coach at Howard University before he returned to Birmingham to coach high school football, including seven years at Briarwood Christian High School. He and his wife, Jean, are raising three boys and three girls, including two sons, Tim and Simeon, who attend the University and play football for Alabama.

"I never dreamed about them playing football when they were smaller. I always thought they should look into doing something else because of the pressure of people comparing them with their father," Castille says. "But it was their decision to play football. It's been good for them, because it was something they choose to do and not something I made them do.

"It's been a real blessing. When your children have dreams and goals it's good to see them work hard and stay focused. It helps them when they face peer pressure, especially when they're teenagers and it helps them stay on the right track, doing what they need to be doing."

Castille is excited to see his boys playing at Alabama, but he often wishes they had been able to meet and play for Bryant. He wishes they could have learned the same things he learned directly from his coach. He hopes they'll come to see that their time in Tuscaloosa isn't just about football, and that it's even bigger than getting an education. He prays they see the bigger picture and come away with something that will make an impact on every aspect of their lives, just as his time at Alabama did for him.

"I know how much going to Alabama helped me and the lessons it taught me," Castille says. "I owe a lot to the University of Alabama and the football program. Coach Bryant helped me grow up and the things I learned from him have helped me raise my children, helped me make the adjustment to life without football. That's what I look at when I look at my boys. Not what happens on the field. I want them to be able to learn a lot of the same lessons and benefit in every area of their life."

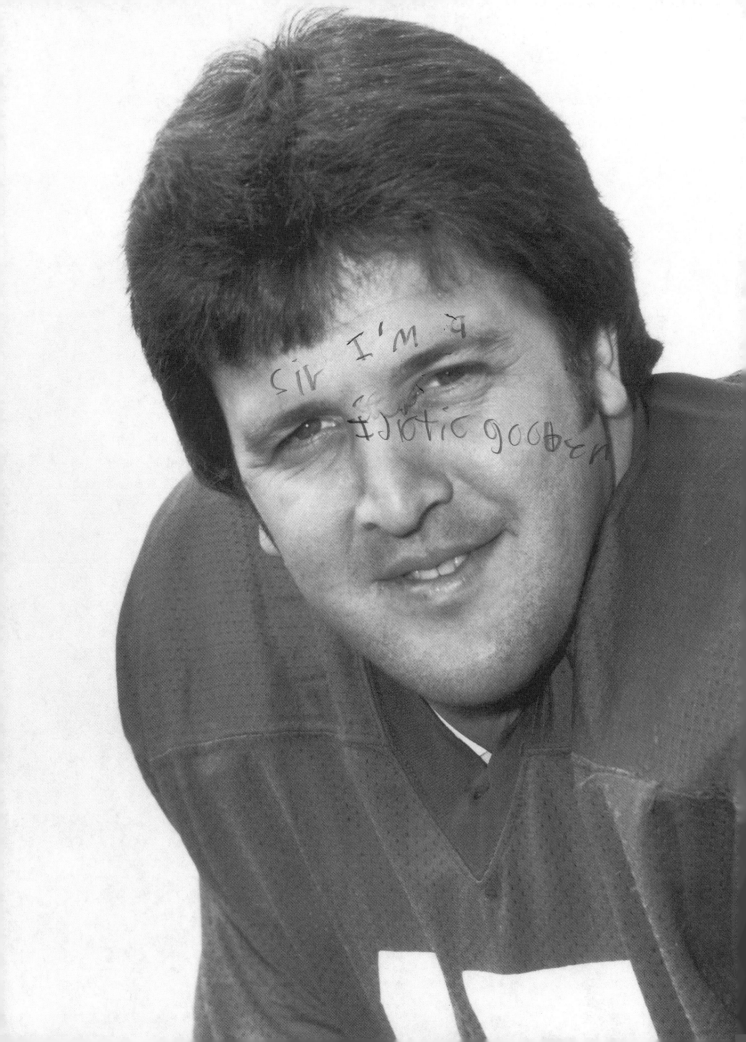

TOMMY WILCOX

DEFENSIVE BACK 1979-1982

I t didn't take much for coach Paul "Bear" Bryant to convince Tommy Wilcox to come to Alabama, but it took Bryant's best to get him to stay.

As a high school senior in Harahan, Louisiana, Wilcox was an option quarterback and a versatile athlete with offers from college football programs throughout the Southeastern Conference and the Southwest Conference, as well as Notre Dame. Of all those teams, one school sparked a special fire in Wilcox's imagination.

"Every now and then in Louisiana, don't ask me how, we could get some of Coach Bryant's TV shows," Wilcox says. "And I can remember every Saturday afternoon after we'd get through playing we'd come in and watch *The Prudential Scoreboard*. I'd always watch that because Alabama was always so good, so they'd have plenty to say about Alabama. And we ran the wishbone in high school, too, so I just fell in love with Alabama."

Moreover, Wilcox was a tough kid, the kind of player who could take a hit, give a hit and keep on hitting. Alabama, he knew, would test him in ways he had never been challenged before.

"I didn't come to the University of Alabama because I thought it would be easy," Wilcox says. "I came because I knew it would be hard. I felt like if I could make it at Alabama and play for Coach Bryant, I could make it anywhere."

The hardest part, it turns out, was staying put until the end of what eventually became a successful college football career. Before Wilcox became a four-year starter, a two-time All-American, a member of Alabama's Team of the Century and one of eight former players to receive a monumental, yet poignant honor, Wilcox came dangerously close to throwing it all away.

When Alabama redshirted Wilcox as a freshman in 1978, it seemed like a good idea to everyone but Wilcox. After being a big fish in a little pond back in Harahan, Wilcox ran the scout team offense against the same defense that held Penn State on the famous goal-line stand in the 1979 Sugar Bowl and paved the way for a national championship season. After getting beat up by players such as Marty Lyons, Barry Krauss, Rich Wingo and Curtis McGriff, Wilcox started to realize he could handle himself against the best Alabama had to offer.

"I really felt like I could play," Wilcox says, "but I didn't feel like they were giving me a chance."

That's when Wilcox found himself back in Harahan in the summer of 1979.

"I wasn't coming back," Wilcox says. "I was homesick, I hadn't played any that year, I got beat up a lot. Between all that I figured I'd just hang around close to home and go to one of those other schools."

Bryant, however, wasn't ready to give up on Wilcox. Bryant called Wilcox and told him to meet him at the airport in three days. Wilcox met him at the airport and walked with Bryant to a nearby Hilton, where Bryant secured a room so he could sit and talk with Wilcox face to face.

"You know they got those little tables with the two chairs in some of those rooms? Well he pulled both chairs away from that table and put one right in front of the other so that when I sat down and he sat down, his legs were on the outside of mine and my legs were stuck close together," Wilcox says.

It was Bryant at his intimidating best.

"He said, 'Boy, what's your problem?'" Wilcox says. "I started talking and sort of looking around the room, and he said, 'Wait a

minute, boy. When you talk to me, look me in the eyes.'"

After Bryant heard Wilcox's story, he told him, "Look, I've been around for so long that there ain't any problems I ain't heard before. You being homesick just reflects on your childhood and your family and what a good job they did raising you. When you miss people like that, there must have been a lot of love in the household."

More than anything, Bryant convinced Wilcox that if he returned to Tuscaloosa and worked hard, he could play for the Crimson Tide. In his own way, Bryant filled Wilcox with confidence and then challenged him to live up to that assurance. When Bryant walked him to the door, he insisted Wilcox wait three days before he answered him.

"Right before I left he said, 'If you'll do what I think you'll do and come back to school and you'll work hard and you'll get after folks like I think you will, I think you have the chance to be an All-American before you leave Alabama,'" Wilcox recalls. "Needless to say, I was back at school in three days."

He was not, however, welcomed back like the prodigal son. Instead, Bryant put him to the test by throwing him back on the scout team. Only this time, Wilcox found himself with the first-team scout team on both offense and defense, which meant now he would take a beating by starters on both sides of the ball.

"He never let me off the field," Wilcox says. "After a week he called me into his office and let me know I had passed the test."

Bryant also opened an important door for Wilcox. Bryant often signed several quarterbacks each year, knowing that many high school programs put their best overall athlete at quarterback. Then he would bring them in and find the right place for them. Two of Wilcox's fellow defensive backs, Jim Bob Harris and Benny Perrin, had come to Alabama as quarterbacks.

At five foot ten, 182 pounds, Wilcox was capable of running the wishbone effectively, but he would probably have to spend the season behind starting quarterback Steadman Shealy. Instead, Bryant guessed Wilcox would be even better in the secondary, and he could compete for playing time and a starting job immediately.

When Bryant presented the opportunity, Wilcox didn't spend much time thinking about his answer.

"I told him, 'Coach, I sat out all last year and got the heck beat out of me,'" Wilcox says. "'I want to play. I don't want sit on the bench anymore. Wherever you want me to play, I'll play.'

"If you're a competitor, you want to play. Would I have loved to play quarterback? Probably so, but I figured if I was going to go anywhere later in life, it wasn't going to be as a quarterback. I figured my future was in the secondary, so why not get a good start on it?"

Wilcox's transition to defense was made easier by its similarity to the system he ran in high school. Wilcox not only earned the starting job as a redshirt freshman safety in the season opener, but Bryant also shocked him by making him a captain the next week for the Baylor game. The next year Bryant surprised him again by taking him on a national speaking tour.

"We had a real good relationship," Wilcox says. "For some reason he always kind of liked me, and I think he knew how I felt about him."

Bryant's affection for Wilcox came as no surprise to Bryant's coaches, including former secondary coach Louis Campbell.

"Coach Bryant always had a soft place in his heart for people who exceeded what other people thought they could do, whether it was on the field or off the field," said Campbell, the current director of football operations at Arkansas. "Tommy was Coach Bryant's kind of player. He was extremely committed to football and to the team. He'd do anything it took to win, and he was an exceptional leader."

Wilcox also played like a coach on the field and made the most of his athletic ability, two more attributes that earned Bryant's approval. Those qualities helped Wilcox become a clutch player with a knack for making the big play in the big game, including an interception in the 1980 Sugar Bowl against Arkansas when Alabama beat the Razorbacks 24-9 and earned Bryant's sixth and final national championship; five tackles on seven plays near the goal line and an interception against Penn State in 1981 when Bryant won his 314th game, tying Amos Alonzo Stagg for the most victories by a college football coach; and an interception near the goal line the next week in Bryant's 315th win, a 28-17 victory over Auburn.

"He had a knack for being at the right place at the right time," Campbell says. "He was extremely smart, had a great awareness, and a great feel for the game. He obviously knew what was going on. Every time you drew something up, you'd wonder if he was fast enough or could he cover this guy or that guy, but the end result was that he always got the job done. He was a lot more productive than his ability level."

Despite the close nature of their relationship, Wilcox never saw Bryant's resignation coming at the end of the 1982 regular season. Four close losses and several disciplinary problems among key players left Wilcox frustrated in his senior season, especially since a painful Achilles' tendon injury limited his availability in two of those losses, but he never thought Bryant would be ready to retire before Alabama played Illinois in the Liberty Bowl.

Bryant told his players not to worry about him, but to win the Liberty Bowl for themselves. The players, however, couldn't help themselves and rallied around the emotions of the moment.

"All year long it seemed like we were in control, and then we'd end up losing games in the fourth quarter, something we'd never done at Alabama," Wilcox says. "I remember players saying, 'No matter what happened in the past, this year we're not leaving this field without winning this football game. We're going to play our hearts out and finish this thing and make sure Coach Bryant walked off the field a winner in his last game.'"

The players did their part by beating Illinois 21-15, sending Bryant off as a winner one final time.

"I was there through two national championships, three SEC championships, Coach Bryant's 314th win and his 315th win and his final game," Wilcox says. "I was fortunate I came in at a real good time. If you'd have told me I was gonna be a part of all that stuff, I'd have told you you're crazy."

Wilcox also played a part in one of the saddest days in Alabama football history. Like his teammates, coaches and Alabama fans elsewhere, Wilcox was fully aware Bryant had spent the night at Druid City Hospital but appeared to be feeling better the next day, January 26, 1983. Wilcox was working out on the practice field preparing for a try-out with professional scouts when a teammate told him the news.

"I forget who it was, but somebody came out running out of the building," Wilcox says. "All of the news reports said he was doing fine and resting comfortably, and then all of a sudden, boom, it just hit him. I thought they were kidding when they told me. He was doing fine that morning. It was just so hard to believe."

Just as Wilcox played a part in so many of Bryant's most monumental accomplishments, he also played a part at his funeral. Along with teammates Paul Ott Carruth, Walter Lewis, Jerrill Sprinkle, Mike McQueen, Paul Fields, Jeremiah Castille and Darryl White, Wilcox served as a pallbearer at the request of Bryant's widow, Mary Harmon Bryant.

"There are thousands and thousands of players who deserved to do what I did," Wilcox says, "and for Mrs. Bryant to pick me, it was an honor."

The characteristics that made Wilcox successful in college carried over to his pro career. The new United States Football League was raiding the NFL for young stars and throwing around good money, so Wilcox jumped at the chance to play for a franchise that started in Arizona and moved to Chicago the next year. He spent two years in the pros before a serious neck injury forced him to the sidelines.

"The [Denver] Broncos bought my contract, but I couldn't even pass the physical," Wilcox says. "They told me if I didn't want to be paralyzed, I should retire."

It wasn't easy for Wilcox to give up the game he had played with so much passion since he was five years old, but he eventually turned his attention to pharmaceutical sales for Bristol-Myers Squibb. He also makes the most of another life-long passion by hosting an outdoor television program, *The Woods and Water Outdoor Show*. The program has allowed him to get together with former teammates and other celebrities for hunting, fishing and reminiscing.

"I still miss football," Wilcox says, "but I'm having fun with the outdoors show."

CORNELIUS BENNETT

LINEBACKER 1983-1986

Cornelius Bennett could never see himself doing the kind of work his dad did to put food on the table and a roof over his family's head. He still can't. Not after watching Lino Bennett leave his Ensley, Alabama, home day after day for 32 years so he could labor at U.S. Steel.

When Lino Bennett passed away at age 81 in November 2003, he didn't leave behind an enormous financial fortune. Instead, he left a legacy of hard work that carried over to his son, who used it to carve out a successful college and professional football career as one of his era's top linebackers.

"If people ever watched me work they'll know I was working with a purpose and not just out there showing off," Bennett says. "I was working to get the job done, just like my father. I never heard anyone say a bad word about my dad. He spent 30-something years working at U.S. Steel and he wasn't just getting up early every morning just to be going.

He was going to serve a purpose. That purpose was to be the best he could be so he could maximize his pay potential and better support his family.

"My efforts on the football field, in high school, in college and in the pros, helped me get paid better. But the ultimate payday was winning."

Bennett made the kind of payday his father could only imagine and secured a foundation of financial security for his own family, but he probably would have fit in well with the NFL of the 1950s and 1960s before the big money started pouring in.

"The pay and the money are awesome, and I'd be lying if I said anything else," Bennett says. "I don't have to work now, and it's put me in position where I can just do charity work the rest of my life if I want to.

"I wouldn't trade that in, and I'm not one of those guys who would tell you I would have played for free, but I did enjoy trying to be the best, regardless of the pay or the situation. I was not going to be outworked by anybody. That was always my mentality. I didn't play the game for the accolades. I played it because I was meant to do it, and I loved doing it."

Perhaps that's one explanation why Alabama, the Buffalo Bills, the Atlanta Falcons and the Indianapolis Colts also enjoyed a measure of success during Bennett's time with those teams. Wherever it was, Bennett did his part to bring a high standard of expectations to every team he played for in his career.

Because Bennett never played on an SEC or national championship team, and because he played on five losing Super Bowl teams, it would be easy to overlook his accomplishments. It would also be a mistake to do so.

In his four seasons at Alabama, the Crimson Tide went 32-15-1, played in three bowls and endured the difficult transition from coach Paul "Bear" Bryant to coach Ray Perkins. For his part, *The Birmingham Post-Herald* chose Bennett the Alabama player of the decade.

In his nine seasons in Buffalo, the Bills made it to the Super Bowl four times. They haven't come close since. In his three seasons in Atlanta, the perennially wayward Falcons went to the Super Bowl for the first time in the franchise's 33-year history. In his one season with the Colts, the Colts made the playoffs for the first time since 1996.

Bennett's teams made the playoffs in 10 of 14 pro seasons, and his teams won 10 or more games in a season nine times. After starting all 16 regular-season games and leading the Colts in tackling in 1999, it finally took a major knee injury at age 34 to end his career.

His college and pro success shouldn't have come as any surprise to the neighborhood kids who called him "Biscuit." Bennett learned his football from his older brother Curtis, who played at Alabama A&M, and he was just 13 playing in a neighborhood tackle football game, with no helmets or pads, when a hit he laid on a 23-year-old player foretold his future.

"He hit him square," Curtis says. "Now, I know he hadn't really been taught how to tackle at that point, but this was a picture-perfect play. He took the guy straight off his feet and put him right on the ground. He actually brought a hush to the field with that hit. We had to stop the game for a while until the guy got his wind back."

Following a standout career at Ensley High School, Bennett didn't have to look very far for trustworthy advice on his choice of colleges. Former Alabama basketball star Reggie King, who was inducted into the Alabama Sports Hall of Fame along with Bennett in 2004, made a considerable impact on Bennett.

"For one thing, Reggie King and I grew up neighbors and we went to the same church, and his mother and my mother were best of friends," Bennett says. "When he was playing basketball at the University, that really made me want to go there because of how he spoke so well of the University whenever he came home.

"Coach Bryant was another reason. I was like a lot of kids back then, growing up watching his television show on Sundays. That and the winning tradition of Alabama football, those were big influences.

"Plus, my mom wasn't going anywhere else to watch me play, so I had to go to Alabama."

When Bennett joined Alabama as part of coach Ray Perkins's first recruiting class it didn't take him long to make an impact. On Bennett's first day of practice Perkins compared him to the NFL's best linebacker of the time, saying, "You're going to be the next Lawrence Taylor."

As if that didn't get people's attention, Perkins hit closer to home when he said, "He might have a chance to be the greatest linebacker who's ever come through here before he leaves."

Bennett spent the next four years adding himself to an Alabama linebacker tradition that also includes standouts such as Lee Roy Jordan, Woodrow Lowe, Barry Krauss, Mike Hall, Leroy Cook and E.J. Junior. As a four-

year starter, he recorded 287 tackles, including 210 solo stops, 16 sacks, two interceptions and 15 pass deflections. He also forced six fumbles, recovered three, earned All-America and All-SEC honors three times each and became just the second linebacker to win the Lombardi Award in 1986.

For all those accomplishments, one moment continues to stand out in the memory of Alabama football fans. Midway through the first quarter against Notre Dame on October 4, 1986, Bennett rushed Notre Dame quarterback Steve Beuerlein from the right side and

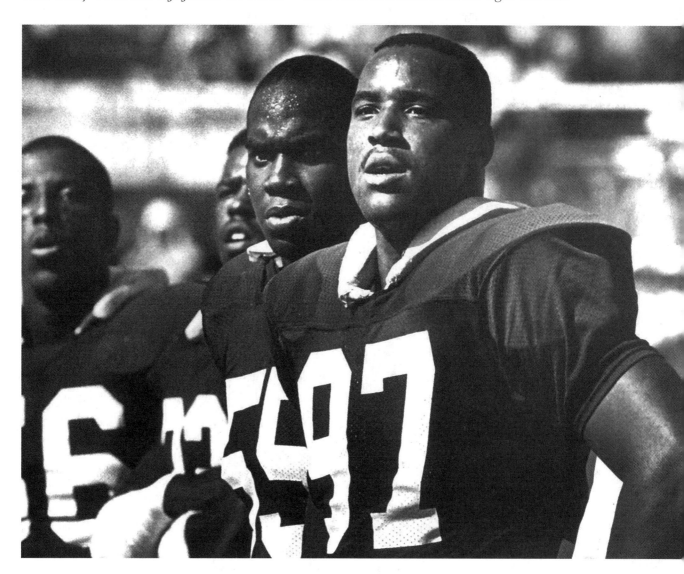

went unblocked. When he met Beuerlein in a massive head-on collision, the ball went flying, and so did Beuerlein. In photographs of the play, both players are horizontal, with the full brunt of Bennett's stampeding weight driving Beuerlein's head and back into the artificial turf at Legion Field.

"He knocked me woozy," Beuerlein said. "I have never been hit like that before, and hopefully I'll never be hit like that again."

Beuerlein, who was later found to have suffered a mild concussion on the play, spent the rest of the day worrying about where Bennett was coming from and Alabama won 28-10. Today, Alabama fans still own posters and paintings of the play that has come to be known simply as "The Sack," and Bennett is constantly reminded of it when he runs into Crimson Tide fans.

"There was a lot more to my time at the University than that Notre Dame game or one particular play," Bennett says. "Memories of that game mean a lot to fans, but to me it's just another tackle. When people talk about it, I try to share their excitement, but the truth is everything I did on the football field I was taught to do. I was taught to get the man with the football as fast as I could and as many times as I could. They called the play for me to get the quarterback and I got him.

"So people look at it and say, 'Aw man, that was a great hit,' but to me, every tackle I made was a great hit, even if I tackled a guy by his shoestring. Either way, I did my job."

Bennett insists he didn't even think much about the hit until the media and fans started asking him about it after the game. Instead, he was thinking about the play after "The Sack."

"I was thinking about me making a block on the punt return so Greg Richardson could score," Bennett says. "That meant more to me—getting a block on a punt return for a touchdown—than making one tackle. I look back on that game and think about Freddie Robinson getting two interceptions and almost getting a third. I think about the defense. In my four years at the University, that was probably the best defense of any game we played. We had a lot of standout plays in that game."

Plays like "The Sack" also caught the attention of NFL scouts. The Tampa Bay Buccaneers had just hired Perkins as their head coach and owned the top pick in the 1987 draft, so Bennett appeared to be on his way to the Bucs. Instead, the Bucs drafted Miami quarterback Vinnie Testaverde, and the Colts took Bennett with the second pick.

When the Colts and Bennett's agent butted heads throughout a prolonged contract dispute that lasted until October 31, the Colts finally traded him to Buffalo for two first-round picks, a second-round pick and a running back. The trade eventually paid off when Bennett became a cornerstone for four AFC championship teams from 1991-94.

Bennett's time in Buffalo was not without its problems. While it was frustrating to lose four consecutive Super Bowls, those defeats barely compare to the embarrassment and shame of Bennett being found guilty of sexual assault in Buffalo and serving 35 days in jail in the summer of 1998. Bennett, by then a Falcon, returned to football a changed man, armed with religion, a new lifestyle and a new start. That season, the Falcons finished 16-3 and reached the Super Bowl.

"Not many things in this world can rock me, and I've had my share of tough times," Bennett says. "I've had some times that I wish were forgettable, but everything that's happened has happened, and what doesn't kill you makes you stronger."

No matter what the reason, Bennett isn't one to look back very often and reminisce about his college and pro career and wonder what if.

"I'm different from a lot of other guys, and people who know me will tell you that I believe what happened yesterday, happened yesterday," Bennett says. "I have some great memories from the University and great friendships, and every year I played was special, but I can't go back and change it. I don't watch a lot of old game films. I've yet to watch the Super Bowls I played in, either. I left a legacy at the University, but I don't go back and try to re-live it.

"But I do like to think about the people and a lot of the great things that happened to me at the University, like just being able to walk around that campus every day and getting to live in Bryant Hall. It still sickens me that the NCAA did away with athletic dorms like Bryant Hall, because that was such a special place to live and grow up. That's something I'll cherish as much as anything, because the players who lived there were so close-knit and together. It was like family. That's what Coach Bryant wanted when he built the dorm."

Bennett also wishes he could change the perception people carry of Perkins and his time at Alabama. Perkins was widely regarded as hypersensitive and caustic by people outside the program, and his image didn't improve when he left Alabama for Tampa Bay.

When Bennett and other players gathered together last year to share memories for the *Alabama Football Legends Reunion* DVD, Bennett spoke up frequently so he could represent his era.

"I didn't want people to jump over that time or Coach Perkins," Bennett says. "I was worried it wasn't going to be talked about.

"When I was at Alabama, we didn't win a national championship or an SEC championship, but at the same time we had some of the greatest players who ever came through the University, and we did something no other team could do by beating Notre Dame. People want to look at it as a dark period in Alabama football, that just makes me want to fight. And I'll kick butt because that's not right.

"I also hate it when people say bad things about Coach Perkins. That's my dude. That's one of my best friends in the whole world. But just like a lot of people want to sit and judge me because they think they know me from reading about me or watching TV, those people think they know Coach Perkins, but they don't. People can't leave out Ray Perkins when they talk about Alabama football. If they talk about me, they have to talk about him, because he was my coach."

As for the game itself, Bennett is done talking about it or watching it—at least for now. He's had his time in the spotlight and has since learned how to live without it. He'd rather commit his time to his wife and two young children, as well as his numerous charitable causes, including the Cornelius Bennett Celeb-Am Classic.

"I've had enough light shining on me," Bennett says. "I'll be in the background, doing whatever I can to help."

DERRICK THOMAS

LINEBACKER 1985-1988

Growing up and playing high school football in a tough Miami neighborhood didn't give Derrick Thomas much exposure to the history and tradition of Alabama football. All Thomas knew was that he wanted to play college football for a program with a national reputation and a habit of winning. When it finally came time to choose between Alabama and Oklahoma, he chose Alabama simply because assistant coach George Henshaw was waiting for Thomas at South Miami High when Thomas reported for school on signing day.

It didn't take long, however, for Thomas to decide that he wanted his own place in Crimson Tide history.

"One of the things that was most important to Derrick was to have his hand and footprints over at Denny Chimes," says former Alabama assistant John Guy, who coached Thomas in 1987-88. "That's the highest individual honor, being a team captain at Alabama

and having his foot and handprints in that concrete, and that meant everything to him."

"He wanted that so badly. He talked about the great players who had come before him. He understood a lot about Alabama's history, and the great players who had played at Alabama. He had a real feel for tradition, and he marveled in that and he wanted to be part of that."

Before his time at Alabama was complete, Thomas achieved his goal of leaving his prints in the captains' walk of fame at Denny Chimes. He also left his own distinctive mark on the Alabama football program as an All-American, a member of the University's Team of the Century and one of the most accomplished linebackers for a program rich in outstanding linebackers.

For all his honors and awards, including 10 All-Pro selections during his NFL career with the Kansas City Chiefs before his untimely death at age 33 in 2000, it was Thomas's spot in the Denny Chimes concrete and his four years at the University that held a special place in his heart.

"Whenever I see those crimson jerseys and crimson helmets, I feel humbled to have played football for Alabama," Thomas told *Alabama Illustrated*. "Other players in the NFL talk to me about their schools and their traditions. I just smile, knowing the immense love Alabama fans have for our school and its football program. I'm proud to be a part of that Crimson Tide heritage."

Lessons in pride and heritage became important to Thomas as a child through the legacy of his father, U.S. Air Force captain Robert Thomas. Derrick was five years old when his father's B-52 was shot down over Vietnam during a bombing run called "Operation: Linebacker Two" in December 1972. Everyone but Thomas was able to bail out on time and survive. Thomas was the last to evacuate, but his body was never recovered and he was declared legally dead in 1980.

Thomas always said he didn't remember much about when or how he heard about his father's crash but still kept his father's memory alive.

"He's a great inspiration," Thomas said. "Everything he set out to accomplish he accomplished. He graduated with honors from high school, he graduated at the head of his class in ROTC, and he graduated with honors at Tennessee State. He was a math teacher at my high school, which I didn't find out until I got there. ... I think he'd be proud of me."

By the time Thomas survived a tumultuous childhood that included three months in a state-run program for disorderly youth, he arrived at high school as a big, rangy kid who had proved he could run, hit and hold his own against the bigger kids in his area, both on the field and in the streets. College recruiters came to see one of his teammates but soon noticed Thomas's athleticism at tight end, running back and linebacker, a position he didn't play until the final game of his junior season.

Thomas turned out to be a natural outside linebacker, a fact that became immediately obvious when he reported to Alabama in 1985.

"The first thing you saw with DT was his speed, but the one thing that jumped out at me was that he just had a knack for making the turn as a speed rusher coming off the edges," says former Alabama head coach Mike DuBose, a defensive assistant when Thomas arrived on campus in 1985. "From the first day, he just had the lean and the ability to get around the corner and get to the quarterback. It's not anything you can coach, but I asked where he learned how to lean the way he did, and he told me it was from running track. A lot of people don't know he was really good in track in high school and he said got that from leaning into the turns.

"When you combine that speed with his understanding of leverage and the fact that he played bigger and stronger than he was and his competitiveness, you knew right away that he was a special player."

Thomas's combination of talent and competitiveness helped him stand out and earn some playing time as a true freshman.

"Like all great players, he fed off competition," DuBose says. "The better the competition, the better he played. In pressure situations DT wanted them to throw the football so he could make a big play or he wanted them to run the football at him so he could make the stop. He was such a competitor that he wanted to make the play in a critical situation."

By the time Guy arrived to coach Thomas

in 1987, Thomas was a starter and a star in the making.

"Derrick was a very athletic guy, and I think in his mind he always thought he was a running back playing linebacker," says Guy, now the director of pro personnel with the Buffalo Bills and godfather to Thomas's son, Darrius. "There wasn't much that he didn't think he could do athletically. But at the same time, he wasn't selfish. He was a team guy and winning was the ultimate thing with him. He wanted to be the best he could be, but he wanted to do it as part of the team.

"He did a lot of little things that would go unnoticed. He wanted to be one of the greatest players in Alabama history, but at the same time he was never bigger than his teammates. Two of his favorites were Byron Sneed and Jimbo Salem, and they both played sparingly. I remember one game when we were winning big and Derrick wouldn't go back in because he wanted those other guys to go in and play. That was important to him that those guys got to play, and he always tried to make them part of his success so they could experience some of that."

For all of his good intentions, it took awhile before Thomas truly understood his potential and the expectations and demands that came with being both a star and a leader.

"Derrick was always late for everything, and it was Byron's job to make sure he got places on time," Guy says. "If he wasn't late, he was getting there in the last few seconds. I remember one time he was running on the practice field with his pants on, his shoes on, his shoulder pads halfway on, his socks in his hands, and this was a guy who wanted to be a captain. I told him, 'If you want to be captain and have your prints over at Denny Chimes, you've got to be on time, you've to be responsible.' It took a major blow-up for him to see that."

Thomas broke Cornelius Bennett's school record with an impressive 18 sacks as a junior in 1987 and emerged as a popular awards candidate. After spending time on the awards circuit in December and not practicing like he should have before the Sun Bowl, Thomas failed to play up to expectations against Army. "To me, that was kind of a warning," Guy says. "He had started believing all those things people said and wrote about him."

Thomas reported for preseason practice in 1988 in good shape, but his attitude was not what it needed to be. "He came in kind of cocky," Guy says. "I had allowed him to do some things other guys weren't allowed to do because he was special and he had exceeded it."

During a preseason team meeting, another coach asked if Thomas was meeting expectations and Guy didn't pull any punches, exposing Thomas's letdown. Thomas got mad to the point of tears, but Guy wasn't done. The next day at practice when Thomas attempted to be a team and position leader by taking the first spot in line for drills, Guy sent him to the back of every drill. That afternoon, Guy did it again, and Thomas continued to fume.

The next morning, Thomas told Guy, "Coach, you can't be doing this to me." Guy responded, "No, you did this to you." Thomas said, "You sold me out in that meeting. You told me I could do the things I was doing." Instead of arguing, Guy simply called for Thomas's backup, Thomas Rayam, and asked Rayam, "What did I tell Derrick he could do?" Rayam looked Thomas in the eye and told him, "Derrick, you were wrong. You went way beyond where you could go."

It was one thing to hear it from a coach. It was another to hear it from a player who looked up to Thomas.

"It was at that moment that a change took place," Guy says. "Derrick knew he was wrong, and he really changed. He got himself back on track. He always wanted to compete, loved to win, loved to be successful, always wanted to be on top, but after that he was really hungry and really wanted to get better and do what he had to do to be successful."

Thomas never did make a consistent habit of being on time, even in the NFL, but he went on that season to break his own school record with an incredible 27 sacks, 12 tackles for losses and 88 tackles overall. He also became a captain as a senior, earned unanimous All-America honors and won the Butkus Trophy as the nation's top linebacker.

After the Kansas City Chiefs selected Thomas with the fourth pick in the first round of the 1989 draft, he became the NFL Rookie of the Year and one of the game's premier pass rushers, following in the footsteps of NFL Hall of Famer Lawrence Taylor by harassing quarterbacks for sacks and hammering their throwing arms to force fumbles and interceptions.

Thomas also became a popular public fixture in Kansas City, using his celebrity status, time and money to serve several causes in the community, including funding literacy

Dick Butkus (left) and Derrick Thomas

programs for inner-city children, reading to children through local libraries, raising funds to feed the hungry and spending time with ill and hospitalized children. His principle cause was the "Third and Long Foundation" to raise money to promote literacy among Kansas City's youth. Thomas also made a regular habit of visiting the University of Alabama whenever he could, especially in the spring.

Along the way he won numerous awards, including the 1999 Veterans of Foreign Wars (VFW) Man of the Year, the Byron "Whizzer" White Humanitarian Award in 1994 and 1995, and the Daily Point of Light Award from former President George Bush in 1992, becoming the only NFL player to receive the honor.

By the time he had reached age 33 Thomas had lost a step off the edge but remained a key player for the Chiefs. On January 23, 2000, he was on his way to the Kansas City Airport so he could attend a playoff game in St. Louis when his Chevrolet Suburban flipped three times on an icy road around 1:30 p.m. Neither Thomas nor his friend Michael Tellis were wearing seatbelts, and both were thrown from the vehicle. Tellis was killed instantly. A third person in Thomas's vehicle was wearing his seatbelt and sustained only minor injuries. Thomas was airlifted to Jackson County Memorial Hospital, where doctors performed four hours of surgery to repair his broken spinal cord and neck by inserting screws, rods and hooks along with grafting bone from his hip. Despite their efforts, Thomas was still paralyzed from the chest down.

Doctors told Thomas he was fortunate just to be alive but would likely never walk again. Football was out of the question. For more than two weeks, Thomas, his family and his friends strived to come to grips with his situation, and he appeared to be making considerable progress when he was transferred to a hospital in Miami. Then on February 8, as he was being wheeled to a therapy session, Derrick turned to speak to his mother, Edith Morgan. Seconds later, he was dead, due to heart failure caused by a massive blood clot.

While the sudden news of his accident and his death shocked family, friends, teammates, coaches and fans, many found solace in Thomas's spiritual commitment and the joy and enthusiasm that marked his life.

"Knowing Derrick gave his life to the Lord, I can stand here in peace," said Kansas City Chiefs fullback Tony Richardson, who played at Auburn. "Giving back to the community is the legacy Derrick Thomas has left for us. What are we going to do to continue this legacy that he's left for us? When I was reading [his funeral] program, the most important date I saw was March 1997. Derrick rededicated his life to Christ.

"Derrick's at rest, he's at peace. If he had an opportunity to come back right now, there's no way he'd trade where he's at right now. I know that, one day, I'll see my buddy again."

In an open letter to family, friends and fans in the days before his death, Thomas put his situation in perspective that helped sum up what so many people appreciated about him.

"I know one day this will be over. When it is, I want to look back on it and know that I enjoyed myself, met many people on my journey and maybe influenced some of them to excel to their potential," Thomas wrote. "I may be sad when it's over because I can't do something I loved. But I don't want to be disappointed."

BOBBY HUMPHREY

HALFBACK 1985-1988

Bobby Humphrey was a good kid, thanks in large part to his mother, Marlene. She tried to keep a tight grip on her four children, raised them at home and church and insisted they be home before the sun went down and the street-lights came on in the Elyton Village section of Birmingham.

"It was the one rule you couldn't break," Humphrey says. "There was no excuse."

Most of the time, mama knew best around the Humphrey home. But if Mrs. Humphrey had been right about everything concerning her son's future path, the closest he could have come to taking the field at an Alabama football game was by playing a musical instrument for the Million Dollar Band.

Marlene Humphrey would simply laugh when her son would watch NFL games on television and say he was going to be playing on TV someday, but she had other plans for her third son.

"She didn't want me to play football," Humphrey says. "She wanted me to be in the band and play the trumpet, like my brother Montte."

Not that there's anything wrong with play-ing in the band, especially the Million Dollar Band, but if Humphrey had listened to his mom about football, he would never have become one of the best backs in Alabama history. If Humphrey had not gone behind his mom's back and signed himself up for a youth football team at 13 years old, he wouldn't have been chosen All-America twice or become an NFL standout.

"It's amazing at how I've gone from a kid selling Cokes at Legion Field during Alabama football games to this," Humphrey said in May 2004 upon his induction to the Alabama Sports Hall of Fame. "For a kid who played football in the eighth grade without his mom knowing it, and now here it is, I'm being inducted in the Alabama Sports Hall of Fame. Sometimes you aim high and hit the moon."

Humphrey wasn't trying to aim or hit anything when he snuck off to play football. He was just being a kid growing up in the shadow of Legion Field in an area where playing football was a measure of youthful manhood.

"Things like the Hall of Fame or playing college football never even entered my mind growing up," Humphrey says. "I just loved the game of football so much that my total attention and focus was on going out and doing everything I could to play football. I never even thought about what I wanted to accomplish. I just wanted to play."

To play football and keep his secret safe from mama, all Humphrey had to do was change out of his uniform after practice and get home before dark. That was the easy part.

The hard part came when the games started. His first one just happened to start in the early evening. By halftime, darkness covered the area, and Humphrey knew he was in big trouble.

"When I got home, my mom was at the door," Humphrey says. "I couldn't tell you what time it was. It was probably eight or nine o'clock. She had a limb, getting ready to spank me."

Before she could take her first swipe at her son's behind, Humphrey hid behind the trophy he brought home from the game. He had started the game at defensive tackle before his coach wised up and listened to his neighborhood friends about Humphrey's athletic ability. When the coach finally put the ball in Humphrey's hand, a star was born.

In that one game, Humphrey scored four touchdowns, tackled quarterbacks for sacks and returned a kickoff and a punt for scores and earned his first football trophy. Obviously moved by her son's accomplishments and his

passion for the game, his mother relented.

"He came home and I saw his eyes all aglow with the trophy," Marlene Humphrey said. "Normally I would have spanked him. They didn't keep anything from me. They don't hide things from me.

"But this time I saw the expression on his face, and I knew I was supposed to rejoice with him. So I put that trophy on the piano, where I kept other little things. And I hugged him and just was happy with him."

Marlene Humphrey ended up becoming her son's biggest football supporter and his most important coach. Good thing, because not everything would go as well for Humphrey as it did in that first game. Still, it meant so much to Humphrey to play football that he played for a losing football program at Glenn High School and still managed to have a successful prep career, gaining more than 7,000 all-purpose yards. The next year, Glenn closed it doors for good.

Glenn's lack of success wasn't enough to hide Humphrey from the eyes of college recruiters throughout the Southeast. Fortunately for Alabama coaches, signing with the Crimson Tide was a relatively easy decision for a kid who grew up parking cars in the yards around Legion Field and selling drinks inside the stadium, imagining what it would be like to be down on the field, playing in those crimson jerseys.

It didn't take long for Humphrey to convince Alabama coaches he could play at the SEC level, and they gave him the ball 99 times as a freshman in 1985. Humphrey responded with 502 yards (5.1 yards per carry) and four touchdowns.

"It was obvious early in his freshman year that he was a very special player," says Rockey

Felker, the direction of football operations at Mississippi State and Humphrey's first running backs coach at Alabama. "He had all the tools—speed, quickness, the ability to change directions. Plus, he's a lot more physical than you might think. He drags tacklers three, four, five extra yards."

As a sophomore in 1986 Humphrey started to turn all that potential into real production, rushing for 1,417 yards (6.2 yards per carry) and 15 touchdowns. He also caught 22 passes for 201 yards and two more scores.

"That year was really when I came into my own and started realizing I could become a good back if I worked at it," Humphrey says.

He continued to work at it, and despite nagging injuries during his junior season he still rushed for 1,255 yards (5.3 yards per carry) and 11 touchdowns to go with 22 receptions, 170 yards and two touchdowns. Along the way, he earned the respect of opposing defenses.

After Humphrey ran over, around and through Penn State for 220 yards and a touchdown on 36 carries and completed a 57-yard pass that set up another touchdown, Nittany Lion nose tackle Aoatoa Polamalu called Humphrey, "The Cadillac of tailbacks. We all knew he was quick as heck, but he had deceiving strength. He truly is a great back."

Penn State defensive back Sherrod Rainge said, "He's strong and fast. He looks like a finesse back, but he's strong enough to run over you. Then when you think he's going to run over you, he puts a move on you and goes around you."

Then, just as he was set to enter his senior season as one of the nation's leading Heisman Trophy candidates, Humphrey missed most of the spring because of a broken foot. At the

time, the injury didn't seem like such a big deal. When he broke the same bone against Vanderbilt in the second game of the season, though, Humphrey admits he started to worry about his future.

"When I got to the hospital, I cried," Humphrey says. "It was my senior year and I thought my career was over, seeing as how I'd broken my foot twice. I didn't know what my next turn would be."

Humphrey made a decisive turn the next spring. He could have returned in 1989 after receiving a medical redshirt for his 1988 season, but instead he made the difficult decision to pass up his final college season and enter the NFL's supplemental draft.

"As bad as I wanted to come back to Alabama," he says, "I just couldn't risk breaking my foot a third time."

Humphrey, who finished his Alabama career as a two-time All-American and owned the school record for rushing yards (3,420) until Shaun Alexander broke it in 1999, did what he had to do and ended up with the Denver Broncos, a strong franchise contending for division titles and the Super Bowl, with stars such as quarterback John Elway and tailback Tony Dorsett. Despite's Dorsett's presence, it was Humphrey who eventually earned the starting job as a rookie and helped lead the team to Super Bowl XXIV. He also produced one of the more memorable Super Bowl quotes when a reporter asked him why he took his earring out during games. Because, Humphrey said, he didn't want a diamond "to be pushed through my ear to the middle of my brain."

After becoming the first tailback in Broncos history to rush for 1,000 yards in each of his first two years in the NFL, Humphrey was on top of the world, ready to cash in on his rising star status. That's when Humphrey's career took a wrong turn. After holding out for a better contract at the start of preseason camp in 1991, Humphrey started taking a lot of things for granted, stopped working and lost his starting job. The next summer, the Broncos traded him to the Miami Dolphins, but knee injuries and bad choices forced him to retire after just four seasons in the NFL.

Those choices all started to add up when Humphrey was jailed in Columbus, Georgia, for possession of marijuana and cocaine and a charge of disorderly conduct. During that time in jail, Humphrey started taking a serious look at his life and made a commitment to change his life when he left jail.

"Since that point, I haven't picked up a joint, I haven't seen any cocaine, I haven't drank beer or wine, and I haven't touched a cigarette," Humphrey says. "I have been clean since that day."

He was not, however, able to break away from his old life until a few days later, when a former teammate shot him in the leg during an argument. Soon after he returned to Birmingham and decided to start over and give his life back to God.

"That's when all the pieces started coming back together," Humphrey says.

After returning to Alabama and completing his degree in social work in December 1998, Humphrey's life took another unpredictable turn. This time, it was an offer to be a head coach for the Birmingham Steeldogs of arena football. After attempting an unsuccessful comeback with the Buffalo Bills in 1995 and going through a period of time in

which he wanted nothing to do with football, Humphrey rediscovered his love for the game in the spring of 1999 as a volunteer coach at Brookwood High School, about 20 miles east of Tuscaloosa. Three months later, he was the Steeldogs' head coach.

"That fire got rekindled," Humphrey says. "At Brookwood, volunteering and helping with running backs, that fire started to come back up into a flame again. The Steeldogs were my first opportunity."

Over the course of his five seasons with the Steeldogs, Humphrey has grown into a successful head coach with a style of his own, built on a foundation of lessons he learned from his mom, his time at Alabama and his experiences with the Broncos and Dolphins.

"I've learned a lot, and I've had some ups and downs," Humphrey says. "When you've had ups and you've had downs, it gives you experience and confidence, knowing that you can accomplish the next task at hand.

"It's just amazing that four years have gone and that I'm on my fifth year now. I appreciate the hard times I've had, because I think it's helped me become the coach I am today."

More important, it's been one more step toward becoming a better man, a better husband and father—the kind of man who can look back and see his mama was right about a lot of things, even if she was initially wrong about football and the trumpet.

"Life is great," Humphrey says. "I'm enjoying what I'm doing. I'm enjoying coaching mostly because I have some input into the lives of these young men. I'm their father away from home. I enjoy helping these guys grow as men."

SHAUN ALEXANDER

TAILBACK 1996-1999

Shaun Alexander has always been full of surprises. From his jersey number to his college choice to the day his daughter was born, Alexander has made a habit of following an atypical path toward successful choices and results.

Somehow, someway, Alexander has made it work on and off the field, during his outstanding high school years in Kentucky, his All-America college career at Alabama and now as a professional with the NFL's Seattle Seahawks.

"I'm always the oddball compared to everyone else," Alexander once told *Breakaway* magazine.

Perhaps the world around Alexander should have seen it coming during his youth football days. Alexander played mostly defense until someone gave him the chance to return a kickoff in fourth grade.

"I think I ran two of them back in the same game, and everybody just gave me so much attention," Alexander says. "I was like, 'I wonder what happens if I play running back or receiver?' The first game I played running back I ran for a bunch of touchdowns and I just thought, 'Wow, this is amazing. Everybody's buying me ice cream.'"

From there, it seemed stardom was just a matter of time for Alexander, even if it wasn't so obvious to other people. Even his choice of jersey number defied his talents. He actually wanted the number 44, but a linebacker already owned that number, so Alexander chose 37 just because it was different. Think about it: when was the last time you saw a great back, besides Alexander, wearing 37?

"He was a skinny kid and he had these glasses on," says Rick Thompson, head coach at Boone County High School in Florence, Kentucky. "He didn't really stand out just looking at him.

"The first thing you saw was that he could run. The first chance he got to run with the football, it was obvious the kid could do some things with the ball in his hands."

That talent carried over from the practice field to the games when Alexander ran for a touchdown on his first high school carry as a sophomore. The first time he started a game, as a junior, he scored five touchdowns in one game. In Boone County's final regular-season game that year, Alexander ran for seven more touchdowns, and by the time he was done with his prep career, he had scored 110 touchdowns in all.

"There's no telling how many he would have had, but there were a lot of games he didn't play in the fourth quarter," says former Boone County coach Owen Hauck. "He had seven touchdowns twice and did it in three quarters both times."

It's no wonder college football programs from all over the nation came calling with scholarship offers. Michigan and Notre Dame appeared to have the inside track until Alabama got involved, with a small boost from Thompson, a former walk-on at Alabama in 1979 and 1980. From the time Alabama coaches first called the high school, Alexander was interested—and intrigued enough to visit the school. Alexander was immediately impressed with coach Gene Stallings and the school's storied football tradition and surprised recruiting analysts by signing with the Crimson Tide.

Alexander, Alabama fans and media with high expectations were then surprised when Alabama redshirted Alexander as a freshman in 1995. He also spent most of the next two seasons sharing the ball with older, more experienced tailbacks and carrying 167 times for 1,005 yards and nine touchdowns in two seasons. Even if those veteran backs were considered less talented than Alexander, they also did the things Stallings wanted them to do, especially when it came to blocking and practicing hard every day.

"We had a system for playing the backs and they understood coming in that they were going to have to pay their dues and take their time," says Mike DuBose, an assistant coach when Alexander arrived at Alabama and the Crimson Tide's head coach from 1997-2000. "There was no question Shaun was an outstanding talent when he got there, and he would have been more productive if he had played more in the early part of his career, but he had to wait for his opportunities. But even then, like the second half of the LSU game, he was a special type of player."

Alexander had rushed for a total of 144 yards and a touchdown during the first eight games of his redshirt freshman season when he dropped a major surprise on LSU, as well as Tide fans and the media, by rushing for 291 yards and four touchdowns in a 26-0 victory at LSU. In the second half alone, he rushed 19 times for 274 yards.

"Those of you who cover us regularly have seen him practice and know it's a just matter of time," Stallings said after the game. "He has speed, he has size. ... I think before he leaves Alabama he'll be an excellent player."

Alexander didn't start proving Stallings's point consistently until his junior year when he finally moved ahead of the pack of Tide tailbacks and broke through for 1,178 yards, 13 touchdowns, 26 receptions and four touchdown catches.

"At times coaches would get mad at him and sometimes the other players would get mad, too, because Shaun didn't look like he was going hard all the time," DuBose says. "They didn't think he was going full speed or working hard, but when you step back and take a closer look at the ground he's covering he is going hard, but he's such a great athlete and ran so effortlessly with great vision that it didn't look like he was having to work as hard to get the job done."

Following Alexander's success as a junior, Tide coaches were justifiably concerned about losing him to the NFL draft. Instead, Alexander defied the skeptics and surprised

coaches, teammates and fans by deciding to stay at Alabama for his senior season. At the time, he simply decided he was having too much fun to leave Alabama and wanted one more season to enjoy college football after completing his degree in the spring before his senior season.

Alexander finally put it all together as a senior in 1999. Injuries limited his availability and performance at times, but he still managed to rush for 1,383 yards and 19 touchdowns and catch 25 passes for 323 yards and four touchdowns. He was at his best in two games against Florida. In the first, a 40-39 upset victory at Florida five games into the season, and just three weeks after a disastrous home loss to Louisiana Tech, Alexander did his part with 106 rushing yards, 94 receiving yards, three touchdown runs and a touchdown catch, and the winning score on a 25-yard touchdown run in overtime. In the second game, a 34-7 victory over the Gators in the SEC championship game, Alexander came through with 97 rushing yards and a touchdown run and opened up the offense for other players, particularly quarterback Andrew Zow and receiver Freddie Milons.

"I don't know if people fully appreciated how competitive Shaun was," DuBose says. "I've never been around a football player who wanted the football more in critical situations than Shaun Alexander. He took that kind of leadership very seriously. He talked the talk, but he walked the walk, too. Some guys would talk about doing things right and then become an entirely different person off the field but Shaun was the same all the time. He knew people were watching him to see if he was going to be a leader and he wanted people to follow him in the right direction and he took

that responsibility very seriously."

In the process of emerging as a more consistent player and a team leader, Alexander also broke Bobby Humphrey's school record for career rushing yards by finishing with 3,565 yards and topped Johnny Musso's career record for touchdowns by scoring 41.

"A guy like Shaun Alexander breaking my record—a good Christian young man, president of the FCA (Fellowship of Christian Athletes)—I mean, records are made to be broken, but if there's anybody I'd like to break it, it's Shaun Alexander," Humphrey said.

Alexander rode his senior success into the first round of the 2000 NFL draft, as the 19th overall pick by Seattle. Of the five running backs selected in the first round of that draft, none have run for more than Alexander's 4,241 yards or 46 touchdowns over the past four seasons.

One of Alexander's best games came under appropriately surprising circumstances. When Alexander's wife, Valerie, went into labor with their first child early on a Sunday morning during the 2003 season, Alexander called coach Mike Holmgren to let him know he might not be available for the Seahawks' home game that day. However, after helping with the delivery of daughter Heaven Nashay at 12:37 p.m. (23 minutes before kickoff) and cutting the umbilical cord, Alexander reached the game in time—thanks to the urgent driving of Seahawks security officials—to find the Seahawks trailing the St. Louis Rams 14-7 in the second quarter.

After dressing and stretching quickly, Alexander ran out to the huddle and immediately set the tone with his teammates, saying, "Okay, watch this." On his first carry, he ran for 12 yards. On the next carry, he went for 17, sparking the Seahawks to a scoring drive. A rugged five-yard carry later in the game to the Rams' three-yard line set up the game-winning touchdown in a 24-23 Seattle victory.

"I wanted to take care of my responsibilities as a husband first and take care of my wife," Alexander said after the game, "and then I wanted to take care of the next thing—and that's my team."

The Seahawks are obviously pleased to have Alexander on their side, but like Alexander's college coaches, his Seattle coaches often struggle to understand him. Alexander still doesn't practice with the intensity NFL coaches prefer, remains somewhat inconsistent in games from week to week and still lacks the pass protection skills of a quality all-around back but has the ability to pull all sorts of surprises out of his sleeve, like the time he set an NFL record by scoring five touchdowns in one half against Minnesota.

"Shaun has all the talents he needs to be a Pro Bowl guy," Seattle running backs coach Stump Mitchell says. "The only thing I have to try to get him to do right now—and that's a big challenge—is to work hard every day."

Perhaps, like his Alabama coaches and teammates discovered, the Seahawks are still learning Alexander has a way of expressing himself that doesn't fit with the football norm.

"I think it drives Coach Holmgren crazy,"

Alexander says. "When a person is fiery, you know what they're thinking. I think Coach Holmgren doesn't know what I'm thinking."

Alexander's religious devotion is one of the big reasons for his more relaxed nature, and his faith is the primary motivation for his widespread charitable activities. Alexander made a habit of speaking to school groups and playing an active role in the FCA during his days at Alabama, but now he's putting his time, effort and money into the Shaun Alexander Family Foundation, a nonprofit organization run by his brother Durran. One of the principle services of the foundation is to meet the needs of impoverished families, particularly during major holidays.

"I've been blessed," Alexander says, "so I want to be a blessing to other people, too."

Alexander says his desire to help people stems from his mother's hard work and devotion as a single mom, as well as the charitable work he witnessed from Stallings and former Alabama standout John Croyle, who passed up a shot at the NFL to establish a home for abused and abandoned children. It's more than evident that even though Alexander wasn't born in Alabama or raised on Crimson Tide football his Alabama roots remain strong.

"Once you're 'Bama, you're 'Bama forever," Alexander says. "You know, there's no getting out of it, and that's the way we like it."

ACKNOWLEDGMENTS

Thanks first and foremost to Our Heavenly Father, who has an amazing capacity for doing the impossible, turning my trash into treasure and not giving up on me; my wife, Karen, a constant source of inspiration and unconditional love, as well as her gentle and compassionate editing; and my sons, Colin and Taylor, who hold me to a high degree of accountability and humility and always seem more concerned with my love and time than the nature of my work. Thanks also to Bo and Grace for wagging tails and sloppy kisses, even in the worst of times.

Thanks to Dad for leading me down this path as a husband, father and man. Thanks to my mom, Jane, a true gift from God in countless ways, and my mother, Lanie, for her selfless love. Thanks to Michael, Casey, Connor, Ryan, Logan, Mom and Dad Hulce, Lori, Greg, Sean, Ron and Dana for loving family support.

Thanks to everyone at Mountaintop Community Church, especially my small group family, Team 45, my high school friends and my trusted friend, Emily Dickinson. Thanks to everyone at South City Theatre for letting me explore and grow.

Thanks to my favorite Alabama fans: Tim King, for being the world's most realistic Tide fan and a true brother; and Norah Gilchrist, for loving me almost as much as Joe Namath and Mike Shula.

Very special thanks for the unselfish assistance of Larry White, Alabama's Associate Director of Athletics for Media Relations, and his staff; Ken Gaddy, coach Clem Gryska and Brad Green at the Bryant Museum, a wonderfully unique and valuable resource of information; and Langston Rogers, the Associate Athletic Director for Athletic Media Relations at Ole Miss. They greeted me with open arms and open archives, so this book would not be possible without them. Additional thanks to Bill Martin of the Alabama Sports Hall of Fame, Michael Bite (Joe Namath's Birmingham-based attorney) and Michael Litman of the Seattle Seahawks.

There are so many outstanding writers and broadcasters, and better men, who must be acknowledged here. Some I've known, such as John Forney, Clyde Bolton, John Pruett, Jimmy Bryan and Al Browning (we should have fished together more). Others, such as Zipp Newmann, Naylor Stone, Bennie Marshall and Mickey Herskowitz, I only know through their work and the colorful stories from people in the business. They covered the Crimson Tide and wrote the stories and the books that paved a foundation of research and understanding for this book. My personal favorite is Bill Lumpkin, the former *Birmingham Post-Herald* sports editor and columnist who took me under his wing and taught me invaluable lessons about Southern football, sports writing and life.

The available research for this book was plentiful, especially through the archives of *The Birmingham News*, *The Birmingham Post-Herald*, *The Tuscaloosa News*, *The Huntsville Times*, *The Montgomery Advertiser*, *The Mobile Register*, *The Decatur Daily* and *'Bama Magazine*. Numerous books were invaluable, including *Bowl Bama Bowl* by Al Browning; *The Crimson Tide: A Story of Alabama Football* by Clyde Bolton; *Talk of the Tide* by John Forney and Steve Townsend; *Coach: The Life of Paul "Bear" Bryant* by Keith Dunnavant; *Bear: The Hard Life and Good Times of Alabama's Coach Bryant* by Paul W. Bryant and John Underwood; *The Legend of Bear Bryant* by Mickey Herskowitz; *Turnaround: The Untold Story of Bear Bryant's First Year As Head Coach at Alabama* by Tom Stoddard; *Century of Champions* by Wayne Hester; and *Legends in Crimson* by Ben Cook. I also made frequent use of *Alabama Football Legends Reunion* by Gabriel Sports Reunion.

Long overdue thanks to mentors and former editors Don Kausler, Jr., Jeff Krupsaw and the late Jimmy Denley for their sense of direction and vision. A special thanks to mentor and editor J. Wayne Fears for giving me a chance and believing in me.

Thanks to editor Gina Sabbia of Sports Publishing for walking me through the process with patience and encouragement.

Finally, and with deep gratitude, thanks to the Alabama players and coaches who made this book possible, as athletes, teammates, husbands, fathers, businessmen and gentlemen. You shared the priceless gift of your time, enthusiasm and memories. You lived the lives chronicled in this book; I just wrote about them. It's no wonder your fans hold you in such high regard.

As for those who didn't participate … well, what can I say? Let me say this: Billy Neighbors and Lee Roy Jordan said they returned my calls because Coach Bryant always returned his calls and told his coaches and players to do the same. Think about that the next time someone tries to get in touch with you for a good cause. The last thing any of us needs to do is to forget the valuable lessons he taught.

—RS

EPILOGUE

Like most successful traditions, Alabama's history of winning is no accident. Someone had to start with a vision. Someone had to construct a plan. Someone had to make a commitment to building a winning program.

Legends put Alabama football on the map in the mid-1920s. A decade later, a new coach and new players had earned two more Rose Bowl wins.

One of those players returned when "Mama called," and the Crimson Tide reclaimed its post at the top of college football, winning three titles each in the 1960s and 1970s.

Then, a backup quarterback from the 1961 squad and assistant on the next six championship squads became the athletic director in 1999, took a plane to Miami at the start of 2007, and hired the coach who brought the program its next three titles at the time of this writing.

At most stadiums across America on Saturdays, fans express their disappointment with the current season and spend their time reliving the great moments on their Jumbotrons.

At Bryant-Denny, fans continue to witness larger than life moments, legends in the making.

In the 1920s and 1930s, fans read from numerous newspapers about the Crimson Tide. In the 1960s and 1970s, the fans turned to radio and the voice of John Forney to bring them the legends of Alabama football. Today, fans access video of the Tide at the click of a mouse, and still some legends are better talked about than seen.

Who will Crimson Tide fans speak of 50 years down the road? Here's a case for a few players and one key administrator.

Mal Moore—In the 10 years since this book was first published, the university renamed the football building in honor of him, the State of Alabama Sports Hall of Fame elected him into its 2011 class, the National Football Foundation's named him the top athletic director in 2012, and Nick Saban, persuaded by Moore to come to Alabama in 2007, led the Crimson Tide to three national championships in a four-year span, giving Moore an astonishing legacy of playing a role in 10 national championships for Alabama.

Moore's presence fills this book, due to his 40-plus years of influence on the university. Alabama football wasn't past its latest title celebration when Moore passed away due to pulmonary problems in March 2013.

"Mal was truly a special person in every sense of the word," Saban said in a university statement. "We can talk about all the championships Mal has been involved with, but I think what will be remembered most was the man he was. He always put the best interests of others ahead of his own, he carried himself as a first-class gentleman, and he helped bring out the best in those around him.

"Mal was an outstanding leader in terms of all he did for Alabama athletics. Most importantly, he was a great friend to me and my family. Mal was the No. 1 reason we decided to make the move to Tuscaloosa."

Moore's connection with people can be seen not only in the coaches he hired and supported, but also in the way he pushed for significant building improvements completed under his watch. Perhaps the easiest way his legacy can be explained is to look at Bryant-Denny Stadium.

Bryant-Denny became a different place to play in the Moore era. Today, the players enter the stadium among thousands of cheering fans at the Walk of Champions plaza that served as a parking lot and fraternity house prior to the expansion in 2006. When the opposing team's quarterback has to burn a timeout because he can't change the play, part of the blame should surely lie with Moore's work to enclose the upper decks and add 18,000 seats.

Moore finished his playing career as a backup quarterback, but he finished his life's work as a legend without replacement.

Julio Jones—Julio Jones crafted his legend after "the" catch. Even as a freshman, Jones seemed like the big kid playing with the little guys. In the 2009 Arkansas game, Jones caught a pass near the sidelines and kept driving as one, two, three, and eventually, all 11 defenders attempted to stop his progress. Not only was he tough after the catch, but also he put together an impressive highlight reel in his three years at Alabama: the one-hand touchdown grab against San Jose State in the 2010 season opener, an Alabama record 221 yards receiving against Tennessee in 2010, and a 73-yard touchdown run off a short screen pass to break open a close game against LSU in the 2009 season—a run that showed off another talent, his speed.

Javier Arenas—Kicking to Javier Arenas was like the evil villain putting TV's "The A-Team" in an "impossible" spot: No matter the odds, you knew they'd get out of it and it would be fun to watch. Arenas finished his career fourth all time in school history for all-purpose yards, and he certainly would've had more if Alabama had needed him on the offensive side of the ball or if other teams had actually kicked to him his junior and senior seasons. Arenas was a talented cornerback—his interception in the 2009 SEC Championship game is proof of it —but his elusive ability as a returner set new standards at Alabama. Arenas holds the career punt return yards mark by over 600 yards, and he holds the career kickoff returns mark by over 900 yards to the closest competitor.

Carson Tinker—The day a drive to Tuscaloosa looks normal is the day when the legend of Carson Tinker needs to be retold. An F4 tornado ripped through Tuscaloosa on April 27, 2011, taking with it the lives of at least 64 people and causing more than $2 billion in damages. That day, Tinker lost his girlfriend, Ashley Harrison, when she was pulled away from him after the tornado blew away the house where they attempted to hide. The effort to rebuild in the aftermath led Tinker and his teammates to the 2011 Disney Spirit Award for the team. The award is given annually to college football's most inspirational player or team.

"Carson Tinker has done a lot of community service, probably lost the most, and has given the most," Coach Nick Saban said in a University release at that time. "I'm very proud to be a part of this, and I think a lot of other people should be, as well. I think it's the way we should do things, and I think I'm proud of the example we try to set in helping in our community, and I'm talking about the university as a whole and the football program as a whole."

The Alabama athletic department donated $1 million to the UA Acts of Kindness Fund to provide relief to faculty, staff, and students who experienced hardships from the tornado. Additionally, linebacker Courtney Upshaw raised nearly $20,000 in his hometown of Eufaula. The team worked collectively to rebuild 13 homes, 14 total, after that year's national championship.

Tinker accepted the award for the team during the ESPN ceremony and said to reporters, "I'm glad that I can come here and win this award on behalf of my team, that the team has won this award, and people can see that when they think I'm sad, I'm not. I'm trying to do everything I can to inspire somebody.... I wouldn't have chosen this role for myself, so I can't say that I like it, but I know it comes with a responsibility."

Tinker and the team's rebuilding effort inspired their performance throughout a 2011 season that contained its own redemptive themes. The Crimson Tide overcame a 9-6 overtime loss to LSU in the regular season to beat the Tigers 21-0 for the national championship. Tinker was rated the top long snapper heading into the NFL draft, and he signed a free agent deal with the Jacksonville Jaguars in the summer of 2013.

Terrence Cody—It seemed only fitting that Mount Cody was the one to stop Rocky Top's attempt to spoil Bama's 2009 undefeated season. Cody, who finished that season as a two-time All-America player, blocked two Tennessee fourth-quarter field goals to preserve a 12-10 Crimson Tide win. The last block came with four seconds remaining, one of those four-seconds-remaining moments that require several CBS TV timeouts that only heightened the anxiety and the prayer life of nearly every Alabama fan. Facing the 44-yard attempt, Cody broke through the Creamsicle orange line to get his hands up and send the ball harmlessly away to the left side—and keep "Rocky Top" from being played at least another 20 times.

Cody was a force in his two years at Alabama. He recalled for *USA Today*'s David Leon Moore that Coach Saban recruited him by saying: "We need a body like yours in the middle, to stop the run, to change the rhythm of the game."

Boy, did he. Georgia Head Coach Mark Richt said in an ESPN report that "I haven't seen anybody who's a match for this guy one-on-one. Nobody playing on Saturdays, or Sundays probably." This was prior to the 2008 "blackout" game between the No. 3 Bulldogs and the No. 8 Tide. The week before, Cody had knocked around Arkansas and its highly regarded offensive line in a 49-14 win. The Crimson Tide and Cody were simply overbearing as they raced out to a 31-0 lead at halftime against UGA. Cody faced against Georgia what he would for most of the rest of his two years: double- and triple- teaming that limited his own work but freed up the rest of the Crimson Tide defense to stay near the top in the nation in scoring defense those two years.

Additionally, Cody served as a fullback in short yardage situations, clearing the pathway for Mark Ingram and serving as inspiration for linemen to follow. Jesse Williams would be used in much the same way his two years at Alabama— and like Cody, no one ever seemed particularly interested on the defensive side in engaging such an imposing force at fullback.

Barrett Jones—A player versatile enough to have played in another era but smart enough to realize a leather helmet wouldn't have protected him, Jones was a four-year starter on the offensive line. Whether at right guard his freshman and sophomore years, left tackle his junior year, or center his senior year, Jones helped to open the holes that Mark Ingram, Trent Richardson, and Eddie Lacy spun through on the way to three national championships. Jones won the 2011 Outland Trophy, the 2012 Remington Trophy, All-America honors two times, and CoSIDA/ESPN Academic All-America accolades four times.

Jones played with a line that protected just two starting quarterbacks for those four years. Since Nick Saban's first year at Alabama, the line has done a remarkable job keeping the starter from being knocked around, injured, and forced into interceptions—a stat that stands out in the record book because three of the top five consecutive pass streaks without an interception have been during the Saban era.

Jones kept his quarterbacks safe, even at his own expense. The Germantown, Tennessee, native tore ligaments in his foot during the first quarter of the 2012 SEC Championship Game. He played through the pain in Alabama's thrilling come-from-behind and run-them-ragged 32-38 win over Georgia and then through the BCS title win over Notre Dame. Jones had surgery after the championship game, and it cost him a chance to work out at the NFL combine.

Jones finished his career as a three-time national champion. He was called by some the "most intelligent" player in the NFL draft, and yet his partner on the line, right guard Chance Warmack, was called the "most athletic." Jones was drafted in 2013, joining Warmack, Mike Johnson, and James Carpenter as other Alabama offensive linemen during Jones' career. Certainly, anyone who remembers Brodie Croyle running for his life or Kenneth Darby running into a wall at the line of scrimmage appreciates what Jones and his group accomplished.

Mark Ingram and Trent Richardson—Together, they form the legend of the two-back system. One change in the Saban era was the introduction of frequent substitutions on the defensive line and at running back. While the line moves out frequently between plays, the backs tend to switch out at the beginning of the series, leaving both sets fresher at the end of games, games the Crimson Tide struggled to finish prior to Saban's arrival.

Ingram came to the Crimson Tide from Michigan, a signee to Saban's first full recruiting class, and became an immediate factor. Relieving back Glen Coffee, Ingram led the team in rushing in his first game and finished 2008 with 743 yards. Coffee left after 2008, an early departure for the NFL draft who started an interesting trend:

Coffee played for three years and departed a year early to be a third-round draft pick.

Ingram ran for three years and departed a year early to be a first-round draft pick.

Richardson ran for three years and departed a year early to be a first-round draft pick.

Eddie Lacy (Richardson's second in the two-back system for 2011 before taking over in 2012) perfects the spin move (he really should have a patent) and runs for three years before departing early to be a second-round draft pick.

And T.J. Yeldon, Lacy's second? All signs point to Yeldon being successful at Alabama and in the pros.

Ingram and Richardson played together for two years, 2009 and 2010, and the two finished their respective three-year careers at Alabama just 131 rushing yards apart from each other. Ingram won the Heisman in 2009, the first Heisman winner in school history. Richardson won the school's first Doak Walker Award as the best back in 2011. Both backs were All-America players, Ingram in 2009 and Richardson in 2011. Both are tied for the single-season record with nine games of over 100 yards rushing.

Ingram had the larger-than-life numbers at the end of games. In 2009, he ran for 246 yards against South Carolina, including a critical 68 in the fourth quarter. With the Crimson Tide up by seven, Ingram took all six snaps directly from the Wildcat formation, the last carry for a four-yard run that put Alabama up 20-6. Ingram was often compared in size and speed to former Florida Gator and Dallas Cowboy running back Emmitt Smith, a comparison that even Coach Saban made on the NFL Network before Ingram's draft day.

Richardson ended his career being compared to Smith as well, in terms of his aggressive style, but in comparison to Ingram, Trent produced the flashier moments in a game. In 2009, he shook off six hapless Hog defenders on the way to a 52-yard touchdown run that helped the Crimson Tide to an early lead. In 2011, he not only made a poor Ole Miss defender miss near the line of scrimmage, but he found that same defender again 50 yards down the field and completed a hesitation move that left the defender dusted—all on the way to Richardson's 76-yard touchdown run and 191-yard and four-touchdown night.

Richardson used his speed as a receiving option and his occasional use as kickoff returner gave him the single-season mark at Alabama for all-purpose yards at 2,083. Richardson finished second to Bobby Humphrey for career all-purpose yards with 4,580. At fifth on the chart, Mark Ingram finished with 3,976 (sixty yards less receiving than Richardson's 730 and just 45 kickoff yards as a returner, to Richardson's 720).

Ingram holds the school record for most career rushing touchdowns at 42, while Richardson finished with 35, but Richardson set the single-season mark for rushing touchdowns at 21 in 2011.

Ingram is currently a member of the New Orleans Saints, and Richardson is a member of the Cleveland Browns.

Since 1915, players have claimed All-American honors while playing for Alabama. With highly touted recruiting classes and administrative support in place, Tuscaloosa seems destined to see plenty more legends in the years to come.